FOR ARGUMENT'S SAKE

A Guide to Writing Effective Arguments

FOURTH EDITION

KATHERINE J. MAYBERRY
Rochester Institute of Technology

New York • San Francisco • Boston
London • Toronto • Sydney • Tokyo • Singapore • Madrid
Mexico City • Munich • Paris • Cape Town • Hong Kong • Montreal

Vice President/Editor in Chief: Joe Terry
Acquisitions Editor: Susan Kunchandy
Executive Marketing Manager: Carlise Paulson
Supplements Editor: Donna Campion
Project Coordination, Text Design, and Electronic Page Makeup: Pre-Press
    Company, Inc.
Cover Design Manager: John Callahan
Manufacturing Buyer: Roy Pickering
Printer and Binder: The Maple-Vail Book Manufacturing Group, Inc.
Cover Printer: Lehigh Press, Inc.

For permission to use copyrighted material, grateful acknowledgment is made to the
copyright holders on p. 203, which are hereby made part of this copyright page.

Library of Congress Cataloging-in-Publication Data

Mayberry, Katherine J., 1950-
    For argument's sake: a guide to writing effective arguments / Katherine J. Mayberry.–
4th ed.
        p. cm.
    Includes index.
    ISBN 0-321-08504-3
        1. English language–Rhetoric. 2. Persuasion (Rhetoric). 3. Report writing. 4. Logic. I.
Title.

PE1431 .M39 2001
808'.042–dc21

2001029753

Please visit our website at http://www.ablongman.com

ISBN 0-321-08504-3

2 3 4 5 6 7 8 9 10—MA—03 02 01

Brief Contents

Detailed Contents

Preface

The focus of *For Argument's Sake* is the process of writing effective arguments. By dividing written argument into its four most common modes—factual arguments, causal arguments, evaluations, and recommendations—and outlining the steps of argument composition, from the earliest stage of invention through audience analysis to final revision, this text provides a comprehensive guide to the creation of responsible and effective written arguments.

For Argument's Sake came out of my own experience teaching a college course in "written argument" at the Rochester Institute of Technology. At the time, my textbook choices were limited to theoretical treatises on logic and reading-focused argument anthologies. But what my students needed was practical advice about how to write arguments. In the absence of such a text, a colleague (Robert Golden) and I decided to write our own. In the first edition of *For Argument's Sake,* we created a practical guide to writing effective argument that is helpful to students from a variety of disciplinary backgrounds, new in its approach to some fundamental issues, and detailed without being unnecessarily complex.

ORGANIZATION

The text is organized around the three major phases of argument writing: focusing, supporting, and reviewing. Chapters 1 through 5 discuss how to bring a developing argument into focus, including finding and focusing a claim, identifying and accommodating the audience, and understanding the relationship between claim and support. Chapters 6 through 9 show students how to support the four different classes of argument (arguments of fact, cause, evaluation, and recommendation). And Chapters 10 through 12 present the reviewing activities necessary to refine and polish an argument: considering image and style, composing openings and closings, and revising and editing the argument draft.

These three writing phases are presented in the order students typically follow when composing arguments, but there are of course perfectly acceptable and effective exceptions to the typical. The order presented is meant to guide, not prescribe. Further, the sequential presentation of phases is not meant to contradict the received wisdom about the recursive nature of good writing; in the real practice of writing, changes made in one phase lead to changes in the others.

SPECIAL FEATURES

The discussion of dissonance in Chapter 2 is unique to argument texts. The question of what moves people to write arguments is a critical one for students that can lead them to make a greater personal investment in their own writing.

The treatment of formal and informal logic is also unique to argument texts; in this book, they are introduced at the point in the argument process where they are most useful: the development and evaluation of support. Too often, argument texts include the theory of logic and examples of informal fallacies without addressing how they are useful in the actual writing process. Chapter 5 presents both formal and informal logic as practical tools for creating reasonable arguments.

The inclusion of an entire chapter on style and image (Chapter 10) enriches the traditional view of argument, which sometimes seems to suggest that effective arguments have more to do with formulas and principles than with using language fairly and effectively. Here, a writer's style—the image he or she projects through the writing—is a fundamental component of argument, not just a lucky accident of talent.

For Argument's Sake contains many examples that today's college students (both traditional and nontraditional) can relate to, as well as examples from a range of academic and career areas. The range of applications helps students see the importance of writing effective arguments not only in college courses, but also in their post-college careers.

Because improvement in writing comes only with practice, the emphasis in all the activities in the text is on *writing*. Each chapter gives students many opportunities to practice what they are learning by writing (and rewriting) full and partial arguments.

NEW TO THIS EDITION

The fourth edition of *For Argument's Sake* retains the overall structure of the first three editions, as well as the emphasis on invention, composing, and overall practicality. My own experience of teaching from the first three editions, invaluable input from colleagues across the country, and the continuing information explosion of the last few years have necessitated some important modifications to this fourth edition.

Among these changes is an expanded discussion of responsible strategies for Internet research. With written argument as dependent as it is upon reliable facts, the ready availability of factual information on the Internet—both good and bad—must be addressed by an argument textbook. In particular, Chaps. 2, 3, and 4 now include discussions of optimizing the Internet's value as a tool for discovering and supporting arguments. Throughout the book, frequent references are made to "cyberarguments," as well as to more traditional text-based arguments.

This edition also contains more examples of student writing, an expanded discussion of documentation styles, and a discussion of reading arguments. The book's contemporary tone is maintained by updated references and examples reflecting changes in the external environment.

This fourth edition contains the most popular features of the previous editions while reflecting the revolutionary changes wrought by information technology. I am pleased to offer it as an even more useful, accessible, and manageable guide for college students at all levels who must write arguments.

SUPPLEMENTS

A new companion website is available to accompany this edition of *For Argument's Sake*. (www.ablongman.com/Mayberry) Features of this site include additional apparatus, chapter summaries, and links for each chapter.

An Instructor's Manual is available to adopters, upon request.

ACKNOWLEDGMENTS

The fourth edition of *For Argument's Sake* remains closely tied to the vision I shared with Robert E. Golden when we began the first edition more than 15 years ago. In addition to Dr. Golden and the many people who contributed to the success of earlier editions of *For Argument's Sake,* I have a new group of extremely helpful individuals to thank. A number of people have served as readers and editors of the manuscript, both from Longman Publishers and from a variety of colleges and universities. Among the Longman folks are Susan Kunchandy, Anne Smith, Lynn Huddon, and Rebecca Gilpin. External readers include: Greg Beatty, North Carolina State University; Bill Bolin, Texas A & M University–Commerce; Jami L. Carlacio, University of Wisconsin–Milwaukee; Kathy M. Heuff, University of Georgia; Ronald F. King, Tulane University; Mary Sauer, Indiana University-Purdue University Indianapolis; and Jennifer W. Spirko, North Carolina State University. I am grateful as well to Peggy L. Richards from the University of Akron, who helped with the identification of new student essays and key Internet revisions.

I

An Introduction to Argument

AN EXTENDED DEFINITION

If you grew up with siblings, or if you and your parents had a particularly stormy relationship during your adolescence, you may think you know all there is to know about argument. And you may be right, if you understand the word *argument* to mean a verbal battle where reason is absent and agreement rarely reached. A teenager engaged in this kind of argument with her mother might proceed as follows:

> Mom, I don't believe you! You are so unfair! Why can't I stay out 'til three? You never let me do anything fun. None of my friends has a curfew. How do you think it feels to be the only one who has to leave a party early? Everybody thinks it's ridiculous, and I bet they're all really glad they don't have you for a mother.

The unpleasant and usually unproductive practice illustrated in this example is not the subject of this book. In fact, the kind of argument focused on in these pages is almost the exact opposite of the preceding illustration. Of concern here is the formal, traditional meaning of *argument:* the process of establishing, through the presentation of appropriate evidence, the certainty or likelihood of a particular point or position (what we call the *claim*).

Another daughter, using the principles of traditional argument, might make the following case about her curfew:

> Mom, I would really like to stay at this party tonight until it's over. I know you have a problem with my being out late, and I understand you're concerned about my welfare. But I'm eighteen now, I'll be leaving for college next month, and maybe it's time you let me start testing my own judgment. You and I both know I'm not going to do anything stupid, and I

I

would really like to get some practice making my own decisions about my comings and goings.

While there is no guarantee that Daughter 2 would succeed with such an argument, it *is* a reasonable argument. Daughter 2 is acknowledging her mother's chief concerns and citing a sensible reason for lifting the curfew: she needs some practice at being grown up while still in the safety of her home environment. Daughter 1, on the other hand, has a lot to learn about making her point successfully; indeed, she commits about every foul imaginable in reasonable argument, including insulting her mother, irrelevantly and probably inaccurately appealing to crowd behavior ("None of my friends has a curfew"), and failing to offer any sensible reason why her mother should change her mind.

Daughter 2's request is an oral argument, and the subject of this book is written argument; yet the principles and practices are essentially the same. The objective of each is to gain agreement about a point through the use of reasonable evidence. When you think about it, much of the writing you will do in college and in your careers following college falls under this definition. Research papers, lab reports, literary interpretations, case studies—all these forms of writing seek to convince an audience (your professor) of the reasonableness of certain conclusions. All these forms of writing, as well as application letters, instructional manuals, and corporate annual reports, are built around the simple objective of making a point.

An argument, whether written or oral, is different from an opinion. An *opinion* is based not so much on evidence as on belief, intuition, or emotion. Argument, on the other hand, is a position supported by clear thinking and reasonable evidence, with a secure connection to solid facts. While arguments rarely prove a conclusion to be absolutely true, they do demonstrate the probability of that conclusion. Opinions tend to be expressions of personal taste that have not been tested by the application of reasonable principles. Your opinion may be that history is a more interesting subject than literature, or that yellow is prettier than red, but these remain only opinions until they are thoughtfully and fully justified.

Effective arguments are ethical as well as reasonable. They make their points openly and honestly, avoiding underhanded methods and false promises, and seeking to remove ambiguity rather than exploit it. We make arguments in order to advance a reasonable position, not to trick a reader into serving our self-interest. As writers of ethical arguments, we recognize the influence that skilled writing can exert over credulous or ignorant readers, and we are committed to exercising that influence reasonably and responsibly.

Of course, what constitutes a reasonable and responsible argument is sometimes up for grabs. When they argue, people disagree about basic assumptions, beliefs, and values, and those disagreements affect their understanding of what is reasonable. Daughter 2 in the previous example is working from the assumption that children should be encouraged to behave maturely. This seemingly inarguable assumption leads her to the conclusion that she should be allowed to exercise her own judgment about curfew. But perhaps her mother believes it is a parent's responsibility to protect her child from harm—another seemingly inarguable assumption. This reasonable assumption leads her to conclude that she cannot put her child at risk by lifting her curfew. Both daughter and mother are being reasonable, but their differing beliefs take them in two very different directions.

So this book will not be able to define what constitutes a reasonable argument for every writer, every audience, and every occasion. But it can introduce you to some concepts, processes, and tools that will help you make informed and effective decisions about how to construct your own arguments. And the many writing samples included at the end of most chapters will demonstrate how the principles and practices of formal argument carry over into a wide variety of writing contexts.

THE CLASSES OF ARGUMENT

Once you begin paying attention to the writing you do for school and work, you will notice how frequently your assignments fit within the definition of argument. You may also notice that the claims, or propositions, of these arguments tend to fall into certain patterns. Papers in economics or history courses may tend to concentrate on identifying the causes of certain events, whereas lab reports in biology or physics focus on describing a particular process and interpreting its results. In fact, argument can be divided into four classes: (1) factual arguments, (2) causal arguments, (3) evaluations, and (4) recommendations. These classes are distinguished both by the type of claim being argued and the degree of agreement expected from the reader.

Factual arguments try to convince an audience that a certain condition or event actually exists or has existed. Factual arguments, though they sound quite simple, are the most ambitious type of argument, for they try to convince readers of the truth or factuality of a claim. Those laboratory reports from biology or physics are examples of factual arguments, and their purpose is to convince their reader (usually a professor) that certain steps were taken and certain things actually happened.

Causal arguments—often found within those economics or history papers—try to convince readers that one event or condition caused another or is likely to cause another in the future. A paper identifying the complex economic reasons for the 1987 stock market crash would be a causal argument. Causal arguments can only rarely claim truth or certainty; most are judged successful if they establish a certain cause or future effect as *probable*.

Evaluations, or **evaluative** arguments, make value judgments. The film critics Roger Ebert and Richard Roeper are in the business of oral evaluations, as they share their judgments about the quality of recent films with their television audience. Because evaluations are often tied up in personal tastes and opinions, they are the hardest of all arguments to make successfully; nevertheless, they *can* be reasonable and effective.

Finally, **recommendations,** as their name suggests, try to get readers to *do* something, to follow a suggested course of action. While the other three classes of arguments aim for armchair agreement, most recommendations want the reader's agreement to be translated into action.

This book will take up the principles and practices of each argument class in isolation from the others, but you should realize from the outset that many of the writing assignments you will do for this course, for other courses, and on the job will *combine* these classes. In fact, the most common type of argument is the combined, or *hybrid,* argument.

ARGUMENT THROUGH IMAGE

An argument's success depends on many things: the clarity and exactness of its claim, the appropriateness and adequacy of its supporting evidence, and the particular *image* it projects. Image is the total impression a reader gets by reading your writing, and it is composed of a number of elements. Among these is the writing *style,* which consists of word choice, sentence length and structure, and the writer's tone of voice. Other elements of image include grammar, punctuation, neatness of the page, and quality of graphics. Together, these elements compose an overall impression of the writer and the work that will influence the reader's final acceptance or rejection of the argument. A positive image will help to secure the reader's confidence, respect, and attention; a negative image inevitably gets in the way of the agreement that all arguments seek from their readers.

Consider the example of an application letter for a job. Let's say that you are the head of the work-study program at your college, the person responsible for placing students in campus jobs. You have whittled the pool of applicants for the desirable job of dean's assistant down to two applicants: Jon Marshall and Becky Quinn. Both students have comparable academic qualifications, and both have been highly recommended by faculty and former employers. Becky's application letter is a well-organized, neatly typed business letter that carefully lists and develops Becky's qualifications for the job. Jon's letter also contains his qualifications, but it is filled with misspellings and faulty punctuation, it addresses you by your first name, and it has a grease spot on the upper-right corner. All other things being equal, which candidate is likely to have the edge? Which image better argues the writer's suitability for the job?

THE ARGUMENT PROCESS

It is one thing to recognize the prevalence of argument in the writing you do but quite another actually to create effective written arguments. While this book contains no single blueprint or recipe for writing effective arguments, it will suggest a practical process, as well as theoretical principles, that will help you reach the desired product of an effective written argument. Unless you are extraordinarily gifted—one of those rare students who can produce a perfectly acceptable essay in a single sitting—your writing process will consist of at least three broad stages: forming the argument, supporting the argument, and reviewing the argument.

In order to explain and illustrate these stages, we have created the hypothetical case of Rob Wade, a journalism major with the ambition of becoming a radio sports announcer—the Vin Sculley of the twenty-first century. In this age of high-tech video, you may find Rob's ambition a bit old-fashioned, but it is based on his belief that television is ruining sports for the American public. After watching the television coverage of the 1998 Winter Olympics in Nagano, Japan, and the 1997 World Series between the Florida Marlins and the Cleveland Indians, Rob's convictions have grown so powerful that he feels compelled to communicate them to a large audience. He decides to kill two birds with one stone: his professor has assigned a "Letter to the Editor" as part of his journalism portfolio, and Rob plans to use this requirement to communicate his strong disapproval of television sports coverage. Let's watch how Rob moves through the three stages of argument composition as he creates his letter.

Forming the Argument

Forming your argument consists of discovering a motive for writing, identifying an audience to address, and discovering and sharpening the point or points to be argued.

Most successful arguments originate in the writer's strong personal interest, which often includes a desire to change the status quo. The origin of Rob's letter to the editor, his *motive* for writing it, is his long and growing discomfort with television sports coverage. He is disappointed in this coverage, angry at how it packages sports for the public; the desire to communicate these feelings and to remedy the harm he sees being done are powerful motives that will energize his writing.

Once Rob has decided to act on these motives, he needs to think seriously about where he would like his letter to be published—in the school newspaper, the city newspaper, the *New York Times,* or *Sports Illustrated?* This decision must be made before he begins writing; otherwise he will lack the necessary sense of audience. *Audience* is an inescapable consideration in writing, yet writers often underestimate its importance, forgetting that argument always consists of one person addressing another person, or a group of people. In Rob's case, a letter to the editor of the school newspaper, whose readers consist largely of young men and women in their late teens and early twenties, would be very different from a letter to the editor of *Sports Illustrated,* whose readers are typically educated males of all ages. Also, *Sports Illustrated* will be more selective in choosing which letters to publish than the school paper is likely to be. Regardless of where Rob decides to send his letter, his argument will gain focus and immediacy if he has a clear sense that he is writing to a particular audience, with particular backgrounds, expectations, values, and beliefs.

Rob also must be clear from the outset about the exact point or points he plans to argue. Sure, he knows he wants to attack television sports coverage, but he will soon find that such a goal is too vague and too emotional to inform what must be a clear and reasonable argument. Before he starts writing, he'll need to compose a clearly focused statement of the point or points he wants his readers to agree with. In most arguments, such a statement is a one- to three-sentence summary of the argument's conclusion--called the *claim*. Some claims come to writers early and easily in the writing process, whereas others are the result of considerable reading, thinking, and narrowing. Though Rob knows generally what he wants to write about, it will take him some time to develop a claim that will interest his readers, that will be clear, and that he can reasonably support.

After more thinking than he had anticipated, Rob finally comes up with the following as his working claim: "While television coverage of sporting events allows us to be armchair spectators of exciting athletic contests that we would otherwise never see, we are paying a price for the convenience of this coverage. For what we are watching from our comfortable vantage point is glossy, high-tech artifice, not *real* sports."

Supporting the Claim

Having identified his claim and his audience, Rob now must decide how to support that claim. An argument's *support* is all the material that turns a tentative claim into a justified conclusion. Support is the most important component of argument. Without adequate and suitable support, a claim remains merely a hunch or an opinion; with appropriate support, it becomes a sound and credible conclusion.

At the very least, Rob can support his claim through his own viewing experience, which is, after all, what led him to the claim. But he's pretty sure that one person's experience is not enough to support an argument, so he knows he has some work to do. Identifying the class of his argument will help Rob select appropriate support, because certain kinds of support tend to apply to certain classes of argument. After careful consideration of his claim, and a thorough review of the four classes to which it might belong, he decides that his claim introduces an evaluative argument: it is making a negative judgment about the quality of television sports coverage.

This identification will help him, but there is more to selecting support than matching it to the class of the argument he is making. Rob will also need to ensure that the relationship between his claim and its support will be *reasonable,* that it will accord with the principles of formal and informal logic. So he will review carefully the material in Chapter 5 of this book, which presents these principles.

Reviewing the Argument

The product of these three steps—identifying an audience, composing a claim, and selecting appropriate support—will be a first version, or *draft*, of Rob's argument. As a journalism major, Rob has a fair amount of writing experience; he knows how difficult it is to evaluate your own writing, particularly when you have no distance from it. So, as he always tries to do, he puts his first draft away for a couple of days, so that when he returns to it, he has a fresh perspective that allows him to see problems in style and organization and reasoning that he hadn't noticed two days ago.

While getting distance from his argument will help to freshen his perspective, there is no fresher perspective than that of a second party who is unfamiliar with the work. In his writing classes, Rob has learned how well the process of "peer reviewing" works. As the name suggests, peer review is getting a friend or classmate or coworker to read your writing before you submit it to your professor, or, in Rob's case, for publication review. Peer review works best when you ask your reviewers to consider certain questions as they read. In the case of Rob's argument, these questions might be listed as follows: Does the argument effectively address its intended audience? Is its claim completely clear, and does it stick to that claim throughout? Is the supporting material reasonable and relevant to the claim? Does the argument project a positive image of its writer? Does the argument convince its audience? Friendly readers of your writing can identify problems and suggest solutions that you yourself are too close to the writing to see. Peer review is not cheating; it is not the same thing as getting someone else's answers to a calculus test. Peer review is a perfectly acceptable form of collaboration, providing an invaluable supplement to the writing process that the writer alone simply cannot supply: a *reader's* perspective. As a college student, Rob is lucky to have plenty of reader perspectives to call on. And his experience tells him that he would be foolish to ignore them, that without this collaboration, the revision process might become nothing more than superficial editing for spelling, punctuation, and grammatical errors. While editing is a necessary part of the review process, it is the final "spit-and-polish" step; revising often entails significant changes.

One addition that Rob will make to the first draft during the revision process is composing an introduction and conclusion. Like many writers, he finds it difficult to write interesting and representative introductions right out of the gate; the problem is partly psychological (first paragraphs are always the hardest) and partly practical (he won't know the exact content of the argument until he has finished a first draft). Likewise, it makes little sense to labor over a conclusion if the content of the first draft is going to be changed substantially during the revision process.

CONCLUSION

Having provided an extended definition of argument and a brief overview of the writing process, let's proceed to a detailed description of the steps involved in creating effective written argument, the reasoning principles that inform effective argument, and the special elements and requirements of each of the four classes of argument.

SUMMARY

An Introduction to Argument

- Written argument attempts to convince the reader of the writer's point of view, using reasonable and ethical methods. Most effective writing contains some form of argument.

- The *image* projected by the argument is the overall impression the writer makes on the reader. Image is created through writing style; correct spelling, punctuation, and grammar; and the physical appearance of the document.

- Argument can be divided into four classes: arguments of fact, cause, evaluation, and recommendation.

- While the process of argument composition varies from writer to writer, most writers follow these three stages: (1) forming an argument, which can consist of discovering a motive for writing and identifying an audience to address, discovering and sharpening a position, and developing an appropriate style; (2) supporting the argument; and (3) reviewing the argument, which can include considering the image projected by your argument, making substantial additions or deletions to a first draft, and adding an introduction and conclusion.

SUGGESTIONS FOR WRITING (1.1)

1. If you are planning on finding a summer job or a part-time job while in school, you will probably need to write a letter of application to your prospective employer. Give yourself some practice by writing a one-page letter of application for a real or made-up job. Try following a sequence like the following:

   Paragraph 1: State the position desired and your primary qualification for it.

   Paragraph 2: Expand on the primary qualification.

   Paragraph 3 and following: Develop other qualifications for the job.

   Concluding paragraph: State your willingness to answer questions and be available for an interview.

   Before writing, be sure to identify to yourself the needs and expectations of your reader—that is, your prospective employer. Then be sure your letter addresses these needs and expectations through such elements as the content of the letter, its level of formality, and the overall image projected by the letter.

2. Find an editorial in your local newspaper or online. With two or three classmates, analyze your responses to the editorial. Do all members of the group find the argument convincing? Why or why not? Do your disagreements reveal anything about your different concerns and values as readers? What im-

age is projected by the editorial? Does the image appeal to all members of your group? Why or why not? Are there ways that the editorial could be changed to be effective for all members of your group?

3. With a small group of your classmates, review an essay examination that one of you has written recently. As a group, identify the expectations of the professor giving the exam. To what extent does the claim, the support, and the overall image of this one essay meet these expectations? As a group, rewrite the essay so that all of these considerations are met.

2

Where Writing Begins: Motives and Audience

Most of us write because we have to, not because we want to. As a college student, you write a research paper because your political science professor has assigned it; a sales rep writes a monthly report because her boss requires it; a mother writes a note explaining her son's absence from school because school policy insists on it. Yet the best writing, the kind we read voluntarily and the kind that endures over centuries, springs from some source other than mere necessity. And even when necessity drives great writing, other motives are also at work. Shakespeare wrote *Hamlet* to make a living, Dickens wrote *David Copperfield* to feed his many children, but these writers were surely inspired by some motive beyond making money.

MOTIVES FOR WRITING

What are these other motives for writing? They are powerful intellectual and emotional drives of enormous variety—from the desire to create a lasting record of some important experience (think of Anne Frank's *Diary of a Young Girl*), to the yearning to express love or joy (a common motive for music through the ages from Renaissance musicians to Tracy Chapman), to the need to disagree strongly or even complain (Harriet Beecher Stowe's *Uncle Tom's Cabin* was written from a deep disagreement with the institution of American slavery). One common motive for writing, especially for writing arguments, is our drive to resolve personal dissonance. *Dissonance* is actually a musical term meaning an inharmonious arrangement of tones that the listener wants resolved into harmony.

On a more general level, the term *dissonance* suggests tension or uneasiness. It is a good word for describing the mismatch between the way we want life to be and the way it is. Dissonance drove the angry voice of the prophets in the Old Testament, the determined defiance of the Declaration of Independence, and the heartfelt challenges in the *Communist Manifesto*. Driven by intense dissatisfaction with the way things were, the writers sought a resolution of this tension by expressing it in writing.

The Value of Dissonance

The principle of dissonance is a useful starting point whenever you are at a loss to discover an argument worth making. If you find yourself doing nothing but staring at a blank page when you are supposed to be writing a ten-page paper for an English composition class, try asking yourself the following questions: "What really bothers me? What do I wish were different? What could be done to improve the situation?" The cause of the dissonance may be anything from parking problems on campus, to the status of women in large corporations, to the chemistry professor you don't understand.

If you begin the process of forming your argument by identifying a cause of dissonance, you will find both a subject to write about and a position to take on that subject (i.e., a claim). Because this position comes from your own interests and experience, developing it into an argument will be interesting to you, and if it's interesting to you, it's likely to be lively and interesting to your reader.

Let's assume that in an English composition class, you are asked to write about the impact of technology on education. An obvious position to take would be that the computer and associated technologies like educational CD-ROMs and the World Wide Web enhance the learning process for children and young adults. A solid position, certainly, but a bit predictable: probably 90 percent of your class will take this or a similar position. Plus, though you know it's a defensible position, it's not one that you find particularly exciting. So put that tentative claim on a back burner, and take some time to probe the general topic for personal dissonance. What discomforts, uneasiness, or inconveniences have you experienced from the new educational technology? Perhaps you were an avid reader as a child, someone who treasured the physical properties of books—the texture of the pages, the shape and heft of the volumes, the warm look of a filled book shelf. As you think about it, you realize that as amazing as educational technology is, it threatens the reader's important physical relationship to books, to tangible texts. Reading about the Byzantine Empire or cell mitosis from a computer screen just isn't the same as learning about them from a volume taken down from your living-room shelf. This could be the beginning of an interesting argument about the losses incurred when screens replace pages, when electronic texts make the comforting tangibility of books obsolete.

This approach has a number of advantages. First, it promises to be different, unusual. In writing, an unusual approach, as long as it is intelligent and not merely eccentric, is often effective: it gets people's attention. Second, working from dissonance lets you get to the core of your discomfort by discovering reasons for it. Turning an opinion into an argument is a great way to challenge and define your unexamined views. And finally, focusing on problems is more useful and productive than ignoring them; neither you nor your readers can improve a situation until you have identified and accounted for its problems.

Don't take this advice to mean that you should turn every writing assignment into an occasion for complaining. Searching for dissonance should help you learn to be a critical and discerning thinker, not a cynic or whiner. And one of the hallmarks of a discerning thinker is the ability to recognize value where it exists: a student writing on the disadvantages of educational technology should acknowledge its obvious positive impacts. To pretend that they don't exist will only make the argument seem nearsighted and unfair. Of course, sometimes balance and fairness are not appropriate; the Declaration of Independence would be much less effective if it presented a balanced view of the British government. But extreme situations calling for one-sided appeals are relatively rare.

Writing Arguments That Are Meaningful to You

Of course, not every writing assignment will allow you to call on your own feelings and opinions; sometimes you are required to write about topics that simply don't interest you. Yet there are ways to make even those assignments more relevant to your interests and experience. The next time you find yourself working with an uninspiring assignment, try these three suggestions for making that assignment more meaningful to you:

1. *Search for the most interesting facets of the assignment.* If you must write on the American Civil War—a topic that holds little interest for you—try to find one aspect of the war that is at least potentially more meaningful to you than any other. You may need to do some research, but your time is well spent if you get excited about the topic. If you are interested in medicine, for example, why not write about the medical treatment of the wounded during the war?

2. *Don't lie.* Express only those opinions you honestly believe in. If you are unsure of your claim despite your best efforts to become comfortable with it, don't hesitate to use qualifiers such as *perhaps, probably, usually,* or *likely.* Never be lukewarm when you can be hot or cold, but don't take a position simply for the sake of taking it. A qualified claim, such as "Athletes who train with professional coaches usually perform better than athletes who do not," is preferable to the unqualified statement "Athletes who train with professional coaches perform better than athletes who do not" because there are bound to be some exceptions to this rule.

3. *Don't be pompous.* You don't want your writing to be too informal and colloquial, but you also don't want to sound like someone you're not—like your professor or boss, for instance, or the Rhodes scholar teaching assistant. Good writing is always genuine writing.

These suggestions apply to any assigned writing, from a monthly sales report to a memo on improvements in office procedures, to a lab report, to an anthropology research paper. You may not have chosen to do the writing in the first place, but energy spent making the project your own will result in a more lively and credible argument.

ACTIVITIES (2.1)

1. Look at the last four things you have written: letters, e-mail, reports, essays, memos, and so on. What were your reasons for writing them? How many of them were not written out of choice? Would these have been better if you had tried to write about what is important to you? Adjust the topic of one of these to make it more meaningful to you, and then rewrite it following the suggestions presented in the preceding part of the chapter.

2. List four aspects of your life or of the world around you that you wish were different. From these four aspects, derive tentative topics for essays.

THE IMPORTANCE OF AUDIENCE

When you prepare writing assignments for a college professor, you are usually writing for an audience of one: a professor who is a specialist in the subject of the paper, who has certain expectations of the paper, and who is obliged to read it carefully. Having such a predictable audience is actually a luxury to students, freeing them from one of the most important steps in argument formation: identifying the audience. But in most of the writing you will do outside an academic setting, you won't be able to ignore this step. Written argument assumes a relationship between a writer and a reader: the writer speaks and the reader listens and reacts. As a writer, your first and most basic goal is simply to engage your audience—to get their attention. Taking the time before you write to consider your audience will help you avoid boring or offending or confusing them. Considering your audience will also add focus and purpose to your writing: you will write with an imaginary "reader over your shoulder," as poet Robert Graves put it, which is vastly preferable to writing into a void.

Audience consideration is important to all writing, but particularly to arguments. Since the purpose of all arguments is to convince someone of something, knowing who that "someone" is is crucial. An argument seeking to convince college students of the need for a tuition hike would proceed very differently from an argument seeking to convince the school's board of trustees of the same claim.

Developing an accurate sense of audience depends in part on experience, but you can sharpen this sensitivity by considering the following questions each time you prepare to write: *Who* is the audience? *Why* will the audience read your argument? *What* should the audience be able to do after reading your argument? You should try to keep the answers to these questions in mind not only as you form the argument, but also as you write it.

Who Is the Audience?

Sometimes this question will be answered in terms of specific individuals (my supervisor, my prospective employer). More frequently, it is answered in terms of categories or groups of readers (readers of a certain magazine, users of a certain product, students in a particular class).

Having identified your audience, you will want to consider how familiar they are with the subject matter. Readers usually know much less than writers about the topic at hand; even readers in the same organization with similar education and experience may be unfamiliar with the subject matter of your report. With this in mind, consider where you might provide background information, what terminology you might define, what difficult concepts you might explain or illustrate. No matter how convincing your argument is, if it baffles its readers it's not going to succeed. Most readers, if they have any choice in the matter, will stop reading a difficult argument before they will struggle through its unfamiliar language and concepts. If you don't know how much your audience is likely to know, or if they have different levels of knowledge, you are better off providing too much explanation than too little. Most people prefer feeling superior to feeling ignorant.

Finally, audience identification also includes considering your readers' probable disposition to your claim. Are they likely to be friendly or hostile to your position? The answer to this question will influence a number of your argument strategies. For example, if you expect your audience to be hostile to your claim, you might give them credit for their views at the outset. In recommending an expensive federal crime prevention program to an audience already frustrated by the cost of crime to taxpayers, acknowledging and legitimizing that frustration may help to neutralize their hostility: "There is something wildly unjust about living in fear of crime *and* having to pay for that crime as well." Once you have conceded that your audience probably won't want to pay more to prevent crime, you could proceed to argue for a new crime bill that, while temporarily costly, offers an excellent chance of reducing crime and its costs to the taxpayer. Telling the audience that they are selfish or pigheaded or shortsighted will not gain you much agreement, but expressing a genuine understanding of their frustration may convince them that your motives and theirs are essentially the same.

When you know that someone in your audience holds a view completely different from your claim, or even when you know that there is a good counterargument to your position, you may need to include a *refutation* of that opposing argument. (Refutations are discussed in Chapter 4, under "Addressing the Counterargument.") Even if you don't refute such a counterargument directly, acknowledging that you are aware of its existence can convince your audience that you have taken time to learn about the issue.

If you are confident that your audience shares your views, your work will be easier, but don't let yourself become sloppy, or you may lose the agreement you started with. To guard against triteness and predictability, try playing devil's advocate (appearing to support the opposing view), or expressing your central claim outrageously, or reminding your audience of the dangers of knee-jerk responses.

If you have no idea how your audience might respond to your claim, perhaps you can get some information about their general beliefs and values, which you can then appeal to in the course of your argument. Some arguments—particularly evaluations and recommendations—depend on successful appeals to readers' values and beliefs. An argument written for the *New Left Journal* recommending the recitation of the Pledge of Allegiance in public schools will succeed only if it appeals to a value held by the *Journal's* politically liberal readers. These readers will not be moved by a "Your country: love it or leave it" approach. But if your claim rests on the principle of free choice, arguing that every student should have the choice of saying the pledge, your argument may succeed with this difficult audience.

In considering these questions about your audience—who they are and what they know, think, and believe—you are considering audience psychology. But it is important that you understand your reasons for doing so. You are not going to the trouble to understand your audience so that you can manipulate them through underhanded, unreasonable, unethical methods. Rather, you are giving your good argument the best chance at success by trying to ensure that the audience will approach it fairly and reasonably.

ACTIVITIES (2.2)

1. Examine a copy of *four* of the following and try to identify the probable audience for each. Estimate the level of education and the kinds of occupations each audience would probably have.

   Example: *Publications of the Modern Language Association* (PMLA). Level of education: usually at least some graduate education. Occupations: primarily graduate students in English or foreign language and literature and college-level instructors in these subjects.
   a. The *Wall Street Journal*
   b. *Time* magazine
   c. *Cosmopolitan*
   d. *People* magazine
   e. The *New England Journal of Medicine*
   f. *Popular Mechanics*
   g. *Soldier of Fortune* magazine
   h. Online "Instructor's Manual" for the Apple Macintosh computer (or some other personal computer)
   i. *Mad* magazine
   j. The *New York Times*

2. The following passage is from a brochure on how employees can use statistics to improve the quality of their organization's products. The intended audience for this brochure is company employees with a seventh-grade reading level and no previous knowledge of statistics. How well does this passage communicate with its intended audience? If you believe the passage would be difficult for its intended audience, rewrite it so that it addresses its audience more appropriately.

   Quality can be best maintained by preventive action in advance of complete tool wear or predictable machine maintenance. If we check characteristics of parts on a sampling basis as they are produced, it is better than sorting through a bin of hundreds of parts looking for the defective parts and then trying to determine which parts can be salvaged.

   Collecting and analyzing data on current operations is essential in supplier and company plants. By studying the data, the causes of defects for each main quality characteristic can be investigated and determined. Appropriate solutions, including redesign or reprocessing, can be developed.

Once problems are identified, a decision can be made whether to analyze past data, to collect new information, or a combination of both.

Why Will the Audience Read the Argument?

Readers can be divided into two broad groups: those who *have* to read the argument (a professor, a supervisor, etc.) and those who are free to read or not read,
depending on the argument's appeal (think of the fickle magazine browsing you
do in waiting rooms). As part of your preliminary consideration of audience, it
pays to determine why your audience will read your argument—because they
have to or because they want to?

If your readers are a captive audience—if they have no choice about reading
your argument—you are not freed from making your writing interesting and engaging. In fact, the captive audience puts considerable pressure on the writer to
be engaging. The professor with piles of student compositions to read, or admis-
sions committee members with hundreds of application essays to evaluate, are
likely to be bored and irritable by the time they come to your composition or essay. Knowing this, you should put more, not less, effort into getting and keeping
their attention. In some cases, this may mean getting to the critical issues quickly
and directly, or it may mean taking care to follow directions exactly, or putting a
unique spin on your argument that will distinguish it from all the others your audience has to read.

When your audience is a purely voluntary one—readers of popular magazines,
for example—they may not approach your work bored and irritable, but they are
under no obligation to read further than your title if they don't find your argument
interesting. Writers who write for daily or weekly periodicals are continually looking for "hooks" that will attract their readers to subjects that are already quite familiar. For example, in the Summer Olympics of 1996, Kerri Strugs's courageous
vault landing received a landslide of positive attention from the international press.
Patricia Dalton, a weekly columnist, wrote one of the hundreds of articles on the
Kerri Strugs "moment." But she distinguished her article from the rest by opening
with a very different take on Strugs's moment of valor: "I wanted to shout to the
millions of kids watching [Kerri's heroics] on TV two weeks ago: This might not be
good for Kerri—and it certainly isn't good for you." A position so different from the
popular one was far more likely to get and keep the reader's attention than one that
took the more predictable route of praise and applause.

ACTIVITIES (2.3)

The following audiences are likely either to be uninterested in or hostile to the following claims. Working with two or three students in your class, rewrite the
claims, and add whatever additional sentences would help to engage audience
attention. Be prepared to justify your changes to the rest of the class.

1. Parents of a college student: Tuition must be increased.
2. A social worker: Because of budget cuts, your caseload will increase.

3. An African-American woman: Affirmative action results in reverse discrimination.

4. An inner-city high school principal: Metal detectors are unconstitutional.

5. A software specialist: Our society looks at too many screens.

What Should the Audience Be Able to Do After Reading the Argument?

All arguments want something from their readers. At the very least, they want to convince their readers that the claim and its supporting material constitute a reasonable position, even though readers may not agree with it completely. Many arguments are more ambitious, looking for their readers' full agreement, which may mean changing readers' minds. The most ambitious arguments want not only full agreement from their readers, but also action taken on the basis of this full agreement. What you expect from your audience will influence the nature and extent of your supporting material as well as the overall tone of your argument.

For example, if you were trying to convince an audience that fraternity term paper files on your campus are a problem, you would argue why and to what extent they are a problem. But if you wanted your audience to take action to solve this problem, your argument would need to include specific steps to be taken, such as applying pressure on fraternity councils, setting up a more rigorous honor code for students, and encouraging faculty to change term paper assignments yearly. Including these steps means convincing your audience that they are likely to be effective: fraternity councils will monitor the problem more carefully if they are in danger of losing campus support; term paper files will be useless if assignments are not repeated from year to year; and so on. Arguments that seek to inspire the reader to action should be specific about the action proposed, show the connection between the claim and the proposed action, and convince the reader that the action will lead, or at least will probably lead, to the desired changes.

The expectations you have of your readers should also influence your argument's tone. If you want to convince gently, the tone can be mild: "Members of the International Students Club need to consider an alternative to their international banquet for raising money for travel." If you intend to exhort, the tone should be more forceful, as in Winston Churchill's famous address to the British people in their darkest days of World War II: "We shall fight on the beaches, we shall fight on the landing grounds, we shall fight in the fields and in the streets, we shall fight in the hills." If you want to command (in which case, you are no longer seeking reader agreement), you can afford to be very blunt: "No smoking is allowed in this computer room."

ACTIVITIES (2.4)

For which of the following occasions should the argument spell out the actions it wishes its readers to take? Why?

1. **Claim:** The flood of no-fat and low-fat packaged foods is turning a generation of kids into low-fat anorexics.
   Audience: High school dietitian.

2. **Claim:** Our college needs wireless computer capability.
   Audience: President or "Information" Administrator of your college.

3. **Claim:** The new mandatory bicycle helmet law is an infringement of personal liberty, depriving the citizen of his or her right of self-determination.
   Audience: Listeners of a local call-in talk show.

4. **Claim:** Bicycle helmets should be made mandatory in this state, just like motorcycle helmets.
   Audience: Your state legislature representative.

5. **Claim:** While I have had some academic difficulties over the past year, my commitment to receiving a college degree and my newfound understanding of study strategies will contribute to my eventual academic success, if only you will agree to waive my suspension.
   Audience: Dean of your college.

SUMMARY

Where Writing Begins

- Dissonance—the mismatch between the way we want life to be and the way it is—is a motive for effective arguments.

- When you write, try to write about what is important to you, expressing only those opinions you honestly believe in and avoiding pomposity.

- Before you write, consider these three questions:

  –*Who* is the audience?

  –*Why* will the audience read the argument?

  –*What* should the audience be able to do after reading the argument?

SUGGESTIONS FOR WRITING (2.5)

1. From your list of topics from the second activity in Activity (2.1) at the end of the first section of this chapter, "Motives for Writing," select one of the topics and write a two- to three-page essay proposing a solution to the problem that bothers you.

2. Write a letter to your parents asking them for something you know they won't want to give you—for example, a raise in your allowance, a charge card, or a round-trip ticket to Europe. What steps can you take to neutralize the objections you know they are going to have?

3. Examine the last report or essay you wrote, and answer the following questions: Who was your audience? Why would they read what you wrote? What did you expect them to do after they finished reading? How well does that report or essay, when viewed in light of these questions, communicate with its intended audience? What changes would you make?

4. To recognize how audience affects the tone and content of an argument, write an informal evaluation of one of your current professors for your student e-mail conference system; then write a one-page evaluation of that instructor for the instructor himself or herself.

5. Attend a lecture or speech sponsored by your college or university. Then write a letter to the speaker evaluating her or his sensitivity to the audience.

3

The Claim

You've discovered a subject and motive for your argument, and you've considered some key questions about your audience. Now you are ready to begin focusing your argument. Focusing—clearly defining the center and extent of your argument—occurs throughout the writing process, from discovering a motive to revising a final draft. This chapter concerns an early and critical stage in the focusing process: formulating, modifying, and positioning your argument's claim.

While some writers compose their claims before they begin writing, others let their claims evolve during an exploratory first draft, clarifying and modifying as they write. You can experiment with the sequence that works best for you, but regardless of how and when you reach your claim, your argument is not focused until you can summarize its principal point within a few sentences.

HOW CLAIMS WORK

An argument's claim is a short summary of its central point or points. All arguments have at least one claim; some longer arguments have more than one. Usually, the claim is stated directly, but sometimes, it is only implied by its supporting material. Regardless of where and whether it appears in an argument, the claim shapes and moves the argument, giving it structure and energy.

Claims can be short and tightly packed, as in the statement "America's youth are entirely apolitical," or they can be long and intricate, reflecting the argument's structure as well as its main points: "Because a capitalist system rewards aggressiveness, competitiveness, and intelligence, it is an almost perfect economic extension of Darwinism. In a capitalist society, the 'fittest' get rich; the unfit stay poor."

Crystal-clear claims are extremely useful to readers. All readers, whatever their levels of interest, knowledge, and intelligence, approach an unfamiliar manuscript clueless about its content and direction. An unequivocal, succinct statement of an argument's chief point or points alerts them to the argument's goal and prepares them to understand the relationship between the parts and the whole.

Good claims also help readers evaluate an argument. Knowing the proposition to be argued, they are equipped to judge how successfully it has been made. A claim such as "Independent Counsel Kenneth Starr's investigation of President Clinton, which cost United States citizens over $60,000,000, certainly should make Congress think twice about setting boundaries and time limits on special investigations in the future" provides a benchmark against which readers can judge the supporting argument. On the other hand, a claim such as "The impeachment procedures were interesting" is too vague, too unfocused, to serve as a useful benchmark.

While claims can be discovered or changed at virtually any point in the writing process, you will probably find that formulating a tentative working claim early in the process is quite helpful. Such a preliminary claim will help you determine the kinds of supporting evidence you will need, will guide your argument's organization and direction, and will keep you from darting off on tangents.

Finding a Claim

Many student writers are insecure about their ability to come up with a position worth arguing. But even experienced, mature writers with a wealth of experience and opinions often have to work to find a claim. For inexperienced and experienced writers alike, claims tend to evolve gradually from reading and thinking (at both the conscious and the unconscious levels) about the subject or from personal discomfort with a particular situation or issue.

On occasion, however, the process of developing a claim can be short-circuited. In many college classes, particularly introductory ones, claims are actually assigned. Students in English composition courses, for example, are often assigned a particular thesis (claim) to develop ("Write a two-page essay supporting your view of the effectiveness of student orientation at this college"). And essay exams offer students at least the foundation of a claim. For example, the question "Was dropping the atom bomb in 1945 on Hiroshima and Nagasaki necessary to achieve Japan's surrender? Support your answer with specific reasons" dictates the form, though not the content, of the claim that will begin the essay: "Dropping the bomb was/was not necessary, for the following reasons."

And some writers do come to their work with their main point firmly in mind. But what usually happens to these seemingly lucky folks is that this main point gets modified, changed, and sometimes even reversed as they go about the business of developing and supporting it. And this is as it should be; clinging to a claim that clearly needs modifying can doom an argument at the outset. So if you find yourself passionately attached to a particular position at the beginning of the writing process, try to treat that position as a starting point, a tentative claim that will guide your research and thinking, not a commandment set in stone.

Some assignment topics cause problems because they are too vague. A literature student assigned a fifteen-page analysis of the early poetry of William Wordsworth will set out with little focus or sense of direction. A new employee asked to evaluate the product quality and cost-effectiveness of a particular supplier would probably be equally adrift.

How do such writers move from vague assignments like these to working claims that will give the developing argument some direction and discipline? There are many answers to this question, because coming up with a claim—indeed, the entire writing process—is a highly idiosyncratic business. Some writers logically deduce claims from the evidence, in Sherlock Holmes fashion, whereas others discover them unexpectedly while daydreaming or jogging or listening to music. Claims can be slowly and painfully dredged from the earth, or they can come like lightning from the sky.

When you find yourself doing more dredging than you'd like, consider the following suggestions:

1. Don't press to arrive at a claim prematurely. More time is wasted following up a forced, dead-end claim that eventually has to be scrapped than in thinking, reading, and taking notes as preparation for deciding exactly what your position is going to be.

2. Instead of rushing the claim during the preliminary research phase (and research can mean nothing more than tapping the contents of your own brain without ever opening a book), concentrate on gradually narrowing your topic. For example, if you're preparing to write a paper on the poetry of Wordsworth, your reading and thinking might lead you originally (and accidentally) in the direction of thematic content, then to the narrower concern of images of nature, then still more narrowly to the recollection of nature as an inspiration to poetry. By the time you have gathered material on this focused subject, you will not be far from imposing a particular point of view on the subject. This point of view on a focused topic will be your claim, which might be something like "Wordsworth as a poet was inspired by nature, but nature sifted through memory, not nature as it is immediately perceived." While you may have accumulated a lot of seemingly useless notes along the way, you should be saved the agony of distorting your paper to fit an unworkable claim you have discovered with too little consideration. As you are closing in on a claim, keep in mind that good claims are rarely too narrow, and that poor ones are often too broad.

3. In the early stages of writing, don't spend too much time polishing and refining your claim. At this stage, a claim needs a narrow topic and the expression of a definite attitude toward that topic. A good working claim could be no more than "Smoking in public places is harmful to everyone." Later, after the first draft, you can refine and shine, adding a summary of supporting reasons if necessary.

4. Today's computer technology offers valuable tools for narrowing a broad topic to a focused position. Most libraries have moved their card catalogs to computer databases and are now adding electronic catalogs and major bibliographic indexes stored in electronic format. You will probably also have access to the

Internet, which contains not only databases, but huge volumes of information in various forms. (Chapter 6 will discuss resource materials and steps to help evaluate credible sources.) Whether we are looking for books or articles, we get at the information we want through *keywords* or *descriptors*—words or brief phrases that describe our subject. Searching for information by keyword can give you good ideas for narrowing your topic.

Say you're planning to write an evaluative essay on the films of Stephen King, and you search several film indexes (e.g., *Film Research: A Critical Bibliography* or *Film Review Annual*), using *King, Stephen* as your descriptor. You get close to a hundred "hits" through this search, and you notice that many of the sources have to do with King's novels as well as his films. You become interested in the whole question of adaptation, so you search other film indexes using narrower descriptors like *King, Stephen, and adaptations* or, even more narrowly, *The Shining*. Through this early search for sources, you have imposed considerably more focus on your initial, broad topic—a focus that would soon lead to a working claim like "The true genius of Stephen King is in his ability to adapt the printed page to the medium of film."

Keeping Your Working Claim Flexible

As you proceed with a rough draft that works from a tentative claim, you may discover that the preliminary claim needs modification. Perhaps the thinking and research you have done on the subject have made you realize that your claim does not apply as widely as you thought, and that there are significant exceptions to your position. Be flexible enough to accept these discoveries and change your claim accordingly. Writing is not simply the recording of previously established thoughts but also a way of clarifying your thoughts, of discovering if what you meant to say can be said in a coherent and defensible way. If possible, take advantage of the guidance offered by a thoughtful claim, while remaining open to those discoveries to which writing and thinking can lead you.

Let's say you begin the composition process with a claim that arises fairly easily out of your own strong opinions about the issue of affirmative action. Your preliminary or working claim is "Jobs should be given to the most qualified applicant, not to the most qualified minority applicant. To reject the best candidate on the grounds of his or her majority status is unjust and inequitable." This claim statement not only summarizes your position toward affirmative action but also points to the main support for that position—that affirmative action is unjust and inequitable. In order to argue this evaluative claim convincingly, to convince your audience that one's minority or majority status is irrelevant to considerations of merit, you will need to demonstrate the injustices of affirmative action.

So far, so good. Even though you aren't personally aware of a wide range of cases, it should be easy to come up with examples of the basic unfairness of affirmative action. In the course of your reading, however, you keep coming up against the stubborn argument that majority candidates are often more qualified for jobs and educational opportunities because they are more educationally and economically privileged than members of minority groups. To reward the most qualified, this argument continues, is to perpetuate this tradition of unequal opportunity. You find this position persuasive and reasonable, though it doesn't change your central view that qualifications, not race, should determine one's success in the job market. Gradually, you realize that this is a more complicated issue than you had recognized; a hard-line position is not completely defensible.

You consider ignoring the counterargument and sticking to your original claim, but you conclude that your argument will actually be stronger if it reflects the ethical complexity of the issue and your awareness of the unfair advantage long given to the majority group. So you rewrite your working claim to read:

> In the United States, all men (and women) may be *created* equal, but for many, that birthright of equality is fleeting at best. Few would argue that, where women and minorities are concerned, inequality in economic and educational opportunity has been our national tradition. The affirmative action legislation of the 1960s was designed to redress the harms resulting from this indefensible tradition. Impeccable in its intent, affirmative action has been problematic in application: hiring on the basis of race and gender with secondary consideration to qualifications does not solve the problem of inequity; it merely changes the victims.

This new working claim is richer and more balanced than the first, reflecting your new understanding of the issue as well as your continuing disagreement with affirmative action laws.

The primary lesson to be learned from this example is that working claims should be seen as starting points, not as immutable conclusions; the thinking and writing processes will inevitably influence the starting point of an argument, shaping and modifying and in some cases even reversing the original position. Your final argument will benefit if you remain flexible about the original claim; always be prepared to alter it in the face of contrary evidence or new ideas.

ACTIVITIES (3.1)

1. With a small group of your classmates, select three of the following topics to work with. For each selected topic, work together to narrow the topic to one that could be written about in a seven- to ten-page essay. From this narrower topic, derive a working claim for this paper. Remember that the working claim is the claim with which you would begin to write the essay, though it might be refined or changed as you write.

   Example topic: The risks of cigarette smoking.
   Narrower topic: The health effects of cigarette smoking in public places.
   Working claim: Cigarette smoking in public places is harmful to everyone.
   a. Japanese automobiles
   b. The voucher system
   c. Women's rights
   d. College education
   e. Television
   f. Unemployment

g. Presidential elections
h. New York City
i. Careers
j. Popular music

2. With one of your classmates, agree on a very broad topic of interest to you both, for example, professional basketball, computer games, or a certain actor. Then conduct independent computer searches on the subject, progressively focusing it (and focusing your keywords) as you get a sense of the information available. When you have reached a focused topic that could be argued about in a five-page paper, compare that topic with your classmate's. How similar or different are the two? Retrace the evolution of your keywords for each other.

Positioning the Claim

Another important decision you'll have to make about your claim is where to place it in your argument. You can make this decision before, during, or even after your first draft, but whenever you make it, it's one that requires careful thought. Different placements will have different effects on your audience, in some cases influencing their ultimate acceptance of your argument. As long as you base your decision on audience consideration and the intended function of the claim, you can put the claim almost anywhere. There are two main points to consider in positioning your claim: first, what is the function of your claim? second, what is your audience's probable disposition toward your argument?

Claim Stated Up Front

Stating your claim within the first couple of paragraphs makes sense

- if your argument is complicated or the subject matter is unfamiliar to readers (an up-front claim will let your readers know what's coming)
- if your audience is likely to be comfortable with your argument (so that its claim will not alienate them at the outset)
- if your claim is particularly engaging, curious, or intriguing (an up-front claim will lure readers into your argument)

The following excerpt from an article on fund-raising in higher education, where the claim (in italics) appears after a brief introduction, illustrates the second and third of these conditions. Readers of the *New York Times* (where this article appeared) are not likely to object to the article's claim, though they may be intrigued by the argument's redefinition of the traditional practice of fund-raising.

As the last mortarboards are flung like Frisbees into the air and the last speaker winds up a peroration on endings and beginnings, at least one campus office marches on into summer on an unending mission: raising money.

The task is ancient but the tools get more modern all the time. Colleges and universities, long seen as aloof from the commercial crush of life, are increasingly willing to pull out all the stops in getting alumni to give.

It's still called fund-raising—or development or even institutional advancement. But it's getting to look a lot like marketing. ("Some Schools Won't Take No for an Answer," Janny Scott, the *New York Times*, June 19, 1994, section E, p. 3; emphasis added)

Claim Stated at the End of the Argument

Delaying your claim until the end of the argument can be effective

- when your audience may find the claim objectionable (readers who accept a claim's support as reasonable before they know precisely what the claim is may be less hostile to that claim once it is stated)
- when your evidence builds directly and inevitably toward your claim, which can then serve as your argument's conclusion

Let's say you write for your school newspaper. An example of the first instance would be your editorial recommending stricter enforcement of quiet hours in the dorm—a position that may not be welcome to all student readers. In this case, you can first present all the problems associated with the nightly bedlam in the dorms. Once you have established the seriousness of the problem, you can conclude the argument with your recommendation for stricter quiet hours. Having been convinced of the seriousness of the problems, your readers will be more likely to accept the final claim as necessary and logical.

Or to exemplify the second case, if you were reviewing a film for your newspaper, you might choose to describe various elements of the film first—acting, plot, cinematography—before summarizing these remarks with the inevitable statement of the central claim: "Find the time to see this film."

Unstated Claim in an Argument

You may choose to omit an explicit statement of your claim in situations like the following:

- when your readers will see red at your claim (because it is so bold or so objectionable) regardless of where you place it
- when the claim is very, very obvious
- when stating your claim will oversimplify your argument
- when stating your claim will break the momentum or shape of your argument

A wise mother might use this strategy in a letter counseling her college-age son to hit the books. She knows that outright directions won't work, but she might tell a story that implicitly makes her point—a story about an uncle who frittered away his college opportunities and always regretted it. She does not end her letter with the point "Don't be like Uncle Jake"; that would be too obvious, too heavy-handed. Instead, she lets her narrative speak for itself.

A word of caution, however, about omitting claims: make sure that you have a very good reason for using this tactic, and that the point or points of your argument are absolutely clear without being stated.

ACTIVITIES (3.2)

1. Read the following essays included at the end of Chapters 7 and 9: "I, Too, Am a Good Parent" (7); and "The Side Effects of Affirmative Action" (9). In a discussion with three or four classmates, identify the central claims and consider the reasons for their placement in each essay.

CLASSIFYING YOUR CLAIM

Once you have come up with a claim—even a tentative one—you'll need to identify the class it belongs to. Knowing at the outset of a first draft that you are working with a factual, causal, or evaluative claim or with a recommendation will simplify the gathering and presentation of support, since each class uses different kinds and arrangements of support. Recognizing your claim's class requires familiarity with the characteristics and functions of each class. The following section offers a full discussion of the different categories and examples of claims from each.

Factual Claims

The purpose of *factual claims* is to convince an audience that a certain statement is factual—that a given condition or phenomenon exists or has existed. The fact can be as basic as "Despite appearances, the sun is the center of our solar system, not the earth," or as unfamiliar as "In 1999, 78,092,940 people flew in and out of Atlanta's Hartsfield International Airport." Writers of arguments introduced by factual claims attempt to convince their readers that their claims are true, although perhaps not true forever and under all circumstances (in the Middle Ages it was a "fact" that the earth was the center of the solar system).

Perhaps you find the idea of arguing facts a contradiction in terms; to you, facts are unchanging statements about reality, not provisional statements requiring support and verification. If it's a fact, why argue it? But a statement becomes factual only if it is accompanied by evidence that makes it extremely probable to its particular audience. Because facts become the cornerstones of so much of what we know and expect of the world, we cannot afford to accept them on faith. In short, factual claims must be supported carefully.

Facts are crucial to argument; indeed, it is hard to imagine an argument succeeding if it doesn't include some facts. In the arguments you write in college and beyond, facts will play three roles:

1. They will sometimes appear as an argument's central claim, as in a laboratory report claiming that "The addition of sulfur to the compound created sulfuric acid."
2. They will function as support for other claims. A general claim such as "All the teachers in the Child's Play Day Care Center have experience working with preschool children" would be supported by facts about the specific experience of each teacher.

3. They will serve as examples or illustrations of difficult, unfamiliar, or abstract ideas. Suppose you're writing an essay on photosynthesis for an audience unfamiliar with the process. You might follow the scientific definition of the term ("the formation of carbohydrates in living plants from water and carbon dioxide, by the action of sunlight on the chlorophyll"— *Webster's New World Dictionary*) by the more familiar description of the yearly cycle of a cherry tree.

The four types of facts that will figure most commonly in your arguments are (1) common knowledge facts, (2) personally experienced facts, (3) facts reported by others, and (4) factual generalizations.

1. **Common knowledge facts** are so widely acknowledged as true that they require no support or proof beyond mere statement.

   Examples: Men cannot bear children.

   Opposite poles attract.

2. **Personally experienced facts** are the events, observations, and conditions that you have personally experienced.

   Example: I have taken countless history courses in my life, and I have never had a teacher who excited me about the subject.

3. **Facts reported by others** are those that you have learned from second- or third-party sources. A second-party source is the person who ascertained the fact. A third-party source is the person or document reporting facts ascertained by someone else.

   Examples: "The 'man shortage' and the 'infertility epidemic' are not the price of [women's] liberation; in fact, they do not even exist" (Susan Faludi, *Backlash,* xviii; second-party source).

   "The mental health data . . . are consistent and overwhelming: The suicide rate of single men is twice as high as that of married men" (Faludi, 17; third-party source).

4. **Factual generalizations** claim that an assertion is true for a large number of subjects or over a long period of time. Factual generalizations can be common knowledge facts, personally experienced facts, or facts reported by others.

   Examples: Most of my friends are interested in sports.

   In 1998, 5.6 percent of American children under 18 lived in the home of their grandparents (*New York Times Almanac, 2000,* 284).

All factual claims are stated as definite and unequivocal assertions, as in the following examples:

- New York City is the banking center of the United States. (The claim makes a quantifiable assertion that can be verified by a survey of the number of banks and banking transactions in major American cities.)

- Our solar system is approximately five-billion years old. (While no individual can verify this claim through firsthand experience or knowledge, it represents the consensus of experts on the subject and can be documented in this way.)
- Steel radial tires last longer than tires made with nylon. (Again, this claim can be verified, though the process may be tedious and time-consuming.)
- Most of my friends are involved in intramural sports. (A statement of fact that can be supported, if necessary, by a listing of the number of friends who are involved and not involved in intramural sports.)

ACTIVITIES (3.3)

1. For each of the factual propositions in the following list, identify the category or categories of fact (common knowledge, personal experience, second- or third-party, generalization) in which the proposition belongs.

   Example: The Cuban Missile Crisis occurred in October of 1962. Second- or third-party for most students; personal experience for older people.
   a. The disappearance of former Teamsters Union leader Jimmy Hoffa is still unexplained.
   b. The risk of getting cancer is decreased by a high-fiber diet.
   c. My communications professor routinely missed her 8:00 class.
   d. Alaska is the largest state in the United States.
   e. An apple a day keeps the doctor away.
   f. I get better grades on the papers I take the time to revise.
   g. Severe air pollution is dangerous for people suffering from lung disease.
   h. Women under age 30 have better driving records than men under age 30.
   i. In Italy, people take more time to enjoy life than we do in the United States.

Causal Claims

Causal claims propose a causal connection between two events or conditions. They can argue that A caused B or, more speculatively, that A may cause B at some future time. Statements such as "The violence represented in movies and television has numbed us to the horrors of violence in the real world" or "High consumer spending will lead to greater inflation" are examples of causal claims.

It is human nature to be curious about cause. We watch the careers of prominent public figures and wonder about the reasons for their spectacular successes and failures. We reflect on a tragedy like the Holocaust and demand to know how such a thing could happen. We look for the reasons behind events to assure ourselves that the world is governed by certain rules, not merely by random chance. We also learn by discovering cause. Knowing what causes higher automobile accidents involving specific vehicles gives us a reasonable chance of preventing similar events in the future. And you can be sure that business entrepreneurs will do whatever they can to reproduce those factors that led to Bill Gates' phenomenal financial success.

Just as we are given to discovering cause, we are also fascinated by predicting *effects*. Stockbrokers must be skilled in this form of causal argument, as they try to enhance the interests of their clients by predicting market activity. Doctors practicing *preventive* medicine are also in the business of predicting probable effects: they tell their patients to reduce dietary fat in order to prevent a future heart attack, or to exercise regularly to maintain bone density. And in business and industry, the long-term health of a corporation often depends on the accurate prediction of future trends. Eastman Kodak, for example, with its enormously successful business of traditional photographic products, had to determine the probable future of those products in the face of electronic imaging.

Under carefully controlled scientific conditions, it is possible to identify cause and even to predict effect with so much certainty that the causality can be established as *factual*. Researchers have determined that smoking increases the risk of lung cancer and that lobar pneumonia is caused by pneumococcus bacteria. But in the causal arguments that most of us make, arguments concerning human behavior—our actions, our successes and failures, our relations with others—certainty is impossible to reach. In these more speculative arguments, the best we can hope for is to establish *probable* cause or effect convincingly.

But because a claim cannot be proven with certainty doesn't mean it isn't worth arguing; if we always waited for certainty before acting, our progress would be slow. An argument that establishes probable cause or effect *can* be a reasonable basis for decisions or actions. In fact, probability is the goal of most of the arguments we write. But even probability isn't easy to achieve; in many cases, it calls for more skill than establishing certainty in factual arguments.

Causal claims are easy to spot because they (1) often contain words indicating causality—*cause, produce, effect, consequence*—and/or (2) involve the relationship between two phenomena occurring at different points in time. The following are examples of causal claims:

- According to social critic Neil Postman, technology is causing the surrender of American culture. (The word *caused* is a dead giveaway of a causal argument.)
- If Sally had written a better résumé, she might have landed that job. (An early event—Sally's poor résumé—caused a later one, her failure to land the job.)
- A balanced budget promises a stable government. (The claim proposes a close causal relationship between a balanced budget and a stable government. The verb *promises* indicates cause.)
- Increasing numbers of two-career families have contributed to the rising divorce rate. (*Contributed to* suggests a causal relationship between the two facts.)

ACTIVITIES (3.4)

1. Look back at the distinction between factual and probable causes. For which of the following causal claims could you establish a factual cause—one that

few people would dispute? For which could you establish only a probable cause—one for which you would have to argue?

   a. If Abraham Lincoln had not been assassinated, he could have lessened the bitterness between the North and the South after the war.
   b. The widespread use of computers in business and industry will increase total employment, not decrease it.
   c. If it had not snowed, Ohio State could have defeated Michigan in that football game.
   d. In most automobiles, failure to change the oil at regular intervals will damage the engine.
   e. The decline in the percentage of the population attending organized religious activities has caused the rise in the crime rate in the past 40 years.
   f. The use of seat belts decreases the number of fatalities in automobile accidents.
   g. If newlyweds had more realistic expectations about marriage, there would be a decline in the divorce rate.
   h. The children of the affluent would be happier if they had to do more for themselves.
   i. Some cold medicines cause drowsiness.
   j. The existence of nuclear weapons has prevented the outbreak of World War III.

2. Write a claim for a causal argument for one of the following; then make a list of all the reasons you can think of that would convince a reader of the cause or effect you identify. Describe these reasons in a paragraph.

   a. The cause of a particular war
   b. A team's victory or loss in a certain game
   c. A change in some aspect of the government's social or economic policy
   d. A change in exercise or dietary behavior
   e. The cause of a person's career success or failure

   Example of (c): "There would be fewer homeless people if the federal government increased its aid to cities."

   Reasons: Money could be used for low-income housing. Money could be used for training programs that would give the poor a means of self-support. Other countries that give substantial aid to cities do not have the problem with the homeless that we do.

Evaluations

When we argue an evaluation, we are proposing our personal judgment of the value of a work of art, a policy, a person, an action, even another evaluation. No doubt you often find yourself making informal pronouncements of personal taste: "Your tie is ugly," "That restaurant serves the best chicken wings in town," "I enjoy playing basketball more than playing tennis." These pronouncements are so purely subjective, so clearly a matter of personal preference, that there is little point in trying to argue them reasonably. We are all inclined to pass judgment on what we observe, and frequently we don't much care whether these judgments are taken seriously.

But sometimes we do care about the impact of these judgments; sometimes we want our opinions to influence others. In these cases, we must understand how to argue judgments of value. And many value judgments, even those originating as unconsidered personal opinion, *can* be convincingly argued. Claims such as "Pornography is an offense to all women" or "The government was mistaken in trading weapons for hostages," if they are serious, carefully considered judgments, can be developed into meaningful arguments.

Evaluations are probably the hardest of all arguments to argue successfully. Not only do they originate in the writer's personal value system, they also speak to his or her readers' equally personal, passionately held, and often unexamined values. Changing someone's mind about an opinion or judgment is an uphill struggle, so your goals in arguing evaluations should be rather modest: to gain your audience's sympathy toward a conclusion that you have reached through responsible and reasonable evidence rather than to change the mind of everyone who reads your argument.

An important variant of the evaluative claim is the *interpretive* claim. Interpretations are *explanatory* evaluations of a person, event, or object: "Dreams of beautiful gardens often suggest a state of profound satisfaction in the dreamer" or "Will's domineering and self-centered style is an expression of his profound insecurity." Neither of these examples is simply factual or descriptive; each reveals something unexpected beneath the visible surface of behavior. Interpretive claims surpass mere opinion only when they are supported by facts and reasoned argument. Reasonable, intelligent people may differ in their interpretation of a person or a situation, but not all interpretations are equally plausible or illuminating. To argue, for example, that Hamlet's actions are the symptoms of gout, when there is no evidence to support that view, is an example of poor interpretation.

The following statements are examples of claims introducing evaluative arguments:

- Many people do not realize that Herman Melville, the author of *Moby Dick*, was also an accomplished poet. (Evaluative claims often contain descriptive modifiers, like *accomplished* in this example.)
- Former president Jimmy Carter may not have been a great president, but he was an honorable one.
- Mary's constant chatter is an attempt to keep people from abandoning her. (An interpretive claim, in that it offers a beneath-the-surface explanation of Mary's behavior. Like many interpretive claims, this one contains causal elements, but what distinguishes it as primarily interpretive is the identification of a *coincidence* between visible and hidden phenomena.)
- For my money, soccer players are the most gifted of all athletes. (*Gifted* is a subjective term: it not only means different things to different people, but it also cannot be conclusively verified. Claims including superlative or comparative adjectives are likely to be evaluative claims.)
- "Human memory is a marvelous but fallacious instrument." (Primo Levi, *The Drowned and the Saved*.) (This claim makes two judgments about memory.)

ACTIVITIES (3.5)

1. Write claims for evaluative arguments for the following subjects.

   Example subject: Theft of library books
   Example claim: Stealing library books is not only a criminal act; it is a serious trespass against the ideals of community.
   a. Political campaign spending
   b. Computer games
   c. Pass-fail grading
   d. A particular television show
   e. Distance Learning courses
   f. Your composition instructor
   g. Rap music
   h. Television sports coverage

2. Give an example of an interpretive claim for the following topics.

   Example of topic (a): The cinematic revival of Shakespeare is an expression of *fin de siècle* anxiety.
   a. The significance of a play, movie, or short story
   b. The importance of a contemporary political figure
   c. The meaning of a current trend in fashion
   d. The attitude of students at your college toward their future careers
   e. The attitude of young Americans toward religion

Recommendations

A common goal of argument is to convince an audience that existing circumstances need to be changed. Some *recommendations* seek only to gain an audience's agreement with an idea or a decision, but others have a more practical (and ambitious) purpose: they try to convince their audience to take a particular action or, more modestly, to convince an audience that a particular action should be taken by others. As a student in English composition, you might write a paper for your instructor arguing that the legal drinking age should be lowered, or you might make that same argument in a letter to your congressional representative with the hope of getting him or her to take action. A lab technician might write a memo to her supervisor suggesting the purchase of new equipment. Or the chairperson of the history department might write to the dean requesting an adjustment in faculty salaries. All of these arguments would be recommendations.

All recommendations are concerned with the future, with what should be done at a later time, but they also imply a judgment about present conditions. Writers propose change because of dissatisfaction with an existing situation. Early in arguing a recommendation, you'll need to determine whether you want to concentrate on the current problem or on the improvements resulting from your recommendation; in some recommendations, you'll emphasize both.

- The main goal of recommendations emphasizing *present* conditions is to demonstrate the problems in the current situation. Because these recommendations argue *that* something needs to be done rather than *what* exactly that something is, they usually don't discuss a proposed change in any detail.

- The main goal of recommendations emphasizing the *future* is to present a plan for change and to demonstrate that it is feasible and likely to produce the desired effects.
- Recommendations with *equal* emphasis on present and future argue the problems of the current situation *and* the likely effects of the proposed change.

You may have noticed that recommendations are hybrid, or combination, claims with elements of both causal and evaluative arguments. That is exactly right. When proposing that an existing situation be changed, you are at least implying a negative judgment of that situation. And implied in the changes you recommend is a positive evaluation of those changes. Furthermore, you will support the recommendation itself through an argument of effect—demonstrating the positive future effects of the change.

Because arguments of recommendation argue for an action not currently in effect, words such as *should, would, must, ought, needs to be, will* or *might* typically introduce these arguments. The following are some sample claims for arguments of recommendation:

- We need more emphasis on science and math in our schools to prepare the next generation for a world of international economic competition. (The claim proposes a *change* in the current curriculum.)
- In order to attract more nontraditional students, this university must review and revise its course offerings. (Again, this claim calls for a change in an existing situation—a change that will have positive effects in the future.)
- If this company is to regain financial health, it must divest itself of all divisions not directly connected to its traditional core business. (The words *must divest* identify this claim as a recommendation—a suggestion for a particular action is being made.)
- Take back the night. (A trenchant recommendation expressed in the imperative mode. In the word *back,* the command implies making a change in an existing situation.)

ACTIVITIES (3.6)

1. For the following situations, write two claims of recommendation, one focusing on current conditions and one on the results of recommended improvements.

   Example: Taking a typing course
   Claim with a focus on current conditions: I need to take a typing course because I can't use the word processor required in my English composition course.

Claim with a focus on future improvements: I need to take a typing course so that I will be ready for the day when every office has its own word processor.
   a. Replacing a television
   b. Requesting a new strict policy on noise in a dormitory
   c. Advocating a freeze on the research for and manufacturing of nuclear weapons
   d. Purchasing a new car to replace your or your family's current one
   e. Increasing the number of police in the most dangerous sections of a city
2. Read the two recommendations at the end of Chapter 9. As you read, consider whether these recommendations emphasize the present, the future, or both. See how well your ideas match up with those of a group of your classmates.

Combination Claims

A brief look at any essay anthology may persuade you that "real" claims in "real" arguments don't always fit neatly into the four categories presented in this chapter. But your experience of writing *and* reading arguments will persuade you that all arguments contain claims that fulfill one or more of these four functions.

In some cases, you will need to recast claims mentally to decide what kinds of arguments they are. For example, the famous claim "The only thing we have to fear is fear itself," which is a forceful, lively claim needing no revision, can be translated to mean "We should beware of the dangers of fear"—a recommendation based on an argument of effect identifying the negative consequences of fear. The claim itself need not be rewritten; having identified the category of the recast version of the claim, you can proceed to support the original claim.

Often, as the preceding example demonstrates, the context of a claim will help you categorize it. This quotation about fear is taken from President Franklin Delano Roosevelt's first inaugural address in 1933, during the heart of the Great Depression, when fear about the future pervaded America. In this context, Roosevelt's remark is part of a broad recommendation to the American people to regain their confidence and to begin to plan for the future with new hope. In a less urgent context, "The only thing we have to fear is fear itself" might be a causal claim meaning "The experience of fear is dangerous because it builds on itself."

If you are arguing a claim that doesn't seem to fit into any of the categories discussed here, and you can't seem to recast it mentally, ask yourself some questions about the function of the argument that will support the claim. For example, is the claim verifiable? If not, it is not factual. Does it make an unverifiable judgment about something or someone? If so, it is probably evaluative. Does it propose a course of action? If so, it is a recommendation. Does it account for or predict a particular phenomenon? Then it is a causal argument.

Some claims actually contain two propositions to be argued, as in the sentence "Acts of terrorism are serious offenses against human freedom and should meet with deadly retaliation." The first claim is the *evaluation* that acts of terrorism are serious offenses, and the second is the *recommendation* that they should meet with deadly retaliation. In supporting this double claim, you would have to defend the value judgment about terrorism before moving on to the second assertion, the recommendation. Ideally, both claims should be defended, though writers frequently assume that their audience agrees with them on the most basic points—that terrorism is abhorrent, for example—and concentrate on one or two more arguable points, such as the need for deadly retaliation.

While space constraints may require this kind of corner cutting, be careful not to assume too much about your audience's position. A writer dealing with the controversial topic of terrorism should at least *consider* whether terrorism is always completely unjustified, even if she doesn't address this question in her essay.

Often, a factual claim is combined with one of the other three kinds of claims. When this is the case, as in the statement "The rise in the divorce rate in the last 30 years may increase the divorce rate in the next generation," you must establish the accuracy of your facts (the rise in the divorce rate) before you go on to speculate about the possible effects of this fact. So, too, with the statement "The flight of business and industry from the Northeast to the Sun Belt will eventually have a damaging effect on the quality of public education in the Northeast." First, the flight of business and industry must be established as a fact, probably through outside research; then the long-term causal argument can be made.

The following are examples of combination claims:

- The recent rise in interest rates may contribute to higher inflation. (This statement combines a factual assertion about rising interest rates, which can very quickly be supported, with a causal argument predicting the effect of the higher rates. This second claim would be the focus of your argument.)
- No nation is truly free that does not offer its citizens equal opportunity in education and employment. (This statement combines a causal argument—lack of equal opportunity results in an unfree nation—with an evaluation judging the degree of a nation's freedom.)
- If the candidate wants to win votes, he must convince constituents that his reputation for moral laxness is undeserved. (This statement combines a recommendation that the candidate make his case to his constituents and a causal argument that making this case will win him their votes.)
- While men seem to be driven to success by a fear of failure, women are made comfortable with failure by their fear of success. (This breathtaking generalization combines interpretation—identifying hidden motives for behavior—with elements of a factual argument. The writer will have to present *many* instances of these gender-linked phenomena in order to warrant the generality of the claim.)

ACTIVITIES (3.7)

Into which of the four main argument types or combination of types do the following belong? Be prepared to support your answer.

Example: Automobiles should be designed so that they get a minimum of 30 miles per gallon of gasoline.

Type of argument: Recommendation
1. Excessive consumption of alcohol can lead to many illnesses.
2. Honesty is the best policy.
3. Cutting defense spending will create a safer world.
4. Tariffs on imports merely raise prices for domestic consumers.
5. Alley cats are a public nuisance in this neighborhood.
6. Politics is the art of the possible.
7. An improved sewer system would solve these flood drainage problems.
8. America should protect its domestic industries with tariffs and quotas.
9. Without a belief in God, life has no meaning.
10. Obesity can help cause heart disease.

SUMMARY

The Claim

- Claims help readers to understand and evaluate arguments, and they help you, the writer, to generate the direction and content of your arguments.

- If you have difficulty coming up with a working claim, you probably need to do more thinking and reading about your topic. When you are knowledgeable enough, a claim should come to you.

- Always be prepared to modify a working claim to fit with new ideas and information.

- Claims can be placed virtually anywhere in an argument. The most effective placement depends on the nature of your argument and its probable reception by your readers.

- *Factual claims* seek to convince an audience that a given object or condition exists or has existed. The four kinds of facts are common knowledge facts, facts experienced by you, facts reported by others, and factual generalizations.

- *Causal claims* assert that one event or condition produces or helps to produce another event or condition. In claiming *cause*, we look for what produced a past or current event or condition. In claiming *effect*, we predict a future occurrence on the basis of certain current or intended circumstances.

- *Evaluations* make a value judgment of a person, activity, or object.

- *Recommendations* argue for a particular course of action in order to change existing circumstances. Recommendations can focus on present conditions, future effects, or a combination of both.

- Some arguments work from claims that combine elements of the four classes.

SUGGESTIONS FOR WRITING (3.8)

1. Read an argumentative essay (hardcopy or online) in a magazine like the *Atlantic Monthly* or the *New York Times Magazine,* and write a one- to two-page essay on what kind of argument it is and why. Be sure to give your instructor a copy of the argumentative essay you are analyzing.

2. Select a familiar document, such as Martin Luther King, Jr.'s "I Have a Dream" speech, Lincoln's Gettysburg Address, the Declaration of Independence, or a famous Shakespearean soliloquy, and identify the class or classes of argument it represents. In a one- to two-page letter to your instructor, support your identification. (Texts of each of the suggested sample documents are available online.) Be sure to give your instructor a copy of the document you are analyzing.

3. Find the lyrics to your favorite song, probably available online, and determine whether or not an argument exists. Support your reasoning in an e-mail message to one of your classmates. Be sure to provide your instructor with both a copy of the lyrics and your response.

4

An Argument's Support

Now that you have a working claim and a good idea about the kind of argument it summarizes, you are ready to begin supporting that claim. The body of your argument, the material that will convert your claim into a conclusion, is your presentation of support. Broadly defined, an argument's support is all the material you insert into your argument to strengthen the probability (and in some cases, truth) of your claim. To argue your claim successfully, you must know how to select appropriate support for your particular claim, how to determine how much support is necessary, and how to arrange that support in the most convincing way.

Once you have a working claim, you will probably find that you have some ideas for supporting it. The more your claim emerges from your experience of dissonance and from your own interests, the more likely you are to have solid support ready at hand, though you will have to do *some* research on even the most familiar topics. On the other hand, regardless of how much research goes into them, claims having no connection with your own experiences, interest, or knowledge will be more difficult to support.

Let's say that you are worried about your grandmother, who, although healthy, is growing increasingly depressed and withdrawn. You know from talking with her that she feels useless, ignored, and aimless. Your concern makes you angry about the way our society treats its older citizens, and you decide to let this concern and anger fuel an argument about age discrimination. Your grandmother's experience has given you a number of specific examples of age discrimination and its effects. Some of these examples will help to support the claim "American society, for all its public attention to human rights, is guilty of systematically depriving its senior citizens of countless 'inalienable' rights." But you know that in order to argue such a far-reaching claim convincingly, you will need to find support beyond your personal observations.

Since different classes of arguments often require different kinds of support, knowing the class of argument that your claim belongs to will help you know what kinds of additional support to look for. Chapters 6 through 9 discuss these specific requirements. There are also more general types of support, not specifically associated with a particular class, that you will want to be familiar with. And you will need to determine how much support will be enough and how to arrange that support strategically. These generic supporting tactics are treated in this chapter.

SOME VARIETIES OF SUPPORT

It is useful to think of supporting material as separate units or building blocks that strengthen a claim in different ways and to different degrees. What follows is a discussion of some of the generic varieties of support commonly used to strengthen arguments.

Secondary Claims

All claims, regardless of their class, are supported by further claims, which will require their own support. Sometimes these *secondary* claims will belong to the same class as the main claim, sometimes to a different class. If you were arguing the factual claim "Students in my major are more interested in learning marketable skills than in truly educating themselves," you would need to support your fairly general claim with individual examples of this phenomenon. You probably would cite conversations in which individual students had expressed this preference to you and/or perhaps a survey asking students in your major to rank their educational priorities. In both cases, you are supporting your main claim with a secondary factual claim, which will itself need to be verified.

A recommendation claiming "This university should offer a pass-fail grading option to its students" may include as support the secondary *causal* argument "Removing the traditional evaluative system of letter grades will facilitate learning by reducing pressure." While not the chief point of this argument, this secondary causal claim still needs to be supported. One way to support it is through a third, *factual* claim. Perhaps the writer has access to a survey taken at another university that offers the pass-fail option, and this survey demonstrates a positive student response to the option. Or maybe the writer has friends at other schools who have spoken favorably about their pass-fail grading policy. Whether these responses are gathered through a large survey or individual conversations, they are facts that will strengthen the secondary claim (provided they are responsibly obtained and accurately reported).

As these examples illustrate, eventually all main claims will come to rest on factual claims that are supported by observations, examples, statistics, studies, and so forth. While some arguments depend more heavily on facts than others, no argument is likely to be convincing if it doesn't at some point refer to verified factual claims. In the previous example, the factual generalization about learning goals is supported by secondary factual claims: the expressed preferences of other students in your major and/or a survey of student learning goals. In the second example, a recommendation ultimately comes to rest on a secondary factual claim: positive student response to the pass-fail option. As you will see in Chapter 6, these fundamental factual claims would be supported by the writer's assurance that they have been gathered, interpreted, and reported responsibly.

ACTIVITIES (4.1)

Supply secondary claims that would support the following main claims of arguments. In each case, identify the class of the secondary and primary claims.

1. The *Boles GRE Study Guide* is an excellent tutorial for students preparing to take the GRE.
2. Television newscasting influences how Americans think about social and political issues.
3. In my high school, food abuse was a far bigger problem than alcohol or drug abuse.
4. Dostoyevsky's *Crime and Punishment* is a ponderous novel of sin and redemption.
5. If we really want to eradicate racism, we must institute within the primary grades curricula that honor diversity.

Comparisons

You can support some claims by citing a comparable claim that has already gained wide acceptance. Note, however, that this supporting strategy will work only if the two claims are truly comparable, not just vaguely similar. In an argument predicting financial difficulties for a new snowboard store in your town mall, you might cite the failure of the three other stores that have rented the same space. Or if you are arguing against proposed cuts in state money for scholarships, you may cite what another state has done to avoid reducing its education budget. This comparison will work only if the fiscal situation of the state you refer to is truly comparable to that of your state. In order to know this, you will have to get considerable information on each and probably present that information in the argument itself.

Appeals to Authority

You can support any claim by referring to a similar view held by a recognized authority in the field. You could support an evaluative argument claiming that Michael Jordan is the most talented professional basketball player in the game today by quoting Charles Barkley pronouncing the same judgment (of course, Barkley has to have made this pronouncement—you can't make it up). Just be sure that the person whose judgment you cite *is* an established expert in the subject of your argument. Even though Barkley is a sports celebrity, his fame does not make him an expert on investment strategies or health care.

Appeals to Audience Needs and Values

Remember the emphasis of Chapter 2 on audience consideration, including an identification of audience needs and values? You can convert this preliminary identification into explicit support for your argument. Obviously, audiences will be more accepting of arguments that they see as likely to satisfy their needs or affirm their values. Many arguments presume these needs and values without referring to them explicitly. But you can strengthen some arguments by directly addressing these considerations, particularly when the match between claim and audience needs or values is not obvious. For example, a recommendation addressed to the administration of your college proposing a change from a trimester to a semester calendar should identify precisely how the change would benefit the administration—perhaps in the form of increased enrollment, higher student satisfaction, or long-term savings.

ACTIVITIES (4.2)

Get together with a small group of your classmates and discuss which methods of support (comparison, appeal to authority, appeal to audience needs and values) could be effectively applied to the following claims:

1. The costs of statewide and national political campaigns will discourage all but the rich from running for office.
2. The study of homosexuality is (is not) appropriate in a college course.
3. Using e-mail to keep in touch with friends who have gone off to other colleges is better than making telephone calls.
4. Parents should recognize how they risk their children's intellectual development by parking them in front of a television.
5. The widespread use of antidepressant drugs has revolutionized the psychotherapeutic community.

Addressing the Counterargument

A defining feature of argument is that its claim or claims are subject to disagreement: they are arguable. Thus, any claim you argue should be capable of evoking a *counterargument*—a position different from and often directly opposed to your claim. Just as you must carefully consider certain questions about your audience before you begin arguing, you must also identify the probable counterargument or arguments. Though this statement may seem counterintuitive, your arguments will be strengthened by your acknowledgment of their most powerful counterarguments. Why? For one thing, it is entirely possible that your readers are aware of the counterargument and even convinced by it. In stating and rebutting this position, you are dealing head on with the opposing view. Second, even if your readers aren't familiar with the alternative view, identifying it in your own argument will contribute to your image as a responsible and well-informed thinker.

The following are approaches to dealing with your argument's counterargument:

- You can omit direct reference to the counterargument when it is a weak position or likely to be unfamiliar to your audience. But note that omission does not mean ignorance: you should keep even the weakest counterargument in mind while you are writing, if for no other reason than that a reader may raise it.
- You can acknowledge or identify the counterargument without directly refuting it. This technique shows your readers that you are aware of the complexity of the issue and the legitimacy of other positions; it gives the impression that you are reasonable and broad-minded. In the following example, Margaret Whitney includes a brief acknowledgment of some predictable objections to her claim that competitive athletics are good for girls:

I am not suggesting that participation in sports is the answer for all young women. It is not easy—the losing, jealousy, raw competition and intense personal criticism of performance.

And I don't wish to imply that the sports scene is a morality play either. Girls' sports can be funny. You can't forget that out on that field are a bunch of people who know the meaning of the word cute. During one game, I noticed that Ann had a blue ribbon tied on her ponytail, and it dawned on me that every girl on the team had an identical bow. Somehow I can't picture the Celtics gathered in the locker room of the Boston Garden agreeing to wear the same color sweatbands.

Whitney has chosen not to refute these objections, probably because of the relative brevity of her argument, but her identification of the objections does suggest that she is reasonable and flexible.

- You should identify and directly refute an opposing position in the following situations:
  - –When you know your audience holds that position.
  - –When you know a credible, often-cited countercase exists, regardless of whether your audience subscribes to that position.
  - –If it is vital to your argument to project a broad-minded, well-balanced image.

The full text of Martin Luther King, Jr.'s 1963 "Letter from Birmingham Jail" appears on multiple Web sites, including "The Martin Luther King, Jr. Papers Project at Stanford University." Some of the links reveal the various rhetorical strategies that King uses to develop his response to criticism by Alabama clergy of his program of nonviolent resistance to racial segregation. The following excerpt from paragraph eight of his letter is an example of direct refutation:

You may well ask, "Why direct action? Why sit-ins, marches, and so forth? Isn't negotiation a better path?" You are quite right in calling for negotiation. Indeed, this is the very purpose of direct action. Nonviolent direct action seeks to create such a crisis and foster such a tension that a community which has constantly refused to negotiate is forced to confront the issue. It seeks so to dramatize the issue that it can no longer be ignored. My citing the creation of tension as part of the work of the nonviolent resister may sound rather shocking. But I must confess I am not afraid of the word "tension." I have earnestly opposed violent tension, but there is a type of constructive, nonviolent tension which is necessary for growth. Just as Socrates felt that it was necessary to create a tension in the mind so that individuals could rise from the bondage of myths and half truths to the unfettered realm of creative analysis and objective appraisal, so must we see the need for nonviolent gadflies to create the kind of tension in society that will help men rise from the dark depths of prejudice and racism to the majestic heights of understanding and brotherhood.

Notice how King identifies the opposition's position and even concedes them a point (they're correct in calling for negotiations) before he refutes their position and moves to an idealistic statement of his own. This pattern of statement-concession-refutation is typical of effective refutations, though you have to be careful not to give away too much in the concession.

Direct refutations should be thoughtfully placed in your argument. If your audience appears to be firmly committed to an opposing position, you're not likely to convince them of the error of their views at the outset. On the other hand, readers without strongly held views are less likely to be swayed by a counterargument if it follows an impressive array of support for your claim. But if you include your refutation as the final piece of support, remember that it may linger in your reader's mind for some time, so make it as strong and convincing as possible. And finally, some very powerful arguments are exclusively refutations of opposing positions; these arguments gain form, precision, and intensity from the position they are opposing.

ARRANGING YOUR ARGUMENT'S SUPPORT

Having accumulated support for your claim, you now have to consider the best way to arrange it in your argument. You can make strong support even stronger by arranging it to have the most powerful impact on your readers. Once again, audience consideration is key: your decisions about the organization of your argument's support should be based on your readers' familiarity with the subject, their ability to follow the path of your argument, and their probable disposition toward your claim.

It helps to think of your support as separate units that can be moved around within your argument. In an essay claiming that "The Student Activities Board should bring Matchbox 20 to campus," the units of support could be listed as follows:

1.   A survey shows that Matchbox 20 is the most popular performing group with students at your college.

2. The college would increase student satisfaction by showing their willingness to please students.
3. Ticket sales would be brisk and therefore would substantially offset the cost of bringing the band to campus.
4. In a letter to the *Chronicle of Higher Education,* the vice president of student affairs at a college in the adjoining state praised Matchbox 20 for their entertainment ability. "This is a band that any school should be proud to host," the letter concluded.
5. The band has a solid reputation for being professional and audience-appropriate.
6. Bringing such a popular band to campus would increase the college's community visibility.
7. Student enrollment would increase as a result of bringing Matchbox 20 to campus.

A good general principle is that the *strongest* support should be presented first, so that you gain some early agreement from your readers. If possible, you should also save an effective supporting point for the end of your argument; it will leave your readers with a positive final impression. In the preceding list, the strongest argument may be Argument 2, particularly if the college in question is, like most schools in today's competitive higher-education environment, extremely concerned about student satisfaction. Argument 6, a secondary causal claim, is likely to be persuasive to the Student Activities Board as well, since community visibility is always a plus to college administrators.

What constitutes strong support? To some extent, this will depend on your audience. A credulous, inexperienced group and a cynical or expert audience will be convinced by different points. However, relevant factual support (figures, examples, and statistics, as in Argument 1) is usually very strong, whereas highly speculative arguments (predicted effects with a remote chance of being realized) are weaker; for example, Argument 7 would be extremely difficult to predict convincingly and probably should be omitted altogether. Citing expert opinion, as in Argument 4, is usually effective, provided your expert is credible and his or her support is documented. In Argument 4, does the opinion of a vice president for student affairs qualify as expert in this context? Does she have an obvious bias that might weaken her statement? How respectable a publication is the *Chronicle of Higher Education?* Are your school and hers comparable?

Sometimes you have little choice about the arrangement of your support. Scientific experiments dictate a certain organization, as do causal chains, where Cause A must be discussed before Cause B, Cause B before Cause C, and so on. In these cases, you'll need to make sure that all supporting arguments are strong and that they fit tightly together, because one weak link can destroy the entire argument.

ACTIVITIES (4.3)

1. The following argument, written by student Sharon Bidwell, contains a number of varieties of supporting material. Pretend that you are the editor of your

school newspaper and have decided to print Sharon's letter. In a two-page letter to Sharon, comment on the effectiveness of her choice and arrangement of support.

> The administration's decision not to allow Dr. Fasciano and his white supremacist group to participate in a roundtable discussion with the students on our campus is clearly an act of censorship and should not be tolerated in a country that prides itself on free thought and expression. Censorship, as defined by the *Encyclopaedia Britannica,* is "the suppression or prohibition of speech or writing that is condemned as subversive to the common good." It is obvious that the administration is making a selective decision of what the "common good" is for the students of this campus.
>
> There is no doubt that the administration has legitimate concerns that need to be addressed. First of all, Mr. Fasciano's visit will raise some eyebrows among those who make regular contributions to the university. Second, Mr. Fasciano's visit is likely to set off active protests which have the capacity to seriously disrupt the campus and even threaten the safety and security of the students.
>
> Despite these very real risks, the administration must make it known that this university supports the Constitution of the United States—namely, the First Amendment—and does not bow to pressure when it comes to suppressing free speech. To paraphrase John Milton in his *Areopagitica* of 1644, we must allow that free and open encounter in which truth may indeed prevail over error.
>
> The argument against censorship has been made by many who fought hard against it—against anything, in fact, that interferes with self-development and self-fulfillment. For example, in his first inaugural address, Thomas Jefferson addressed the necessity of free dissent: "If there be any among us who would wish to dissolve this Union or to change its republican form, let them stand undisturbed as monuments of the safety with which error of opinion may be tolerated where reason is left free to combat it."
>
> The administration must give the students the freedom to be the best guarantors of quality and fairness. We rely on these institutions of higher learning to *teach* future generations by allowing them to choose *freely* and make difficult decisions. For those who oppose Mr. Fasciano and his views, let there be an open forum with a free exchange of ideas. Our forefathers fought for this privilege. Let's not let them down.

DEFINITIONS

Obviously, readers can't agree (or reasonably disagree) with what they don't understand. Clarity is the result of many different elements in written argument: precision of ideas in the writer's mind, an understanding of the relationship among these ideas, careful organization of claim and supporting material, clear transitions among parts of the argument, reliance on the conventions of grammar and punctuation, and comprehensible, unambiguous language. It is this final element—the clarity of your language—that concerns us here. Ideally, writers of argument would use only those words that they knew their readers would understand. But arguments can't always rely on simple language, and even the simplest words mean different things to different people. This is where *definition* comes in: the careful delineation of the intended meaning of a potentially troublesome word or term.

Knowing when and how to define terms is critical to successful argument. Because effective and strategic definition strengthen any argument by making it more accessible to readers, it can be viewed as a form of support. In some cases, definition moves from its clarifying supporting function to that of a secondary claim, where the writer must convince the reader to understand a term in a particular way before the central claim can be argued. Sometimes definition of a key term is so crucial and controversial that it becomes a central claim in itself.

When to Define

You should plan on defining the following types of language in your arguments:

- *Unfamiliar terminology.* Any specialized or unusual terms that may be unfamiliar to your readers must be explained. If, for example, you aren't sure whether your readers will have heard of "Maxwell's Demon," or a "net revenue model," or "dysthymic disorder," provide a clear definition.

   Unfamiliar terminology includes *jargon* (specialized vocabulary and idioms). Generally speaking, jargon should be avoided, but there are times when it is the best language for the job. If you must use phrases like "the dialogic principle of feminist discourse," don't assume that everyone in your audience will know precisely what you mean; provide a definition.
- *Nonspecific language.* In general, avoid vague, fuzzy terms, particularly in statements of evaluation and measurement. If you claim, "The Dave Matthews Band is the most popular band in contemporary music," consider how little this statement tells the reader about the nature and extent of that popularity. Popularity based on CD sales? Popularity based on money earned? On concert attendance? And popularity with whom? Certainly they are not the most popular band with people over 65. A more specific statement, such as "The Dave Matthews Band has sold more CDs in the last year than any other contemporary band" is far more useful to the reader.

   And when you use nonspecific words like *poor, excellent, large, grand,* or *considerable,* make sure you explain the meaning of your modifier as precisely as possible.
- *Abstract terms.* While you should try to make your writing as concrete as possible, sometimes you can't avoid using abstract terms in argument, especially in evaluations. The problem with abstractions is that they can be understood in different ways; that is, they can be *ambiguous.* If you must use a term like *popular,* or *talented,* or *conservative,* be sure to pin down explicitly your understanding of the term. While your readers may not agree with your definition, at least they will understand how you intend to

use the word and will judge the success of your argument within those parameters.

- *Controversial terms.* Some terms have been at the center of heated public debate for so long that they are emotionally and politically loaded. Their meaning is ambiguous—that is, it can be interpreted in more than one way—and people tend to argue over which interpretation is correct. *Euthanasia* and *gay marriage* are examples of such controversial terms; how one defines them often determines one's position toward them. When you use such terms in your arguments, you will almost certainly need to clarify what you mean by them.

Sometimes such terms are so controversial that your definition, because it implies a position on the subject, becomes the point of the argument. Consider, for example, an essay on doctor-assisted suicide: a carefully delineated definition of what the practice *is* (or is not)—the prescription of lethal amounts of medication to a dying patient at the patient's request, for example—would take you a long way in an argument supporting the practice.

Or, consider the implications of denying or justifying gay marriages in terms of the "Defense of Marriage Act," which is what student Doug Edwards did when Hawaii seemed about to authorize gay marriages (see Chapter 8). Later, the Vermont legislature removed the religious issue of the "sanctity" of marriage from the debate by legalizing same-sex civil unions, and perhaps redefined "gay marriage" as a result.

Types of Definitions

Terms requiring clarification can be defined briefly or extensively, depending on the needs of your audience and the importance of the term to your argument. The four types of definition you will most commonly use as support for your argument are the shorthand definition, the sentence definition, the extended definition, and the stipulative definition.

Writers often resort to *shorthand* definitions when the term in question requires only a quick explanation. A shorthand definition substitutes a familiar term for an unfamiliar one, as in the following example: "Acetylsalicylic acid (aspirin) is an effective medicine for most headaches."

A *sentence* definition, similar to a dictionary definition but written as a grammatical sentence, consists of the term to be defined (the *species*), the general category to which it belongs (the *genus*), and those characteristics that distinguish it from all other members of that general category (the *differentiae*). A sentence definition has the following structure:

SPECIES = GENUS + DIFFERENTIAE

An example of this form of definition is "A heifer [species] is a young cow [genus] that has not borne a calf [differentiae]."

An *extended* definition includes this basic sentence definition *and* any additional material that would help a reader understand the term being defined. The following are strategies for extending a sentence definition.

Evolution of Definition.   Sometimes an understanding of the historical development of a word's usage will illuminate its richness for readers. The word *queer,* for example, means strange or out of the ordinary. Thus it was eventually coined as a derogatory term for a male homosexual. Recently homosexuals have embraced the term, converting it from a slur to a compliment. There is now an academic field called Queer Studies.

Comparison.   Readers can gain a better understanding of a term if it is compared to something with which they are familiar. An argument that needs to define the term *docudrama* might explain that a docudrama is similar to a movie, except the events depicted are based in fact.

Example.   Offering specific examples of unfamiliar terms is an excellent way to explain them. To define what a *haiku* is, for example, you would almost certainly present an example or two.

Definition by Negation.   Sometimes you can explain a term by telling your reader what it is not, what it should not be confused with. For example, at the beginning of this textbook, we defined the term *argument* by distinguishing it from *opinion,* a term often mistaken as being synonymous with argument.

Etymological Definition.   Providing the etymology of a word—the meanings of its original roots—can also help to explain its meaning. The word *misogynist,* for example, derives from the Greek *miso,* meaning "hate," and *gyne,* meaning "woman."

Definition by Description.   Unfamiliar or abstract terms can often be explained or introduced by a physical or figurative description. If you were defining a Phillips screw, you might explain what the screw looks like. Or in defining contrapuntal music, you could describe the sound: the listener hears two distinct melodies going on at exactly the same time.

Functional Definition.   You can explain some unfamiliar terms by telling readers what the object or person does or how it operates. It would be helpful for a reader unfamiliar with the meaning of *provost* to learn what duties that academic officer performs. Functional definitions are particularly helpful in explaining unfamiliar *objects* such as tools. After describing the appearance of a particular drill bit, for example, you could explain what that particular bit is used for or how it is used.

The following extended definition of "poetry," from Laurence Perrine's *Sound and Sense,* contains many of these strategies of extended definition:

> Between poetry and other forms of imaginative literature there is no sharp distinction. You may have been taught to believe that poetry can be recognized by the arrangement of its lines on the page or by its use of rime [*sic*] and meter. Such superficial tests are almost worthless. The Book of Job in the Bible and Melville's *Moby Dick* are highly poetical, but

the familiar verse that begins: "Thirty days hath September, April, June, and November . . ." is not. The difference between poetry and other literature is one only of degree. Poetry is the most condensed and concentrated form of literature, saying most in the fewest number of words. It is language whose individual lines, either because of their own brilliance or because they focus so powerfully on what has gone before, have a higher voltage than most language has. It is language that grows frequently incandescent, giving off both light and heat.

This definition uses a sentence definition ("Poetry is the most condensed and concentrated form of literature"), a definition by negation (indicating what poetry is *not*: poetry has little to do with line arrangement or rhyme or meter), comparison ("Between poetry and other forms of imaginative literature there is no sharp distinction"), and figurative description ("It is language that grows frequently incandescent, giving off both light and heat").

Stipulative definitions *argue* that a particular definition should be assigned to a term. In other words, a stipulative definition argues a claim about meaning. While all definitions can be seen as claims, in that they propose meaning, and meaning is never fixed, the types of explanatory definitions discussed so far record meanings that most audiences would agree on. Stipulative definitions, on the other hand, argue for a particular meaning rather than record a consensual one. Sometimes stipulative definitions are made for convenience and clarity: "When we use the term *argument,* we are referring only to its primary meaning of demonstrating the reasonableness of a proposition." In this example, the writer is clarifying, not arguing.

But extended stipulative definitions are often fully developed arguments supporting an arguable, often controversial, claim about meaning. Think of the often-repeated argument "Abortion is murder." This short sentence definition opens a Pandora's box of controversies about meaning. First, there is likely to be disagreement over the meaning of the term *murder* in this context. The dictionary tells us that murder is the "unlawful and malicious or premeditated killing of one human being by another" *(Webster's New World Dictionary of the American Language).* But abortion is not illegal, so an antiabortion argument would have to reject this definition and stipulate its own. Or to open another controversy: is the fetus a "human being?" Is there consensus about the meaning of this term? Clearly not: a prochoice advocate would want to restrict or stipulate the meaning of *human being.* Through your stipulated definitions of *abortion, murder,* and *human being,* you are actually arguing your position on the issue of abortion.

Extended stipulative definitions are essentially interpretive arguments: in proposing a restricted, possibly unusual, definition of a concept, you are arguing a particular interpretation or understanding that is suggested and supported by the context of the argument. Stipulative definitions can be supported through a variety of supporting methods. One of the most useful is an argument of effect—that is, demonstrating the positive effects of adopting your particular definition of the term. For example, if you were proposing a new definition of the word *minor* as a way of making a case for lowering the legal drinking age ("The traditional definition of *minor* as someone under the age of 21 leaves out those 18–20 year olds who are considered old enough to die for their country, to get married, and to terminate their education"), you might introduce a supporting argument of effect that money could be saved if police didn't have to enforce the current drinking age. Or if you were arguing that education is a lifelong process, you might base your argument on a stipulative definition of *education,* supporting that definition through the secondary causal argument of the positive consequences that education, so defined, can lead to.

Chapter 10 of this book, "Writing and Image," begins with a stipulative definition of the word *image* as applied to written argument. This definition serves more of a clarifying than an argumentative purpose, but it does make the claim that despite the largely negative popular understanding of the term, a writer's "image" is positive and important.

ACTIVITIES (4.4)

1. Examine an extended definition in an online encyclopedia, reference guide, or textbook, and write a one- to two-page essay that describes what elements (sentence definition, examples, history of the object or concept being defined, comparison or contrast, and so on) have been included in the definition, and speculate on why they have been included. Are there other elements you believe should have been included to help the definition? Are there any elements that could have been omitted?

2. Write your own stipulative definition of *beauty, murder,* or *friendship.* Compare your definition with those of your classmates who define the same term.

SUMMARY

An Argument's Support

- An argument's support is all the material that transforms your working claim into a reasonable conclusion. Knowing the class of the argument you are making will help you determine the appropriate support, but there are some generic varieties of support that can be used to strengthen any class of argument. These are

  – secondary claims

  – comparisons

  – appeals to authority

  – appeals to audience needs and values

  – addressing the counterargument

  – defining key terms

- When possible, arrange your support to have the greatest impact on your readers, with strong support placed at the beginning and end of your argument.

- Any terms in your claim or the body of your argument likely to be unfamiliar to your readers should be defined by a sentence definition, an extended definition, or a shorthand definition.

- Stipulative definitions, which restrict the meaning of a term to one of the term's possible meanings, can be used to clarify an argument or to make an interpretive argument.

SUGGESTIONS FOR WRITING (4.5)

1. Write a claim that comes out of a position or belief you hold strongly (about a political issue, a policy at your university, or your relationship to your family, for example). Identify the category of your claim, and make a list of all the points you can think of to support your claim. Give your list to a classmate and see if he or she can add any supporting reasons you haven't thought of.

2. Write a two- to three-page extended definition of some concept or object, making sure your definition includes a formal sentence definition. Your instructor may have suggestions for this assignment, but other suggestions include entropy, eugenics, amber, ecosystem, and e-commerce.

5

Making Reasonable Arguments: Formal and Informal Logic

In Chapters 6 through 9, you will learn the most appropriate supporting methods for each class of claim. But before you begin working at the specific levels of claim and support, you should have some understanding of the principles of logic. The primary definition of the term *logic* is "the science of correct reasoning." The many and complicated rules of formal logic do, in fact, make up an intricate mathematical system that yields absolutely right and absolutely wrong answers. But this system does not dominate the fuzzier province of written argument, where variations in context, occasion, audience, and purpose make absolute conclusions exceedingly rare. Nevertheless, the fundamental principles of formal logic and their less formal derivatives do have their use in written argument: they are excellent tools for testing the reasonableness of the relationship between claim and support, for measuring the probability of an argument's conclusion. Think of it this way: you can't write successful arguments without some familiarity with logic, but this familiarity will not ensure that your arguments will be successful.

FORMAL LOGIC

The principles of formal logic were identified by the Greek philosopher Aristotle (384–322 B.C.). Today, almost 2,500 year later, these principles continue to influence what we mean by *reasonable* thinking. Just as children learn to speak their native language unaware of its underlying linguistic and grammatical principles, so we learn to think reasonably with little understanding of those complex principles informing reasonable thought. At some point in their education, children must learn the rules of grammar in order to refine their language skills; similarly, as educated adults and certainly as writers of argument, we must become familiar with the principles of logic to refine our reasoning skills.

Formal logic comes in two broad varieties: induction and deduction. *Induction,* or inductive reasoning, involves reasoning from observed evidence (the support) to a general statement (the claim or conclusion). *Deduction,* or deductive reasoning, involves reasoning from premises (assertions accepted as true or probable) to a conclusion or claim.

Induction:

> **Observed evidence:** In the 20 years I've lived in New York State, warm weather has begun every year between March and May.
>
> **General statement:** In New York State, warm weather begins between March and May.

Deduction:

> **Premise:** All human beings are mortal.
> **Premise:** Jane is a human being.
> **Conclusion:** Jane is mortal.

In the first example, notice the movement from specific examples (every spring for 20 years) to a very general assertion. But notice also that the specific examples suggest only that the general assertion is likely or probable, not necessarily true. The move from specific examples to a general conclusion is often referred to as the *inductive leap,* a term which underlines the large gap between the truth of the individual instances and the truth of the generalized conclusion.

In the deductive example, on the other hand, the statement that Jane is mortal is *necessarily true* if the premises preceding it are true. If certain conditions are met, deductive arguments *can* lead to necessary, or absolute, conclusions. But the "if" is a big one; in reality, the principles of deduction will enhance the reasonableness of your argument, but they will rarely ensure its absolute truth.

As you'll see in the next four chapters, some logical principles are more useful with one kind of argument than with another. The remainder of this chapter offers a general introduction to the principles themselves.

Induction

In inductive reasoning, we make generalizations on the basis of individual instances. For example, if you observed repeated instances of male students dominating class discussion, you might conclude that at your school, male students participate in class more than female students. Your conclusion is useful not because it represents the absolute truth, which of course it doesn't (there are exceptions to any generalization), but because it summarizes a set of similar events that you have observed. Inductive reasoning comes naturally to all of us, whether we're highly trained in Aristotelian logic or don't know the difference between a reasoned argument and a shouting match.

But the process does carry risks. For one thing, irresponsible induction can lead to harmful misconceptions. There is a world of difference between the conclusion "Male political science majors at Miller College tend to dominate class discussion" and one claiming "Men are more skillful speakers than women." You can avoid making irresponsible conclusions if you heed the following three cautions: (1) be sure you have *enough* individual examples to warrant the conclusion (your experience in one political science class is not enough to warrant even the preceding first conclusion); (2) provide the context of your examples and conclusion—in this case, your observations of students in a particular major at a particular college; and (3) always qualify your conclusion by using verbs or modifiers that limit the degree of certainty you're insisting on ("Male students often dominate class discussion").

A second risk of inductive reasoning concerns the use to which we put its conclusions. Inductive conclusions are safest if they are used *descriptively,* as a way of summarizing a set of observations or facts ("Male political science majors at Miller tend to dominate class discussion"). But induction is more commonly used to *predict* events or behavior. Many of the predictions we make on the basis of induction are perfectly harmless. If you know that the shopping mall is usually crowded on Saturday afternoons, your decision to shop Saturday morning is a harmless and quite useful prediction based on inductive reasoning. But predictive inductive reasoning can lead to harmful stereotypes. It may be true that women in your major do not participate in class discussion, but if you assume, on the basis of these limited observations, that all the women you associate with will be quiet and unassertive, your false conclusion may put you in personal and political hot water.

Responsible inductive reasoning depends in large measure on recognizing and arguing factual claims, since induction involves supporting a general claim by individual factual instances. For this reason, a full discussion of induction is reserved for Chapter 6, "Arguing Facts." The following essay, "Ally McBeal's Younger Sisters," by media critic Jane Rosenzweig, uses both inductive and deductive reasoning to support its generalized evaluative claim that today's adolescent television heroines are more mature than "their adult counterparts." Underlying the evaluative claim is a syllogism that could be represented as follows:

> **Major premise:** Maturity consists of assertiveness, self-reliance, and independence.
> **Minor premise:** Television's adolescent heroines display assertive, self-reliant, independent behavior.
> **Conclusion:** Television's adolescent heroines are mature.

Of course, both the major and minor premises must be demonstrated to be true, or at least highly probable, in order for the underlying syllogism to be sound.

Because her argument generalizes about television heroines in general, Rosenzweig also relies upon the methods of induction in her argument. In order to support her evaluation of a *group* of heroines, she must offer numerous supporting examples of individual cases.

ALLY MCBEAL'S YOUNGER SISTERS

JANE ROSENZWEIG

In the premiere of Wasteland, ABC's new prime-time soap by the creator of the WB network's Dawson's Creek and the film Scream, 26-year-old Dawnie theorizes that her generation is experiencing a "second coming of age" in which twenty- and thirty-somethings face uncertainties of growing up that used to be the exclusive province of adolescents.

"Look at me," she says. "I've spent my entire life in school, my parents still support me, human relationships baffle me, and I am acutely self-aware—to the point where I am clueless and slightly suicidal." (She is also, in an interesting twist on television's conventional mores, a virgin.) Whether or not Dawnie's hypothesis is applicable to real people—and with any luck for ABC, this will be a subject of fervent water-cooler debate around the country—it certainly applies to the young women of prime time, who are trapped in the most protracted adolescence in television history.

It is perhaps no accident that at a time when youth sells (advertising slots for shows about teenagers, like Dawson's Creek, can command more money than those for the consistently top-10 rated Touched by an Angel), American pop culture has become preoccupied with our collective inability to grow up. People are staying single longer, and the beauty industry is constantly coaxing us to make ourselves look younger if we want to stay in romantic business.

But the proliferation of teen shows is one thing; the packaging of female adulthood as an extended adolescence is something else altogether. Indeed, what's most interesting about this infantilization of twenty- and thirty-something women—a trend started by David Kelley's Ally McBeal and perpetuated by the women of Wasteland, Providence, and to varying degrees a number of new fall programs—is that it co-incides with a flood of shows about teenage girl characters who are more assertive, more independent, and more interesting than their adult counterparts. I'd say Ally McBeal ought to grow up—except the real problem seems to be that she already has and is still less mature than the average television teenager.

Q: What makes your problems bigger than everyone else's?
A: They're mine.

—Ally McBeal

Most of the people here have been saved by you or helped by you at one time or another.

—A classmate speaking to Buffy Summers, Buffy the Vampire Slayer

The preoccupations of young women are not new to television; women have always been the key audience for advertisers. A teenage girl in 1963 could flip on the TV to look for facsimiles of herself on The Patty Duke Show and Gidget. Young adult women, of course, have a long history of television "role models": think of June Cleaver, Donna Reed, and Laura Petrie—or more recently, Mary Tyler Moore. And the history of television is rife with ambiguous portrayals of women: Are they empowered or trapped in traditional roles (think of I Dream of Jeannie and Charlie's Angels)? Can brains and femininity be reconciled in a single character, or must they always be dichotomized into either Cagney and Lacey or Baywatch? Or if they can be reconciled, must the result be Xena: Warrior Princess? But for all this history of mixed messages, there has never been a time when the girls were more like women and the women more like girls than right now.

True, the conventional wisdom these days is that the line between adolescence and adulthood is blurring: the young are getting older, the old younger. Though if that's the case, shouldn't our television counterparts be meeting in the middle? Why, instead, do television teenagers have more mature relationships with men than the thirty-somethings do? Why are Buffy the vampire slayer, Felicity, and the girls of Party of Five and Dawson's Creek so much more emotionally intelligent than the grown-ups on other shows? Harvard psychologist Carol Gilligan and others have observed that the confidence and self-esteem of young girls diminish when they reach adolescence, at which point girls start downplaying their intellects and compromising their personalities in order to adapt to society's expectations—and to be attractive to boys. If current television is any indication, the cultural manifestation of this trend now occurs twice (Wasteland's Dawnie may be onto something bigger than she knows): if girls go ditzy when they reach adolescence, they seem to be going ditzier still as they pass into young adulthood.

This phenomenon, I think, can be explained at least in part by our cultural preoccupation with women's biological clocks, a preoccupation that has clearly constrained the imaginations of today's television writers. Can't they conceive of any other kinds of lives for women? If we succomb to the creative failure represented by the latest crop of television shows, the danger is that we, as viewers, will find ourselves accepting these same constraints in our own lives.

> I want to save the world. I just want to get married first.
>
> —Ally McBeal

It has become fashionable to loathe Ally McBeal. Her contribution to the putative death of feminism, her diminutive cuteness, her short skirts, and her perky pouts all combine to make her an insult to any actual Harvard law graduate—or any graduate of any school in any field, for that matter. While the show is still at times clever and even resonant in its focus on the lonely

search for a soul mate, Ally is a hard character to sympathize with. It may be kind of funny when she says, "I'm tempted to become a street person cut off from society, but then I wouldn't get to wear my outfits," but it's also pathetic. By the end of last season, when she schemed to win back her boyfriend by hiring a gigolo to make him jealous and then propositioned the gigolo, she'd lost all credibility as an adult character. Mary Tyler Moore wouldn't be caught dead messing up her life like this.

While originally hailed as whimsical and imaginative, and even as it continues to garner accolades (most recently, in September, an Emmy for Best Comedy Series), Ally McBeal is well on its way to being the biggest failure of the imagination in prime time. But because of its early critical and ongoing ratings success, Ally has basically created a new category of women on television: pretty young things who, in the guise of successful career women, are actually completely defined by an inability to find a husband and have children. Ally is stalked by a holographic dancing baby meant to remind her (and us) that her biological clock is ticking. While there are women in her age group on television who do care about their careers in some workplace-centered shows—most notably Carol Hathaway on ER—most of the dramas and comedy-dramas that focus on personal lives feature immature women who share more with Ally McBeal than with the people we know in real life. Lindsay Dole on Kelley's The Practice throws tantrums in court; her unhappy housemate, played by Lara Flynn Boyle, appears more anorexic than Calista Flockhart's Ally and seems even more ill-equipped to handle her personal life. It's as though you're supposed to look at Boyle and think, If only she had a nice husband to take care of her, maybe she would eat.

Perhaps the worst example of TV's confused conception of the single woman is Dr. Sydney Hansen of NBC's Providence, which debuted last season. After coming home to find her boyfriend in the shower with another man, she left her lucrative job as an

L.A. plastic surgeon and moved home to practice medicine at a free clinic in Providence. Sleeping once again in the room she grew up in, she regularly wakes, sweating, from dreams in which her dead mother is chastising her about her inability to find a man. Syd consistently makes dating decisions more worthy of a teenager than a smart, adult woman, which is what she is theoretically supposed to be. And her skirts are as short as Ally McBeal's; most real doctors and lawyers, it's safe to say, don't dress like that.

Unfortunately, the new fall season offers more of the same. In addition to Dawnie on Wasteland, there are the women of NBC's Cold Feet, one of whom strikes a blow to sexism by marching into her husband's business meeting to demand, for once and for all, a nanny. (And never mind that the husband appears to have no interest in either wife or child.) Another of the main characters in Cold Feet runs off to sulk at her mother's house when she argues with her husband. These characters are like early adolescents who relate to one another by screaming, pouting, and stamping their feet.

Funny thing is, turn the channel to the WB Network, which has made the strongest effort to stake out the youth market, and you find that the characters who actually are adolescent girls do not stamp their feet. They are calm and collected, surprisingly analytical. Television's message: only when they're not worrying about their biological clocks can women have fully developed characters. It is really the case that only women who are still in high school have the luxury of thinking about things other than themselves without constantly being interrupted by thoughts of their own reproductive limits?

I need to find out if I'm capable of being a whole person without you.

—15-year-old Joey Potter to her boyfriend Dawson on the WB's Dawson's Creek

Don't get me wrong: teenage girls on television are not ideal role models. They all have clear skin and shiny hair and don't seem afflicted by any of the maladies of girlhood described by experts. It's not hard to see how some critics would assert that these characters are the primary contributors to body image problems of ordinary girls. (The actress who plays Buffy, Sarah Michelle Gellar, is a spokesmodel for Maybelline cosmetics, whose ads run throughout the show.) And some characters are perhaps more sexually active earlier than we would like the role models for our children to be. But I would rather have my girls watch Dawson's Creek or Buffy than Ally McBeal.

Say what you will about the fanciful premise of Buffy, in which Buffy Summers fights the evil denizens of hell in order to save her town. But Buffy is neither man obsessed nor self-absorbed, and she refuses to see her problems, like Ally McBeal does, as bigger than everyone else's. In fact, she balances her personal life quite elegantly with her responsibility to protect her community from evil vampires (okay, so that sounds ridiculous on its face; nevertheless, the lesson it conveys is a worthy one). The problems are of a different scale. She misses out on her own prom in order to make school safe for her friends; she gives up something but earns loyalty and respect in return. Also, her best friend Willow is intelligent, sensitive, principled, and the least stereotypical Jewish woman on television.

Similarly, peel away the music-video veneer from Dawson's Creek or Party of Five and you'll find some young women who clearly have their feet planted firmly on the ground, even in the context of formulaic television plots. Joey Potter, for example, in spite of having a dead mother and a jailed father, has enough self-awareness to realize that there is an asymmetry between her boyfriend Dawson's passion for filmmaking and her own passion for Dawson. After some initial sadness, she pulls herself together enough to think about what she really wants out of life—and to realize the folly of a self-definition that requires always having a man. Ally McBeal never shows this kind of independence. The tragedy is that, assuming television convention holds, if Joey graduates from college without having landed a husband, she'll be reduced to jabbering preadolescence. (The self-reliant title character of the WB Network's Felicity suggests that college women still have their own identities and therefore that it is sometime after college that life begins to be about having babies.)

Sometimes the divide between adolescent maturity and post-adolescent immaturity is starkly evident even within a single show. Party of Five, for instance, depicts both teenage girls and twenty-something women. The differences are striking. (Originally about a family of orphans trying to raise themselves, the show has turned into a fairly formulaic soap about adolescents and young adults coexisting in an adult-free San Francisco universe.) Sarah—whose character, now 19, is spinning off this season to a new show called Time of Your Life—was one of the first TV characters I saw with the self-awareness to realize that her coquettish attempts to win her boyfriend's heart (in a batch of episodes a few years ago) were not only a waste of her time but also a challenge to her self-esteem, and that she shouldn't have to compromise her intelligence to win love. In an episode at the end of last season, Sarah, now older, attempted to teach this lesson to 16-year-old Claudia while at the same time struggling to maintain her own interests as her life was increasingly overtaken by her boyfriend's responsibilities.

In contrast, twenty-something Kirsten, the girlfriend of the show's oldest sibling, is a unidimensional character painted almost entirely in terms of her inability to have children. The chain of events that followed her learning this fact was over the top: she plagiarized her Ph.D. thesis, had a nervous breakdown, married a man she didn't love, and spent several seasons obsessing about how she would hold onto a man if she couldn't bear children. Meanwhile, the only other twenty-something women on this show have been a stripper who doesn't love her child, an alcoholic who depends on a 19-year-old man to take care of her, and a hard-edged and independent—but, alas, unlovable and unappealing—social worker.

What is it in the logic of television that demands that self-possessed girls full of possibility must evolve into women who are defined entirely by their marriage status and act like spoiled children? To the extent that television reflects or defines many of our central preoccupations as a society, this is a question to take seriously. Mightn't television capture some more complex way of thinking about the role of women in society? Or must television continue to make women into one-issue vessels when they reach childbearing age? The women I know lead richly textured lives, and the ones who do feel the loneliness of being single do not deal with it by throwing tantrums in court or moving home to live with their parents; surely it's the same for the women you know, too. But that's not the impression your daughters would get—or your sons, for that matter—from watching TV.

Sadly, shows featuring teen girls are becoming more and more formulaic, their lead characters more and more flat and conventional. Television producers are like sheep; thus a few dramas about teenagers from the last two seasons have generated a trend that will feature as many as 10 such shows this season, not counting the returning sitcoms Moesha and Sabrina the Teenage Witch, or the Moesha spinoff The Parkers. As the new season starts, it will be worth watching to see which of these teen girls can sustain their level of maturity as they age and which will become ditzy stereotypes. We can only hope the girls don't lose character definition as these shows become the norm. One thing is certain: if Buffy Summers grows up to be Ally McBeal, there will be hell to pay. Literally.

Deduction

The basic form of the deductive argument is the *syllogism:* a three-part argument consisting of a *major premise* (a premise is an assertion or proposition), a *minor premise,* and a *conclusion.* The earlier sample of deductive reasoning is a classic example of a syllogism:

> **Major premise:** All human beings are mortal.
> **Minor premise:** Jane is a human being.
> **Conclusion:** Jane is mortal.

This syllogism is an example of thinking in terms of classes. The major premise establishes two classes—a larger one of mortal beings and a smaller one of human beings—and it asserts that the smaller class belongs in the larger. The minor premise establishes that a still smaller class—in this case, one individual (Jane)—belongs in the smaller class of the major premise. From there it necessarily follows that Jane will also be a member of the largest class, mortal beings. The syllogism can also be displayed visually.

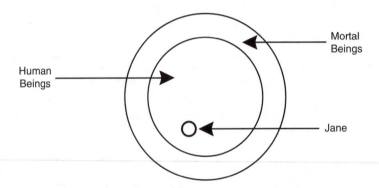

Thinking in terms of classes can be misleading if the process is done incorrectly. Examine the following syllogism:

> **Major premise:** All Catholics believe in the sanctity of human life.
> **Minor premise:** Jane believes in the sanctity of human life.
> **Conclusion:** Jane is a Catholic.

At first glance this argument may seem plausible, but as the diagram on page 61 shows, the argument is seriously flawed because the minor premise puts Jane in the larger group of those who believe in the sanctity of life but not in the smaller group of those who are Catholics. All the argument can really tell us is that Jane and Catholics share this one trait. They may differ in everything else.

This sample syllogism leads us to an important distinction in deductive reasoning: the distinction between validity and truth. A syllogism is *valid* when it's set up correctly, according to the rules of formal logic. You can look these rules up in a logic textbook, but in many cases, you can tell when a syllogism doesn't follow them correctly because, as in the case of Jane's religious persuasion, you recog-

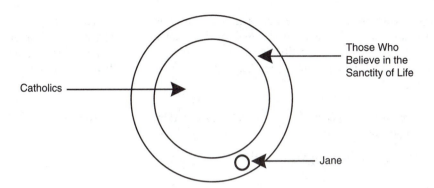

nize instinctively that the conclusion doesn't make sense. On the other hand, a syllogism is *true* only if its premises are true. The syllogism about Jane's mortality is both valid and true. But consider the following syllogism:

> All women are feminists.
> Jane is a woman.
> Jane is a feminist.

Clearly, the generalization that *all* women are feminists is untrue; so, though the relationship between premises (support) and conclusion (claim) is valid, the conclusion is untrue because it works from a false premise. On the other hand, while the premises of the syllogism about Jane's religion are true, the syllogism is not valid because the relationship between premises and conclusion is incorrect.

Deductive arguments that are both true and valid are *sound.* Deductive arguments that are untrue, invalid, or both are *unsound.* Whether reading or writing arguments, you'll need to be on guard against the seductions of the valid argument built on false premises, and of the invalid argument luring you with the truth of its premises or conclusion.

Conditional Syllogism. The conditional syllogism, sometimes referred to as the *if-then syllogism,* takes the following form:

> If John drops the glass on the sidewalk, then the glass breaks.
>
> John drops the glass on the sidewalk.
>
> The glass breaks.

This syllogism is valid, and if its premises are true, it is also sound.

With conditional syllogisms, however, you need to watch out for a very common error, usually called *affirming the consequent,* where the "then" clause of the major premise is turned into an affirmative statement in the minor premise:

> If John drops the glass on the sidewalk, then the glass breaks.
>
> The glass breaks.
>
> John drops the glass on the sidewalk.

The argument is invalid because the major premise merely claims that John's dropping the glass causes it to break; it does not exclude other ways of breaking the glass, such as hitting it with a hammer. Given this major premise, we cannot conclude that John has dropped the glass simply because the glass is broken.

Disjunctive Syllogism.   The disjunctive, or "either-or," syllogism takes the following form:

> Either the doctor gave the patient oxygen or the patient died.
>
> The patient did not die.
>
> The doctor gave the patient oxygen.

Note that this argument is invalid if the alternative is affirmed—that is, if it turns out to be true—rather than denied, or declared untrue, as in the preceding example:

> Either the doctor gave the patient oxygen or the patient died.
>
> The patient died.
>
> The doctor did not give the patient oxygen.

The major premise merely asserts that we can assume that the first alternative occurred because the second one didn't. (In other words, if the doctor hadn't given the patient oxygen, the patient would surely have died.) But if the second one, the patient's dying, did occur, we can't turn around and assume that the doctor failed to give the patient oxygen. Again, the patient could have died from a number of other causes even if the doctor did his "duty."

Making Use of Deduction in Written Arguments.   For writers of argument, classical logic offers a good way of "checking your work." Familiarity with the basic principles of deductive reasoning will probably not help you *create* arguments, but it will help you test the reasonableness of your claim and support once they are composed. Of course, the writing and thinking we do every day do not come packaged in classical syllogistic form, so that detecting sound and unsound reasoning is a little more difficult than in the preceding examples. But with a little practice, you can become adept at recasting your claim and support into the syllogistic model.

Let's say you are writing an argument claiming, "Your name does not determine your destiny." You plan to offer the following support for your claim: (1) students with common names receive higher grades than students with unusual names, but there could other issues operating here; (2) studies of prisoners reveal half of the inmates in prisons undergoing psychiatric evaluations have uncommon names; and (3) many successful people have unusual names. To determine whether your claim and support are logical, you'll need to work with each supporting claim separately, finding the place it would occupy in a formal syllogism that concludes, "Your name does not determine your destiny."

ACTIVITIES (5.1)

1. Identify the major premise of the following incomplete syllogisms, as in the following example.

   Conclusion: My physics professor is a skilled teacher.

   Minor premise: My physics professor knows her physics thoroughly, uses imaginative examples, is concerned that her students learn, and is an excellent speaker.

   Major premise: A skilled teacher knows his or her subject matter thoroughly and can present it imaginatively, is concerned that students learn, and speaks clearly and compellingly.

   a. **Minor premise:** Mack's résumé was poorly written.
      Conclusion: Mack did not get the job because his résumé was poorly written.

   b. **Minor premise:** Jessie made faces at the refs behind their backs, cursed members of the other team, and refused to congratulate them on their victory.
      Conclusion: Jessie is a poor sport.

   c. **Minor premise:** Professor Callahan constantly interrupts his students.
      Conclusion: Professor Callahan does not respect his students.

   d. **Minor premise:** Young people of today do not value family or community.
      Conclusion: Our young people will not grow up to be good citizens.

   e. **Minor premise:** Bill Clinton is a master of the art of compromise.
      Conclusion: Bill Clinton is a fine statesman.

   f. **Minor premise:** There is no way I can write my final research paper for this class.
      Conclusion: I will not pass this class.

2. With a small group of your classmates, discuss the extent to which the major and minor premises of three of the preceding syllogisms would need to be argued.

3. Examine an essay you wrote recently and present its major argument as a syllogism. What are the argument's major premise, minor premise, and conclusion? Are any of these components implicit rather than explicit in your essay? Is the syllogism sound and valid?

THE TOULMIN MODEL:
A MODERN VARIANT OF FORMAL LOGIC

Formal deductive reasoning yields necessary or certain conclusions, yet written arguments about our complex, provisional, and messy world rarely presume to discover absolute truth. It is in this mismatch between the goals of formal reasoning and those of written argument that the limitations of deduction are exposed. The fact is that most of the arguments we judge to be worth making are worth making *because* they are arguable, because they admit the possibility of more than one reasonable position. Few people waste time, for example, arguing about whether the sun will come up tomorrow, but they do argue about whether the problem of ozone depletion in the atmosphere warrants strict regulation of pollutants.

Recognizing the limitations of Aristotelian logic for practical rhetoric, the twentieth-century philosopher Stephen Toulmin identified and formalized a slightly different relationship between an argument's claim and its support. Toulmin's model is a useful way to judge the reasonableness of many of the arguments you construct.

According to the Toulmin model, a claim is linked to its support through what is called a *warrant*. A claim's warrant indicates how one gets from factual support (which Toulmin calls *data*) to the claim. It is the general belief, convention, or principle that permits the data to support the claim.

Suppose you were proposing that your college major institute a junior-year-abroad program. You have a number of supporting reasons for this claim: the program will attract students to the major; it will be an invaluable educational experience for students; it will allow the department to establish important international connections. The Toulmin model requires that each supporting reason be linked to the claim through some assumption or principle acceptable to the audience. Using the last support cited, a diagram of this argument would look like this:

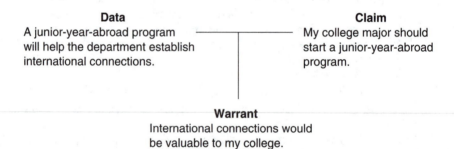

Data
A junior-year-abroad program will help the department establish international connections.

Claim
My college major should start a junior-year-abroad program.

Warrant
International connections would be valuable to my college.

We can identify an argument's warrant (which is not always stated explicitly in the argument itself) by asking, "What is it about the data that allows me to reach the claim?" In this case, it is the *value* of international connections that makes the claim desirable. Just as major premises are sometimes left unstated in real arguments, warrants are sometimes only implied. If you have any reason to suspect that your audience will not accept the warrant as generally true or at least reasonable, you will have to support it with what Toulmin calls *backing*. In this case, one backing for the warrant might be identification of the benefits of international connections in a world where more and more college graduates will be working for international organizations.

A fifth element of the Toulmin model, which makes the concept particularly useful to written argument, is the *qualifier*. The qualifier is a word or words that modify or qualify the claim. In our example, that qualifier is the word *should*, a word that makes the recommendation less strong than *must*, but more strong than *might want to consider*. Unlike the syllogism, the Toulmin paradigm gives the writer room to entertain claims that are less than necessary or certain. Adding the backing and the qualifier to our example, we come up with the following diagram:

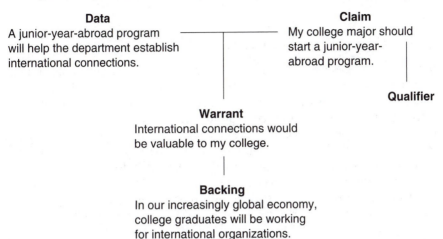

Data
A junior-year-abroad program will help the department establish international connections.

Claim
My college major should start a junior-year-abroad program.

Qualifier

Warrant
International connections would be valuable to my college.

Backing
In our increasingly global economy, college graduates will be working for international organizations.

Applying Toulmin's model to your own arguments can help you flush out the assumptions that generate your claim and evaluate their reasonableness. You may find that this model is most useful in making recommendations (as in the preceding example) and causal arguments. The most useful point in the composition process at which to apply both the Toulmin and the Aristotelian models is after you have formulated a claim and collected some support. Fitting these elements into one or the other paradigm will help tell you what is missing, what needs further support, and what is patently unreasonable. Don't *begin* the argument process by trying to fit ideas into the models; this will only frustrate your thinking and limit your inventiveness.

ACTIVITIES (5.2)

1. Identify the unstated warrants for each of the following pairs of claim and support.

   a. **Claim:** Secondary smoke is harmful.
      Support (or data): The Surgeon General's report on smoking establishes this.

   b. **Claim:** Celebrities who stand trial for capital crimes are not likely to get fair trials.
      Support (or data): The media focus unrelentingly on celebrity suspects.

   c. **Claim:** If you have the flu, you should stay at home.
      Support (or data): This year's strain of the flu is highly contagious.

   d. **Claim:** Writing is a dying art.
      Support (or data): My freshman students don't know the difference between an independent clause and Santa Claus.

   e. **Claim:** Mick is an unorthodox runner.
      Support (or data): Mick holds his arms high when he runs, and his heels never touch the ground.

2. Which of the previously supplied warrants would require some backing in order to be acceptable to readers? What kind of backing might you supply?

INFORMAL FALLACIES

Unfortunately, even when we pay careful attention to the logical principles discussed in this chapter, our reasoning can still go awry through any of a number of *informal* fallacies. Like the principles of formal logic, informal fallacies usually involve a faulty relationship between an argument's claim and its support. Familiarity with these flaws in reasoning is especially useful during the revision stage, when, with these fallacies in mind, you examine the relationship between your claim and its support. Since an inclusive list of these fallacies is a very long one— as inexhaustible as human inventiveness—included here are only those fallacies that frequently turn up in student writing. For each fallacy, the category or categories of argument in which it is most likely to occur are also indicated.

Ad Hominem Argument

An *ad hominem* argument is against the arguer (Latin *ad hominem* means "to the man") rather than against the argument: "Smith's argument against increasing taxes on the rich is worthless because he himself is rich." This fallacy, which substitutes irrelevant judgments of an individual for reasonable evaluations of an issue, is most likely to occur in evaluative arguments.

Ad Populum Argument

Ad populum is Latin for "to the people." One commits the *ad populum* fallacy when supporting a claim by referring to popular opinion or behavior to justify it. A teenager trying to convince her parents to remove her curfew because "everybody else's parents have done it" is attempting to convince her parents through an appeal to popular behavior rather than to reason. This fallacy is a corruption of the legitimate tactic of appealing to established authorities to strengthen a claim.

Circular Argument

A circular argument (also known as *begging the question*) is one in which the claim is already contained in the support: "John did not succeed on the track team [the claim] because he did not do well in track events [the support]." In this example, "did not do well in track events" really only restates "did not succeed on the track team"; it adds no new information about *why* John didn't succeed. Another common version of circular argument, or begging the question, assumes what has to be proven, as in the statement "This film should be banned because it contains immoral scenes." This claim requires a definition of *immoral* and evidence that the film meets this definition. Lacking such material, the claim begs the question of the immorality of the film. Evaluative, interpretive, and causal arguments seem to be particularly subject to this fallacy. One giveaway that your argument is circular is that your supporting statements repeat a key term from your claim.

Distraction

Distraction is bringing in irrelevant points to distract attention from the issue being argued: "Sure I cheated on my income taxes, but I've never broken any other laws." It is also known as the *red herring,* from the practice of dragging a dead herring across a trail to distract hunting dogs from the scent of their prey. Distraction is frequently used to deflect unfavorable evaluations.

Either-Or Argument

The either-or argument is setting up two extreme positions as the only alternatives and denying any possible middle ground: "The painting is either a masterpiece or trash." The painting could be something in between. Also known as *bifurcation* or the *fallacy of the excluded middle,* this fallacy can occur in any category of argument, though it is probably most frequent in evaluations (as in the claim about the painting) or in recommendations, where extreme solutions are sometimes seen as the only options: "Either we build a new computer facility or we give up on using computers at this school."

Emotive Language

The fallacy of emotive language involves making a case through slanted, value-laden language rather than through reasonable support, as in the statement "Smelling blood, the media will attack and destroy any candidate with a newsworthy weak spot." This claim, in its implicit identification of the media with carnivorous beasts, presumes a value judgment about the media that the claim does not justify. Writers of argument should try to refrain from using prejudicial language, at least until their claims have been reasonably made. Emotive or slanted language can be used in any kind of argument, but it is most common in evaluative arguments.

False Analogy

The false analogy supports a claim by comparing its subject to something not *essentially* similar: "Offering courses in gay and lesbian theory is no more defensible than teaching pedophilia or necrophilia." While both sides of the comparison refer to noncustomary sexual preference, there are more *differences* between gay theory and pedophilia than there are similarities, and comparing them attempts to prejudice the reader against gay and lesbian theory. As pointed out in Chapter 10, analogies can be useful in generating and illuminating arguments, but they can never prove a point. Just as legitimate comparison can be used to support any kind of argument (see Chapter 4), analogies can be misused in all of the four classes of argument. If you find that you have introduced an analogy to *support* rather than explain or illuminate a claim, you have probably committed this fallacy.

Hasty Generalization

Basically a misuse of the inductive method, hasty generalization consists of a general claim based on an insufficient sample: "Young professional people tend to be self-centered and materialistic. My friends Eric and Melanie certainly are." This fallacy typically occurs in factual arguments and in the supposedly factual support for evaluative statements about entire groups of people: "Women are sentimental"; "Asian-American students are good in mathematics."

Non Sequitur

A *non sequitur* claims a logical relationship between a conclusion and a premise where none exists: "Henry should make a good governor because he is tall and handsome." *Non sequitur* in Latin means "it does not follow"; *non sequitur* reasoning is behind almost all fallacies. The term is really a generic one that has been specifically applied to cases where the relationship between a premise and a conclusion is seriously askew. The term is also used to cover some fallacies in causal analysis: "I performed poorly on that speech because I wore my green tie rather than my red one." This is an example of our next fallacy—*post hoc, ergo propter hoc. Non sequitur* reasoning can occur in any category of argument.

Post Hoc, Ergo Propter Hoc

Post hoc, ergo proper hoc is Latin, meaning "after this, therefore because of this." It means claiming that because one event preceded another, it must have caused the subsequent event to occur: "I performed poorly on that speech because I wore my green tie rather than my red one." This fallacy is at the root of much superstition, as in the case of a pitcher who carries a red handkerchief with him whenever he pitches because he had one with him the day of his no-hitter. It is a serious risk in any causal analysis, and a writer can guard against it by following the principles of causal reasoning presented in Chapter 7.

Slippery Slope

Designating a first and a last step in a causal chain, when the intervening steps have not occurred, constitutes the slippery slope fallacy: "I didn't get the first job I interviewed for, so I guess I'd better forget about a career as an engineer." In this simple example, the speaker creates a worst-case scenario (forgetting about engineering) based on a series of events that has not yet occurred and will not necessarily occur, that is, repeated failure to be hired in engineering jobs. This fallacy appears most commonly in arguments of effect, usually when the writer wishes to prove that the consequences of a particular action are likely to be negative.

Strawperson Argument

A strawperson argument involves attacking a view similar to but not identical with that of an opponent: "How long will America tolerate softheaded opponents of gun control who want only criminals to have guns?" Advocates of gun control vary in their views, but they do not want only criminals to have guns. The adjective *soft-headed* is an example of emotive language; in this sentence, it is designed to arouse a particular emotional response. Negative loaded terms are frequent in strawperson arguments. This fallacy is a common but misguided tactic of evaluative arguments.

You can improve your ability to analyze your own and others' arguments by familiarizing yourself with the kinds of fallacies previously defined, but you need to remember that what is considered "correct" thinking depends on your context. What may be incorrect in one context may be perfectly acceptable in another: *ad hominem* arguments are frowned on in academic writing (though they do occur), but they are perfectly acceptable in a court of law, where questioning and at least implicitly attacking witnesses' backgrounds and motives are frequently practiced. In addition, some of these fallacies are only a slight step off the path of correct reasoning. For example, there is nothing inherently fallacious about either-or reasoning, but this kind of reasoning goes wrong when either-or alternatives lead to excluding other, real possibilities.

ACTIVITIES (5.3)

Identify the informal fallacies committed in the sentences that follow. Select from the following list:

ad hominem argument	false analogy
ad populum argument	hasty generalization
circular argument	*non sequitur*
distraction	*post hoc, ergo propter hoc*
either-or argument	slippery slope
emotive language	strawperson argument

1. Legalized abortion puts us only a step away from legalizing murders of anyone we deem undesirable or inconvenient.
2. If you can't beat them, join them.
3. I strongly disagree with your proposal to allow women to join fraternities. Fraternities are men-only clubs.
4. Those traitorous, draft-dodging youths who preferred deserting their country to serving it should never have been granted amnesty.
5. Discrimination should be fought on every front—whether it's practiced against members of a certain race, a certain sex, or those who bear arms.
6. I spent two weeks at a military academy and realized that private school is just not for me.
7. It is unfair to penalize Eastman Kodak for harming the environment when it has been such a strong supporter of the local economy.
8. *Supercop* had the highest ratings of any television movie. Clearly it was a superior film.
9. Tom Hanks is a brilliant comedian; he should leave heavy drama alone.
10. Opponents of the Equal Rights Amendment believe that women should stay barefoot and pregnant.

SUMMARY

Making Reasonable Arguments: Formal and Informal Logic

- Understanding the principles of formal logic will help you link claim and support reasonably.

- The principles of inductive logic—moving from specific instances to general conclusions—are important to all writers of argument and are particularly applicable to factual arguments.

- The syllogistic formula, common to most deductive reasoning, can be applied to an argument's claim and support as a way of determining the reasonableness of their connection.

- The Toulmin model of claim-warrant-backing is particularly useful to writers of argument, as it does not make absolute certainty a requirement of the claim.

- Informal fallacies are any of those errors in reasoning that can undermine the credibility of a claim. The best time to consider the possibility of informal fallacies is during the revision process.

The following article by Leslie Knowlton (*Psychiatric Times,* XII, 9, September 1995) contains a number of claims supported in a variety of ways. One important claim is Knowlton's explanation for the lower incidence of eating disorders in males as compared to females. The reasonableness of this causal claim can be tested by applying the Toulmin method. Placed within the Toulmin structure, the assertion that fewer men than women experience eating disorders would be the claim, and the data would be that men are subjected to less social reinforcement of thinness than women. As is often the case, the warrant—that principle linking claim and data—is unstated, but it would read something like "social reinforcements influence behavior."

EATING DISORDERS IN MALES

LESLIE KNOWLTON

About 7 million women across the country suffer from eating disorders including anorexia nervosa and bulimia and, as a result, most research into those two diseases has been conducted on females. However, as many as a million men may also struggle with the diseases.

One of the nation's leading researchers on eating disorders is Arnold E. Andersen, M.D., a professor of psychiatry in the University of Iowa College of Medicine. In addition to his academic and clinical work—some of it conducted as director of the Eating and Weight Disorders Clinic at Johns Hopkins—Andersen has edited a book of studies, *Males with Eating Disorders* (Brunner/Mazel 1990), and is writing another for families faced with the problem. His most current research project involves tracing and comparing the development of attitudes about body shape and weight among fifth- and sixth-grade males and females in the United States and India.

Speaking by telephone, Andersen said that despite being mentioned among the first case presentations in the English language three centuries ago, males with eating disorders have been "relatively ignored, neglected, dismissed because of statistical infrequency or legislated out of existence by theoretical dogma."

"There's a need to improve our recognition of eating disorders in males and to provide more adequate treatment," he said. "In addition, the category of males with eating disorders presents intellectual challenges regarding the etiology and mechanism for this gender-divergent abnormality of human-motivated behavior."

Andersen said that although the disorders look the same for men and women, the paths for getting there are quite different.

"The twin spotlights of empirical scientific studies and broad clinical experience can be brought to focus on either the similarities or the dissimilarities between males and females with eating disorders," said Andersen. "When individuals are very ill, suffering from emaciation or abnormal electrolytes and other medical complications, they appear very similar and require similar treatment."

But as patients become medically more healthy and the symptoms are "deconstructed," the individual life story behind each patient unfolds to reveal differences between the sexes in predisposition, course and onset, Andersen explained.

"We have to go back to where the roots are formed and look at gender diversity," he said.

For example, while women who develop eating disorders *feel* fat before they begin dieting, they typically are near average weight, whereas the majority of men who develop the diseases actually *are* medically overweight. Males with eating disorders are also more likely than women to have alcohol-related conditions and obsessional features.

Also, whereas women are concerned predominately with weight, men are concerned with shape and muscle definition. Additionally, more males than females diet in relationship to athletic achievement or slimming to please a homosexual lover.

"More men who develop anorexia or bulimia were seriously teased as overweight children," Andersen said, adding that about 21 percent of males with eating disorders are gay.

Finally, more men diet to prevent medical consequences of being overweight than do females, said Andersen.

So why do fewer males than females develop full-blown eating disorders?

Andersen said definitive answers are not available, but sociocultural influences have a lot to do with it.

"There's clearly less general reinforcement for slimness and dieting for males than for females, with only 10 percent as many articles and advertisements promoting dieting in magazines read by young males as compared to those read by young females," he said, referring to a study he conducted. "But when subgroups of males are exposed to situations requiring weight loss—such as occurs with wrestlers, swimmers, runners and jockeys—then a substantial increase in the behaviors of self-starvation and/or bulimic symptomatology follows, suggesting that behavioral reinforcement, not gender, is the crucial element."

Therefore, he continued, there's an apparent "dose-response" relationship between the amount of sociocultural reinforcement for thinness and the probability of developing an eating disorder, with the intermediate variable being dieting behavior.

"The process of transition from a normal behavior such as dieting, which is not in itself abnormal, into a fixed illness meeting

DSM-IV criteria for an eating disorder has not yet been well-defined," he said. "But it probably involves a transition from psychosocial to biomedical mechanisms."

Andersen said men who develop eating disorders can generally be divided into three groups: those in whom the onset was preadolescent, those in whom it was adolescent or young adult and those in whom it was adult. As in females, most male onset is adolescent.

While diagnostic criteria for anorexia and bulimia in men are similar to that in women, doctors often are less likely to think of making a diagnosis of eating disorders in males than in females. Likewise, the patient and his family and friends may not recognize it.

One reason anorexia may elude diagnosis in men more than in women is that men don't experience the on-off phenomenon of loss of menstrual periods, which can alert professionals and others to the problem, Andersen said. Rather, testosterone is gradually reduced, with an accompanying decline in libido and sexual performance.

Binge eating disorder may go unrecognized in males because an overeating male is less likely to provoke attention than an overeating female.

"And men are hesitant to seek medical attention for a disorder they fear will be seen as a girl's disorder or a gay guy's disease," Andersen said.

Source: *Psychiatric Times*, XII, 9 September 1995

SUGGESTIONS FOR WRITING (5.4)

1. Pay attention to the informal conversations and discussions of your friends. Start a list of all the generalizations you hear them make. Then write a one- to two-page letter to your friends telling them what information and evidence they would need to support their generalizations reasonably.

2. Focus on three advertisements you see repeatedly on television or in print. Write a one-page essay on each advertisement, discussing your application of the syllogistic and Toulmin models. How would the advertisement look within the format of each model? What premises or warrants are only implied? Are those claims true? What would have to be argued in order to make the advertisement more reasonable? Finally, rewrite the ad so that it conforms to the principles of deduction and the Toulmin model.

6

Arguing Facts

An argument's claim can be supported in a number of ways—some common to all arguments, some particular to specific classes. As is mentioned in Chapter 4, one common form of support for a claim is another claim. For example, if you were arguing that students graduating from your major have had trouble finding jobs, you could support that claim with job placement figures for students in your major, and/or with anecdotes about the employment woes of your friends. In both cases, you would be supporting a central factual claim by further factual assertions.

But take a slightly more complicated example. Suppose that in arguing the claim "First-time DWI offenders should have their driver's licenses revoked" (a claim of recommendation), you cite as support the secondary claim "The threat of license revocation would deter many from driving while intoxicated." This secondary claim is causal (predicting the *effect* of the change) and would require support appropriate to causal arguments. Among others, one piece of support you might use for this secondary causal claim is a factual assertion about the effectiveness of similar laws in other states.

There are two points to be taken from these examples: first, arguments almost always consist of a central claim supported by secondary claims, which themselves must be argued appropriately; second, sooner or later, all argumentative claims will come to rest on factual assertions. Because so many of the assertions we consider factual are themselves debatable, the facts holding up your arguments are not necessarily bedrock. Furthermore, even gathering the most reliable facts available seldom means that you will arrive at absolute truth. But some factual assertions are more solid than others, and it is the purpose of this chapter to show you what constitutes a reliable factual assertion or claim.

WHAT IS A FACT?

The New College Edition of *The American Heritage Dictionary* defines a fact as "Something known with certainty." According to this definition, a fact is a statement that is known to be true and about which there can be no debate or doubt. Assertions like "My physics teacher is a woman," "George Washington was the first president of the United States," and "Human beings are mortal" would fall under this definition; they are inarguable, unambiguous, proven facts that in most arguments would require no support beyond their simple assertion. Facts like these often come from your own experience or have been confirmed by your experience; sometimes they fall under the heading of "common knowledge." In any event, they can be accepted as indisputable.

But what about statements like "Beta-carotene is a carcinogen," "Secondary smoke is not harmful," or "The FDA-established minimum daily nutritional requirements are inadequate"? While these claims are stated as if they are known with certainty, careful readers might hesitate to call them indisputable. For one thing, they come from fields in which most of us are comparatively ignorant; we lack the expertise to judge their accuracy. Second, anyone who reads the newspaper regularly knows that these are the kinds of "facts" that seem always to be retired or revised when new evidence or new research methods emerge. Indeed, each of these statements is a correction of an earlier assertion that claimed to prove the opposite: beta-carotene was for years thought to be cancer-inhibiting; the known dangers of secondary cigarette smoke have just recently been moderated; and millions of perfectly healthy people have based their diets on the minimum daily requirements suggested by the FDA.

Assertions like these fall more properly under the dictionary's secondary definition of *fact:* "Something asserted as certain." Such statements are made in good faith, based on the best available evidence, and stated with conviction, but they are the findings of incomplete and ongoing research in comparatively dynamic fields and thus are always subject to revision and correction as newer, more inclusive, more reliable evidence is gathered. In other words, such factual assertions are *believed* to be certain, but not *known* with certainty; they are more like state-of-the-art educated guesses.

Finally, there is the assertion that is stated with certainty, dressed up as factual, and credited to a seemingly impeccable source, but that is nonetheless utterly preposterous. Some of these impostor facts are easy to detect; we know never to trust anything we read in the *National Enquirer,* for instance. But in more cases than we'd like to admit—particularly with the rush by the media to be the first on the scene—these preposterous facts can sneak right by you without your even suspecting that they are unreliable. You may find yourself particularly vulnerable to accepting (and circulating) false facts if they will strengthen your own argument.

The more your argument relies on the first and second type of facts, the more solid it will be. Your job in presenting facts supporting your argument's claim will be to convince your readers of their truth or likelihood, to convince them, that is, that your supporting facts are "known with certainty" or "are based on the best available evidence." The principles that follow should help you with this crucial job.

SUPPORTING FACTS REPORTED BY PRIMARY AND SECONDARY SOURCES

Most of the arguments you will write will depend on facts you find in your reading and research. Sometimes these facts will be reported by what are called primary sources, sometimes by secondary sources. A primary source is the individual or group that determined the fact in the first place—for example, a manager reporting that sales declined 5 percent in the last quarter or a research oncologist summarizing the findings of her study on cancer remissions in a medical journal. A secondary source is the person or document reporting facts discovered by someone else—for example, a biology textbook describing some little-known facts about Darwin's work on the HMS *Beagle,* or a member of an electronic listserv summarizing information heard at a professional conference.

Electronic listservs are e-mail discussion groups set up to cover specific educational and technical topics, among others. If you want to know more details about Darwin's work in this area, you can use your favorite search engine (*AltaVista, Metacrawler,* etc.) to find listserv groups that might cover this topic. One provider, L-Soft (http://www.lsoft.com), reveals a group that might be perfect for your needs. The listserv is hosted by St. John's University and gives you a description of the topics they cover:

> The Darwin-Med list (Darwin/Evolution Medicine mailing list) is a [sic] open discussion list for anyone interested in a Darwinian/evolutionary perspective on medicine, mainly people who have read "Why We Get Sick" (British edition: "Evolution and Healing") By Randolph M. Nesse & George C. Williams.

Most listservs, like the Darwin-Med list, allow you to look at their archives to see whether or not the subject you are interested in has been covered. If not, but you feel the group is where you can find answers, then you can subscribe to the list and join the discussion. If you do sign up, be sure to save the instructions for having your name removed from the list in the event that you do not want to continue to receive mail from this list after you have completed your research. You will also need to know how to cite the listserv in your list of references if you use any information you obtain from the list.

Because reliable facts are critical to successful arguments and because so many of the statements paraded as facts are unreliable, you'll want to be extremely discriminating about selecting facts from primary and secondary sources, recognizing that whenever you include a fact in your argument, you are tacitly saying to your audience, "I believe this to be a trustworthy statement." When your sources are printed texts (e.g., books, journals, newspapers), you have some assurance that the factual material has been reviewed by someone, though this assurance does not relieve you of responsibility for further evaluating the reliability of your source. But when your material comes from the Internet, that assurance may be completely missing. For both print and electronic sources, there *are* certain steps you can, and should, take to assure yourself—and thus your audience—that the facts you're presenting are relatively trustworthy.

Evaluating Print Sources

The first thing to look at when evaluating print sources is the identity of the author. Books and journal articles are almost always published under the author's name. If you are familiar with the author and know he or she is an acknowledged expert with a proven track record in the field, you have some assurance that the facts you wish to cite are reliable. You are probably safe trusting the facts given out by your college career counselor on postgraduate career opportunities, or facts about astronomy contained in an article by the noted astronomer Carl Sagan, because both have established professional reputations. But you should be wary of advice on the stock market obtained from a staff writer of your school paper. It's not that information obtained from nonexperts can't be reliable, but you should always be skeptical of these sources.

If you're not familiar with the author of the facts in question, it often pays to do a little digging. Your library has a number of professional biographical dictionaries either in its reference section or on-line. It pays to spend a little time looking up the author's qualifications. One thing to consider is the objectivity of your author. If Tiger Woods writes that Nike makes the best running shoe in the world, accept that pronouncement with a good dose of suspicion.

If you can't discover anything about the reliability of the author, or if the author isn't identified (as often happens in reference books, magazines, and editorials), consider the reputation of the publisher. Most university presses, for example, are considered careful reviewers of the material they publish, and certain journals and periodicals have established a reputation for accuracy. The publisher's good reputation will not ensure that the material in question is accurate, but it does make the odds of accuracy relatively high. Certainly a report found in the *Wall Street Journal* is more credible than one found in *Star* magazine or the *National Enquirer.* If you don't know anything about the reliability of your source's publisher, ask a professor in the field.

You also want to be sure to check the date of your source's publication. While a book on Abraham Lincoln dated 1966 might not be considered outdated, a 1966 book on computer technology would be barely worth reading, unless you were doing a historical survey of the field.

Evaluating Electronic Sources

The huge growth in electronically accessible information is both a blessing and a curse to writers who must work with reliable facts. On the one hand, finding information has never been easier. Hundreds, even thousands, of sources on a given topic are available with a few keystrokes. But the sheer volume of information can make us lazier and less effective researchers. Furthermore, because anyone with the proper equipment can post information on the Internet, there is a lot more unreliable information on-line than between the pages of a book or journal that has gone through some kind of review process (The article " 'Vonnegut Speech' Circulates on Net" at the end of this chapter shows how quickly misinformation can circulate on the Internet).

For the most part, evaluating electronic sources isn't all that different from evaluating print sources. Begin by trying to determine the author's reliability—again, through biographical dictionaries or perhaps the *National Dictionary of Addresses and Telephone Numbers*. While you're on the Internet, try a search through the World Wide Web using the author's name as your keyword; you may find some useful information on his or her reputation.

Checking the electronic address of your source gives you some generic information about its origin and thus at least a hint of its reliability. *Edu* means it comes from an educational institution; *gov* is a governmental organization; *org* is a nonprofit organization; and *com* is a commercial organization.

Make sure to check the date of the material if it's available. Much of the material on the Internet has the virtue of being very current, but in quickly moving fields, information may become out-of-date in a matter of days.

If you read useful factual information on a listserv, try communicating with the author (whose name and e-mail address are included on the listserv posting) to get information about the sources of his or her information. Or if you find nonattributed information on a Web site, try following up some of the related "links" on the site; these may lead you to the background you need on the sources of the Web site material.

Citing the Source in Your Text

Another way to support the primary and secondary facts you present is to cite their source within your argument. Providing the source is not only a courtesy to readers who may want to examine the subject in more depth, but also avoids the possibility of plagiarism. Including the source assures your readers that your argument is a responsible one—that your facts are not fabricated for the sake of argument but come from legitimate sources. Failure to cite the sources of the facts on which your claim rests will weaken your argument considerably.

In most cases, your citation of a source will take the form of a footnote, an endnote, or, increasingly, inclusion of the work in a "Works Cited" list at the end of your argument. The subject matter of your argument, and the discipline you are writing for, will determine which citation form you should follow. For example, many education programs require students to follow *The Chicago Manual of Style* footnote format, whereas sociology will probably rely on *The Publication of the American Psychological Association*, more commonly known as APA. Many English professors insist on MLA, the Modern Language Association's format, whereas some may require APA. Scientific notation and documentation procedures can vary widely, so you should ask your instructor which format he or she wants you to follow if it is not specified in the assignment.

You can find models of these forms in most college writing handbooks, CD-ROM handbooks like *Take Note*, and on-line through your library and many college writing lab pages. Purdue, Washington State University, North Carolina State University, and Dakota State University are only a few of the universities who have published their OWLs (Online Writing Lab) and made them available to the public through the Internet.

In addition to a footnote or bibliographic reference, you can also include a brief reference to your source within the text of your argument. For example, "According to the *Oxford English Dictionary,* the word *flick* at one time meant 'thief.'" In this case, the source would also appear in a works cited or bibliography section at the end of the argument.

If your readers are not likely to be familiar with your source, you may want to provide credentials briefly within your text. For example, "In his book *The Mismeasure of Man,* Stephen Jay Gould, the noted Harvard paleontologist and popularizer of science, argues that the results of standardized intelligence tests can be misleading and also misused by those in power."

A note on citing electronic sources: works on the Internet are copyrighted, so you must give full citations (including the Web address and the path, or URL, needed to obtain the file).

ACTIVITIES (6.1)

Write a one-page analysis of the credibility of two of the following passages. Consider the issues of expertise, bias, and currency of facts. You may need to do some research on the credentials of the author or of the publication in which the passage appeared.

1. Mailer had the most developed sense of image; if not, he would have been a figure of deficiency, for people had been regarding him by his public image since he was twenty-five years old. He had in fact learned to live in the sarcophagus of his image—at night, in his sleep, he might dart out, and paint improvements on the sarcophagus. During the day, while he was helpless, newspapermen and other assorted bravos of the media and literary world would carve ugly pictures on the living tomb of his legend. Of necessity, part of Mailer's remaining funds of sensitivity went right into the war of supporting his image and working for it. (Norman Mailer. *The Armies of the Night.* New York: Signet Books, 1968. 15-16.)

2. Chow chow, powerful NONSPORTING DOG; shoulder height, 18–20 in. (45.7–50.8 cm); weight, 50–60 lb (22.7–27.2 kg). Its coat has a soft, wooly underlayer and a dense, straight topcoat that stands out from the body. It may be any solid color and is the only breed with a black tongue. A hunting dog in China 2,000 years ago, it was brought to England in the 18th cent. (*Concise Columbia Encyclopedia.* New York: Columbia University Press, 1983. 168.)

3. A SPECTER is haunting Europe—the specter of communism. All the powers of the old Europe have entered into a holy alliance to exorcise this specter: Pope and Czar, Metternich and Guizot, French Radicals and German police spies. (Karl Marx and Friedrich Engels. *The Communist Manifesto.* Ed. Samuel H. Beer. New York: Appleton-Century-Crofts, 1955. 8. Originally published in 1848.)

4. Many devices have been used in the attempted measurement of interests. The interest inventory is the most important of these both from the standpoint of the number of counselors using them and the number of investigators working with them. The inventory approach consists of the comparison of likes and dislikes of individuals through questionnaire items. Since the individual

is asked to estimate his feeling, the method may be said to be subjective. A complete discussion of interest inventories is given by Fryer [Douglas Fryer. *The Measurement of Interests*. New York: Henry Holt, 1931]. (Harry J. Older. "An Objective Test of Vocational Interests." *Journal of Applied Psychology*. 28, 1944: 99.)

5. People who have a good sense of humor *suffer less constipation, acid stomach and sensitivity to cold* than those who don't get the joke, according to a study presented at the American Psychosomatic Society annual meeting. ("Medical Flash." *Self*. July 1994: 59.)

6. In a report presented to the House of Representatives, Marnie S. Shaul, the Director of Education, Workforce, and Income Security Issues noted that voucher school programs have not been "rigorously evaluated" to determine whether or not the programs are achieving what they claim they can achieve for students. (U.S. General Accounting Office. *At-Risk Youth: School-Community Collaborations Focus on Improving Student Outcomes*. Washington, GAO-01-66. Oct. 2000. Accessed 02 Jan. 2001. Available: http://www.gao.gov/)

SUPPORTING PERSONALLY EXPERIENCED FACTS

Sometimes you'll need to support a fact obtained through your own experience or observation rather than from a second- or third-party source. Personally experienced facts are supported by a credible and objective description of the experience or observation.

Describing the Experience

Let's say you are writing a report for a psychology class on phobias and you want to demonstrate how extreme and irrational phobic behavior can be. As evidence for this position, you cite your observations of a friend who is terrified to fly: "Traveling with a friend on a short domestic flight, I observed firsthand what phobic panic looks like." Because this statement suggests extreme behavior, it requires a careful and accurate description of the panic as support: the pallor, the tremors, the hysteria you observed in your friend. (At this point, we are not talking about explaining or interpreting the fact, but about presenting it in such a way that your reader will accept that it happened.)

The principle holds in more complicated contexts. Take the scientific laboratory reports that are written in all lab courses from ninth grade through graduate school. The writer's basic purpose in these assignments—to report an experience in the lab—is achieved through a careful, detailed description of the steps followed and the results obtained.

Establishing Your Own Credibility

Writers of argument must appear credible to their readers, projecting an image that inspires confidence and trust. This requirement applies to all components of your argument, but it is particularly relevant to the presentation of personally experienced facts. Since you, the writer, are usually the sole support of a personally experienced fact, you must give your readers no reason to mistrust your description of the experience.

If your readers have any reason to suspect that your description is dishonest or inaccurate, your argument is going to fail. For example, if you referred to your 85 year old grandmother as support for an argument against mandatory retirement, citing her daily five-mile runs, her ability to bench-press 300 pounds, and her current prize-winning research on recombinant DNA, your readers would be very suspicious of such obvious exaggeration, and your credibility as an observer would be seriously questioned.

In presenting facts derived from personal experience, you must also guard against the inevitability of your own bias. Without realizing it, we often see only what we want to see and ignore what is convenient to ignore. Ask two politicians on opposing sides of an issue their perceptions of a stormy meeting and you will almost certainly get two very different stories about what happened. They are not necessarily trying to falsify evidence, but their biases color their perceptions. In some contexts, such as sportswriting about the hometown team or essays on the opinion page of the newspaper, readers expect and even welcome a certain bias, but they tend to reject open manifestations of it in other contexts, such as front-page news, academic projects, or business reports. One way to avoid excessive personal bias when you report facts you have observed is to ask yourself whether a person making a different claim would have observed the same things; if the answer is no, you should aim for more neutrality in your description. Another way to guard against the possibility of bias in reporting fact is to consult other people who observed or experienced the same event to ensure that your view is essentially a shared one. If it is not, you must consider whether your own bias accounts for the difference.

SUPPORTING FACTUAL GENERALIZATIONS

Any claim, regardless of the class it falls into, can be stated as a *generalization.* For example, the factual claim "*People* magazine and *USA Today* use much the same format as television news shows" becomes a factual generalization when the communications scholar Neil Postman tells us that "the total information environment begins to mirror television." Similarly, the claim "Frank is a successful sales representative because his father was also a good sales representative" (introducing a limited causal argument with an element of evaluation) can be extended to the following generalization: "Successful salespeople tend to have other good salespeople in their families."

To support any generalization, you need to apply two sets of principles. First, you must convince your readers that your original claims about *People* and *USA Today* or about Frank and his father are plausible—that significant similarities do exist between the television news show *20/20* and *People* magazine, or that there is a demonstrable *causal* connection between a father and a son who are both sales reps. How you support your claim will depend on the category to which it belongs. The first example is a largely factual claim, and the second is a causal claim.

Second, you must show that your generalization is reasonable—that what you've observed about Frank and his father can be plausibly applied to salespeople and their children all over the world. We will use factual generalizations to illustrate this second principle, but it applies to all categories of argument.

Applying the Principles of Induction

All generalizations, even the most informal and sweeping, begin on a specific level. We see something a few times and assume that it happens frequently or even all the time. That is, we move from specific observations to general conclusions; from the particular, we infer the general. In traditional logic, this process by which we assume the widespread existence of particular instances is called *induction*. Conclusions drawn by inductive reasoning are always somewhat risky because they are based on incomplete evidence. You assume that because you have never seen or heard of a flying cat, no such creature exists, yet unless you have seen every cat that ever existed, your claim "There is no such thing as a flying cat" has made a rather staggering leap from the particular to the universal. Yet these leaps are the nature of induction.

Support for a generalization consists of identifying a number of specific, verified instances or examples. If you claim, for example, that American films increasingly show the dangers of casual sexual relationships, you will have to cite individual films to support your claim. Or if you write, "Many young American novelists find universities a supportive and economically secure place to work," you will need to point to specific examples. If the generalization is a factual generalization, the specific examples will be individual facts, which in some cases may need verification. What makes a factual generalization "factual" is not the absolute truth of the generalization, which can never be proven, but its foundation in singular factual instances.

The most credible generalizations are those supported by the most, and best, examples. You cannot reasonably conclude that all algebra teachers are women if your experience is limited to one or two teachers, but you can reasonably conclude that many teenagers like rap music if you have known hundreds of teenagers in many different settings who like rap. In supporting generalizations, you need to know how many examples are enough, whether they are representative of all the available evidence, and which examples to include. Unfortunately, no simple formula exists that answers these questions, but the following general rules of thumb are helpful.

How Many Examples Are Enough?   First, the more sweeping your claim, the more examples you will need. You can position a generalization at any point along a continuum of frequency: "*Some* business majors are good in math"; "*Many* business majors are good in math"; "*All* business majors are good in math." Although the word *some* does constitute a generalization, it is a very limited generalization, a safe one to make if you don't have abundant evidence. To support "some," you need only a handful of examples. "Many" requires more than a handful of examples, certainly, but is far easier to prove than "all." In fact, absolute statements using words like *all, everyone, never,* or *always* should be avoided in written argument unless every constituent in the group referred to can be accounted for. Otherwise, the claims these words make are too grandiose to be credible. The following passage supports its factual generalization with carefully chosen examples:

> A number of fraternity members on this campus contradict the broad and usually unflattering stereotypes circulated about "brothers." While I am not a fraternity member myself, I know a number of members well, and none of them fits the popular image of the beer-swilling, women-chasing party boy. For instance, my friend Judd, a dean's list electrical engineering major and obviously a dedicated student, says that fraternity living gives him the supportive environment he needs to excel in a difficult major. Two of my roommates from freshman year who have joined fraternities have become respected student leaders: Brad is vice president of Student Council, and Kelly is the student representative to Faculty Council. Both Brad and Kelly are well-rounded, academically successful students. Finally, I know that the entire pledge class of one campus chapter received the mayor's commendation for public service for their renovation of an inner-city recreation center. Of course, there will always be individuals who confirm the stereotype, but my observations question its widespread applicability.

In this passage, three examples, the last involving a large group of individuals, are presented to support the claim that few fraternity members fit the campus stereotype. In a more formal academic argument, we would probably insist on more rigorous, less personally observed evidence, but we would very likely accept these examples as adequate in a short, informal essay. As a general rule, three is a good number of examples for a short essay, since one or two examples may seem to be merely exceptions, whereas four or more would become tedious.

The less familiar your readers are with your subject matter, the more specific examples you should supply. If your readers are very comfortable and familiar with your topic, they will often accept sensible generalizations that are only minimally supported. If you refer in an internal business report to the "widespread problems with our new computer system," those familiar with the problem will accept the reference and not demand that it be supported. But a reader unfamiliar with this problem may demand evidence that the problem really exists. Of course, some readers unfamiliar with your subject area will accept dubious generalizations simply because they don't know any better. If these readers are misled, however, some of them will probably eventually learn that you were wrong in your generalizations, and they will then suspect your reliability in other situations, even when you are correct in your claims.

Do Your Examples Represent the Evidence Fairly?   In selecting which evidence for your generalization to include in your argument, you should make sure that the examples you choose fairly represent all the available examples, including the ones you omitted. Imagine, for example, that you support the statement "Fraternity hazing is obsolete on our campus" with examples of changes in the rules and practices of the three largest fraternities, but in the course of your research, you discover that there are significant exceptions to this generalization. You are misrepresenting the evidence if you fail to tell your readers about these exceptions. True, you may have provided enough examples to satisfy your readers, but you are misleading them by excluding the contradictory evidence. The best way around this problem is to qualify the claim in such a way that the evidence you omit is not contradictory. If you rewrite the claim as "Instances of fraternity hazing on our campus have decreased significantly in the last ten years," your three examples will perfectly support the claim, and the omitted evidence will no longer be contradictory.

Is Your Conclusion Too Broad for Your Examples?   Inductive reasoning always requires that the breadth of your conclusion match the breadth of your supporting evidence. If your generalized claim is very broad ("Art majors are the most politically liberal of all college students"), it must be based on proportionately broad examples—in this case, instances taken from a number of different colleges in different areas of the country that offer majors in art. If your claim is more limited ("Art majors at my college are the most politically liberal students"), you are justified in citing examples taken only from your college.

But even in this second, narrower case, you still must guard against generalizing on the basis of instances drawn from too narrow a context. If the art students at your school come from all over the country, yet you use as examples only those who come from the New York City area, your support is not broad enough to justify your conclusion. You will either need to limit your claim further ("Art majors from the New York City area are the most politically liberal students at my college") or to collect examples drawn from a broader geographic group.

ACTIVITIES (6.2)

1. The following conclusions are generalizations derived through inductive reasoning. What kinds of examples, and how many, would you need to make each one plausible?
   a. Most librarians are women.
   b. High school librarians tend to be women.
   c. In my experience, librarians have been pretty evenly divided between men and women.
   d. I have attended two major universities and have been struck by the number of librarians who are women.
   e. Library science departments tend to attract more women students than men.

2. Write a generalization that is adequately supported by the examples listed for each of the following cases.
   a. John, Susan, and Jim prefer chocolate ice cream, whereas Jane prefers strawberry, and Henry prefers vanilla.

b. Last Saturday night I sat alone at a showing of the new film *Anxious Hours,* and I saw no line for the film when I walked by the theater just before show time on Sunday.
c. It is January 15 here in Minnesota, and so far this winter, we have had two snowfalls that just covered the ground and then disappeared.
d. There were 25 Mercedes-Benz automobiles parked in the lot the night of my high school reunion, and as I recall, there were only about 70 students in my graduating class.
e. When I returned from winter break to my classes here in Vermont, I noticed that Jack, Jeff, Mary, Matthew, Carrie, and Megan all had deep tans.

STATISTICS

Statistics are derived from the practice of drawing conclusions about a large number on the basis of a limited number of instances. Statistics are factual information compiled and reported numerically. The following are examples of statistical claims:

- Thirty percent of the American people believe a woman should never be president.
- The unemployment rate is 11 percent.
- One-quarter of all bridges in this state need repair.

In our world, statistics are an inevitable and integral part of our lives. We judge the quality of our manufactured products and of many of our services through statistics; we constantly encounter statistics on the health of our economy, our educational system, our sex lives, our souls. We tend to suspect claims that lack statistical support, and we use statistics in virtually every field in our society, from weather forecasting to managing baseball teams. But these general conclusions inferred from a limited number of instances are reliable only if the original process of information gathering was conducted according to certain principles. Whether you are conducting your own statistical studies as support for your argument or citing statistics obtained from other sources, you must be sure of the following:

1. The smaller group surveyed (or *sample,* as statisticians refer to it) must be *known.* If you read that eight out of ten women think they are overweight, but no reference is made to the source of the survey or who or how many were surveyed, you should not accept or use the figure. For all you know, only ten women were questioned, and they were picked from a list obtained from a weight reduction clinic. Every cited study should be identified and the sample group defined. Without such information, the figures are suspect.

2. The sample must be *sufficient,* or sufficiently large, in order for you to accept the conclusion drawn from that sample. That both of your roommates prefer classical music to rock does not justify the conclusion that classical music is more popular with college students; you need a much larger sample. Trained statisticians sometimes use small samples, but only under very specific conditions and with very specific mathematical models. Our inability to evaluate the use of these statistical for-

mulas makes it hard for us to judge whether statistics are actually being used correctly. In such cases, it's important to learn as much as you can about the context of the studies and the methods by which the samples were gathered before relying on the figures completely. For example, researchers often critique each other's studies, and their analyses provide valuable information about the reliability of the results.

3. The sample must be *representative.* If a figure is given about the political inclinations of all Californians, the sample surveyed must represent a cross section of the population. If the 2,000 people questioned all have incomes of $40,000 and up, or if they're all over the age of 45, your sample is slanted and not representative of the variety of the population as a whole. Professional polling organizations like Gallup and Harris (groups hired to identify the preferences of large populations based on small samples) choose either a representative or a random sample. A *representative sample* is one that guarantees in advance that the sample will reflect the major characteristics of the population—for example, that the sample will have a percentage of Californians earning over $40,000 that is equal or nearly equal to the percentage of Californians earning over that figure in the total population. In a *random sample* on political attitudes in California, every adult Californian would stand an equal chance of being questioned. When chosen randomly, in 95 out of 100 cases, a sample group of 1,500 people will be within 3 percentage points of duplicating the answers of the entire adult population. In evaluating the usefulness of any poll, you should know the method by which the sample was selected.

When you include in your argument statistics obtained from other sources, not only must you test them for the preceding three principles, you must also be certain they satisfy the requirements of second- or third-party facts. The source should have a reputation for expertise in the field and for objectivity, and the figures themselves should be recent. It is unwise to accept as support for your own argument any statistical data not credited to an authoritative source. If you cannot identify the instrument, individual, or organization through which these facts were obtained, chances are good that those facts are not reliable.

When using statistics in your argument, you also need to be aware of the variety of terms used to report large figures and of the way these terms influence the impact of the figures. A study on high school literacy could report its findings on extracurricular reading habits in a number of ways. It could say that out of 500 high school seniors surveyed, *100* had read at least one unassigned novel in the last year, or the same fact could be reported as *20 percent* of the students. Of those 100 readers, one could report the *average* number (or *mean*) of novels read (the total number of novels read divided by the 100 readers), the *mode* (the number of novels most frequently read by individual students), or the *median* (the midpoint of the range of frequency of novels read). The mean, mode, and median for this sample of students follow:

	Students	Novels Read	Total Novels
	25	4	100
	10	3	30
	45	2	90
	20	1	20
Total	100		240

Average = 2.4 novels (total number of novels read divided by total number of students)

Mode = 2 novels (the most common number)

Median = 2 novels (the midpoint of the list of number of novels read according to the frequency of the number. Imagine the 100 students standing in a line, starting with all of those who read four novels, then those who read three, then two, and so on. The midpoint of this line of 100 would occur in the group of students who had read two novels.)

Statistics can be powerful tools in argument, but again, it is crucial to realize that they cannot *prove* claims; they can only *support* their likelihood. A recent poll indicating teenage hostility toward adult society is not proof that it was a teenager who attacked your English teacher or even that the students in a particular high school have hostile feelings toward their parents. It merely indicates that out of a sample of so many teenagers a certain percentage indicated feelings of hostility toward the adult generation. Responsibly gathered statistics are not suspect, but the use to which we put these figures may be.

You should also be restrained in your use of statistics; if scattered profusely throughout a written text, they have a deadening effect on the audience. Often, a visual display of statistics in a chart or a table is more valuable to your audience than a verbal summary; graphic representations can clarify the meaning of the statistics and reinforce their significance. With statistics, it is easy to lose track not only of the "big picture" but also of any picture at all, and visual displays can give the reader the necessary perspective.

ACTIVITIES (6.3)

1. For two of the following statements based on statistics, discuss with a small group of your classmates the kind of information necessary to ensure the statement's reliability.
   a. Over 50 percent of the doctors surveyed in a nationwide study recommend Brand A medicine over any of the leading competitors.
   b. Brand C: the best built truck in America, according to a survey of truck owners.
   c. Over 60 percent of all Americans favor the president's plan for peace, whereas 85 percent oppose Senator Flag's call for more offensive weapons.
   d. Despite competition from television and VCRs, moviegoing is still popular in America. When asked how much they enjoyed going to the movies, 88 percent of moviegoers responded that they enjoyed moviegoing a great deal.
   e. A survey of leading economic forecasters indicates that a mild recession will occur in the next six months.

2. Conduct a survey of some of your classmates or of some friends. Ask them one or two questions that can be summarized in statistics, such as how many hours they studied last week. Compute the mean, mode, and median of these statistics. Write a one-page description of the results of your survey, and also present this information in visual form. Also state how representative you believe this group is of some larger, similar group, such as all students who studied last week.

SUMMARY

Arguing Facts

- All arguments rely on factual claims, either as their primary claim or as a form of support for the primary claim.

- To support facts reported by others, you must be satisfied of their accuracy and provide in your argument a brief reference to the source of the fact.

- To support facts founded on your own experience, you must describe the experience accurately and clearly and establish your own credibility through a responsible, objective, and accurate rendering of the experience.

- To support a factual generalization, you must cite a number of the verified facts that have led you to the general conclusion. The more sweeping the generalization, the more examples you will need to cite. If your readers are likely to be unfamiliar with the subject matter, you should provide several examples as evidence. The examples cited must be typical of all the evidence discovered. The breadth of the examples cited must match the breadth of the generalization.

- Statistics can effectively support arguments, provided they are not overused and their significance is made clear.

- When including a statistical generalization, you must be satisfied of its reliability. It is reliable if the sample cited is known, sufficient, and representative.

- You must be aware of the exact meaning of the terms used to report statistical conclusions, particularly *average, median,* and *mode.*

TWO SAMPLE FACTUAL ARGUMENTS

The following analytical report was written by a student in a "Tools For Engineering" course. Unlike most lab reports, it is primarily a factual generalization. The hypothesis in Paragraph 1 is the unsupported claim, which, by the final paragraph, has been converted into a supported conclusion. The writer supports his claim by reporting analytical facts: the procedure he followed and its observed results. Through his attention to detail, his fully developed discussion of the graphics supplied, and adherence to the conventional lab report format, he implicitly demonstrates that he is a reliable reporter.

Advantages of Matlab

Purpose: To discuss the ability to create and run scripts by Matlab. The programmable nature of this application makes it ideal for engineering and many of its repetitively analyzed functions. It combines the power of mathematical software such as Maple or Mathematica with the programming advantages of a language such as C++.

Discussion: An application of this inherent advantage is one working with the function:

$$y = px^2 + qe^{x/5} + r \ln[x]$$

By creating a function that asks for input values of the constants (p, q, and r), one can quickly compare different cases with four plots.

One of the features of such a function that both scientists and engineers would be interested in is that of curve fitting. When scientific data is collected, scientists often try to summarize their results by noticing characteristics such as linearity in their results. Microsoft Excel's charting includes curve fitting options that aid in deciding if a set of data is best fit by a linear, quadratic, logarithmic, or exponential type of curve. This Matlab script gives you a similar advantage.

The supplied constants that best test this and their graphs follow:

Case 1: The values of $p = 1$, $q = 0$, and $r = 0$ yield an equation proportional to the quadratic and produce the graph of:

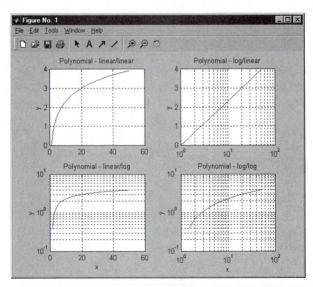

Case 2: The values of $p = 0$, $q = 1$, and $r = 0$ yield an equation proportional to an exponential curve and produce the graph of:

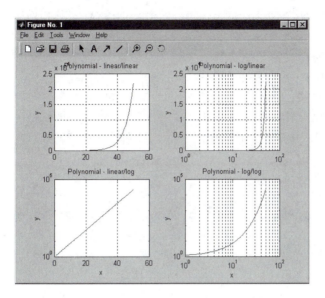

Case 3: The values of $p = 0$, $q = 0$, and $r = 1$ yield an equation proportional to the logarithmic curve and produce the graph of:

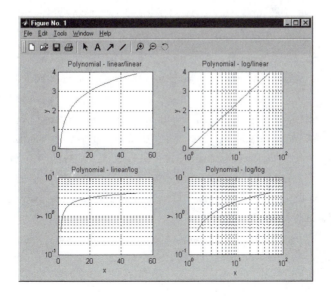

When analyzing these graphs, one needs to note the nature of each of the four subplots. The upper left gives the straightforward linear graphical representation. The upper right offers a graph with an x scale that is exponential. This is characteristic of a logarithm. The lower left is reversed; this time the independent variable remains unaltered while the dependent variable is exponential. This is characteristic of an exponential function. The last plot, the one appearing in the lower-right corner, is exponential on both axes. This plot would be useful to see overall trends of a function.

Applying this information to the three cases allows us to see how each set of data could be fitted. For the graph produced by *Case One* data, the most linear is the third graph. This indicates that the function is neither exponential nor logarithmic. Inspection of the component producing the data verifies this. *Case Two*'s data is most linear in the lower-left subplot. This would indicate that it would be best fit by an exponential function. Once again, inspection verifies this. In regard to the *Case Three* data, the most linear graph is the upper-right graph. This means that the data would be best fit by a logarithmic function, which is again verified.

Conclusion: Matlab has many applications and the ease of creating functions is one of its greatest. Although only three cases need to be considered in this instance, sometimes the best cases are not always apparent. They can only become apparent after trying several different values and inspecting the results. Because of the repetition involved, the ability to create a function to quickly reproduce your results for different values is a highly powerful feature with innumerable applications.

"VONNEGUT SPEECH" CIRCULATES ON NET

DAN MITCHELL

A copy of Kurt Vonnegut Jr.'s recent MIT commencement address made heavy email rotation on Friday. The characteristically pithy, funny, thoughtful speech was passed from friend to friend stamped with such comments as "worth a read" and "check this out—it's great."

And it *was* great. Trouble is, it wasn't Vonnegut's. "Kurt Vonnegut Jr. had never given a commencement address at MIT," said Robert Sales, associate director of the school's news office.

It turns out the "speech" was actually a column penned by the *Chicago Tribune*'s Mary Schmich. The column ran on 1 June—five days before UN Secretary General Kofi Annan delivered the actual commencement address at MIT. That speech "was a lot longer and maybe not as clever" as the purported Vonnegut address, Sales said.

Much of Schmich's column—which consists of advice for graduates—sounds like stuff Vonnegut might say: "Don't be reckless with other people's hearts. Don't put up with people who are reckless with yours. . . . Remember compliments you receive. Forget the insults. If you succeed in doing this, tell me how. . . . Keep your old love letters. Throw away your old bank statements. . . . Do one thing every day that scares you."

Nobody—least of all Schmich—can figure out why Vonnegut's name was slapped onto her column. "Some prankster apparently decided it would be funny. Why is it funny? If you can figure that out, you're a genius," she said Monday.

Perhaps the act itself wasn't funny, but some of the fallout has been. First of all, there's the fact that (ahem) Wired News ran part of the column as its Quote of the Day on Friday. Also, Schmich says she's gotten as much attention from the incident as just about anything she's written. "My email's just flooded with messages," she says. And she says she's actually been accused of plagiarizing Vonnegut—and vice versa. On Friday, she managed to reach Vonnegut, who, Schmich says, said the whole thing is "spooky."

In her column on Monday, Schmich writes that she wrote the piece "one Friday afternoon while high on coffee and M&Ms." And, she insisted, "It was not art."

In part, Schmich blames the "cyberswamp" of the Internet for all the trouble. "At newspapers, things like this have to go through a barrier before they go out to the world," she said. But on the Net "anybody can put anybody's name on anything."

Nonetheless, she added, "No one involved in this did anything bad, except the person who started it."

SUGGESTIONS FOR WRITING (6.4)

1. Write a two- to three-page essay supporting a fact that runs counter to popular opinion. This fact can come from your own experience, from your studies in college, or from your general knowledge. Examples of such surprising facts

are "Despite predictions to the contrary, the increasing use of computers has created more new jobs than it has eliminated existing ones"; "Milk does not always do a body good." This surprising fact can be about yourself, your family, your friends, your hometown, your college, your job, your major, or whatever else comes to mind.

2. Stereotypes are misleading factual generalizations that make the false claim that all members of a group have a certain trait: "The English people have stiff upper lips in times of crisis"; "American men like to watch football." Take a prevalent stereotype and analyze to what degree the stereotype is true and how the stereotype is misleading. Make sure the stereotype is one you can deal with in a three- to four-page essay, such as "Engineering students of my college don't get involved in extracurricular activities." You don't have to do a statistical survey to gather data for this essay, but you should carefully examine and present examples to support your claim.

3. Analyze either a newspaper or a television news show for examples of bias or misleading generalizations (for the television news show, you may have to videotape the show so that you can view it two or three times). How objective is the reporting of the news? Are there any examples of misleading generalizations? What kind of news is *not* included? Write a two- to three-page essay addressing these questions.

7

Arguing Cause

The goal of causal argument is to establish a probable cause or effect for a given condition. A claim arguing "Many teenagers abuse alcohol because they are desperately disappointed by their 'real lives' " will establish the *cause* of teen alcohol abuse, whereas the claim "Today's generation of college students will be far more successful in marriage than their parents have been" argues the *effect* of certain conditions. In order to convince your readers that the cause or effect you argue is reasonable, you must have a good understanding of the nature of causality and of the processes used to determine and report causes and effects. Written causal arguments are essentially reports of the process the writer followed to determine causes or effects.

The first part of this chapter concentrates on arguments of *cause:* arguments that identify and support the cause or causes of an existing situation. As you'll see in the last part of the chapter, the principles and processes involved in arguments of cause are identical to those you'll rely on when you write arguments of *effect* (arguments predicting the probable future effects of an existing situation).

DETERMINING CAUSE

Any single effect is the consequence of a number of causes—some powerful and direct, others less influential but still contributing. For this reason, arguing cause usually involves more than isolating *the* single cause of a given effect: most extended causal arguments discover and support those causes most useful to the context, purpose, and audience of your argument. If your goal is to give as full a causal explanation as possible for the effect in question, you will identify and support a number of causes, both direct and indirect. But if the point of your argument is to assign responsibility, you will address only the most immediate causes (such as who did what, regardless of why). If the purpose of your argument is to instruct, or if you want some future action taken or avoided on the basis of the causality you demonstrate in a comparable situation, you are likely to emphasize both the immediate and the more remote causes of the current situation. For example, if you wish to improve your GPA, you might try to reproduce as many of the habits of a successful student friend as you can: careful budgeting of time, keeping up with assignments, regular class attendance, and so on.

Brainstorming for Possible Causes

Whether or not you begin with a particular causal claim in mind, it is a good idea to begin the argument process by listing all the facts and conditions you can think of that seem to be causally linked to the effect you are explaining. Depending on your subject, this list may come from your own thinking and brainstorming and/or from any reading and research you might do. The list should include as many facts or conditions you can think of that seem even remotely connected to the effect. The next step will be to apply your knowledge of causal principles to this working list in order to identify the most influential causes.

Let's assume you are arguing the reasons for the high student dropout rate at your college. Part of your argument will consist of a discussion of individual cases: why particular people you know decided to leave school. You know one student (we'll call her Emma) who explains her plans to drop out of school by saying, "I just don't like college." But you know this is not a satisfactory explanation. Why doesn't she like college? What events and conditions have made her unhappy enough to make this extreme decision? So, in a couple of long conversations, you press Emma further, and you talk with some of the people who know her well. The result of these discussions is a list of more specific possible reasons for her decision.

For one thing, Emma's grades have not been very good. Though her grades were good in high school, Emma can't seem to pull her GPA above a 2.0. It's clear to you from talking to her that she's the kind of person who expects a lot from herself, so her undistinguished grades have to be a blow to her self-esteem. It makes sense that she would want to leave a place where she doesn't feel good about herself. You also learn that Emma is the first person in her family to go to college, and her parents have made many sacrifices to give her every educational advantage. Their ambition for Emma puts a lot of pressure on her, which has probably made it even harder for her to relax and do her best. And Emma's family situation has worked against her in another way: it offers no close role models to emulate, no family tradition of academic success. Add to these factors Emma's crazy roommate and their closet-size room, and you begin to wonder how Emma lasted through the first semester.

Your examination of the situation has identified a number of possible causes for Emma's decisions—all much more specific and useful than her vague claim that she doesn't like college. Some of the possible causes on your list seem directly influential, like her mediocre grades, their blow to her self-esteem, and her crazy roommate; others are more remote, like her parents' lack of a college degree. But you conclude that, one way or another, each of these factors may have influenced Emma's decision.

Only a thorough investigation like the one you have conducted will yield a full explanation of the causes of a particular effect. The next step is to determine more precisely the relative influence of each point in this cluster of causes, and in order to take this step, you must know something about the causal properties of the different points on your list.

ACTIVITIES (7.1)

1. For the following effects, brainstorm a list of possible causes:
    a. The popularity of John Grisham's novels
    b. The success of Japanese products in the American market
    c. The popularity of disaster movies
    d. An increase (or decrease) in the size of the student body at your school
    e. The popularity of a particular major at your school

Necessary and Sufficient Causes

Understanding the concepts *necessary cause* and *sufficient cause* will help you identify which of the causes from your original list are likely to have been most influential in bringing about the effect you are explaining. To qualify as a cause for a given effect, a causal candidate *must* satisfy the conditions of a necessary or sufficient cause, or both. If it does not, it is not a direct cause of the effect, though it may well have contributed to the effect in some way.

A *necessary* cause is a cause without which the effect could not have taken place. One cannot get typhus without the introduction of a rickettsia, or gram-negative microorganism, into the bloodstream. This rickettsia is necessary to the contraction of the disease. Thus you can be certain that anyone who has contracted typhus has been infected by this particular microorganism. But while introduction of the rickettsia is necessary to the contraction of typhus, it doesn't guarantee that the disease will result. People with a vigorous immune system or those who have been inoculated against typhus will be safe from the disease.

Necessary causes are usually easy to identify: if we know the effect, we know that certain causes or conditions had to be operating. To use a nonscientific example, if you had not parked your car next to a construction site, it would not have been hit by falling debris. Parking your car in that spot was necessary to the effect. In the case of Emma, the cause necessary to her withdrawing from college is her unhappiness there. Presumably, if she were happy and liked college, she would stay.

Sometimes identifying the necessary cause will not be particularly helpful in your attempt to explain an effect. Necessary causes can seem like redundant restatements of the effect itself: the necessary cause of a company's filing for bankruptcy is that it ran out of money, but that doesn't tell us very much about the significant factors that led to the bankruptcy filing. In the case of Emma's planned withdrawal from college, the necessary cause—her unhappiness with college—

does not shed much light on the question of the student dropout rate. In order to understand her decision, we have to work backward from the necessary cause, identifying those factors that set it up.

Sufficient causes, on the other hand, are always helpful in causal analyses. A sufficient cause is one that by itself is capable of producing a particular effect. A person's decision to join a health club can have a number of sufficient causes: for example, winning a year's membership in a raffle, wanting to meet new people, or wanting to become physically fit. Any one of these motives would be enough to prompt an individual to join a health club, but none of them *has* to exist for that decision to be made; that is, they are all sufficient to the effect, but not necessary. In Emma's case, a number of sufficient causes are operating: her poor self-esteem, her crazy roommate, and her distaste for dormitory life. Any one of these might have been enough to prompt her decision, but none of them was necessary to that decision.

Sometimes a single cause combines the properties of necessity and sufficiency. The example of the rickettsia demonstrates this combination. Not only *must* one be infected with that microorganism to contract typhus (the necessary cause), but this infection is by itself enough to cause the disease (the sufficient cause). For every effect, we can expect at least one necessary cause and any number of sufficient causes.

In determining which factors on your initial list have been most influential, you need to identify those that are necessary and those that are sufficient. Unless you are writing a full causal analysis, you will usually find yourself concentrating on the sufficient causes for the effect in question.

Identifying Sufficient Causes

The ability to identify a factor as causally sufficient depends on your good sense and your personal experience of causality. There is no rule or formula to follow in isolating sufficient causes, yet most of us have little difficulty answering the question "Is this factor by itself sufficient to have caused this effect?"

When your subject involves human behavior as either cause or effect, there is a useful test you should apply to those factors you think are sufficient. Actions performed by an individual or group are linked to their causes by some commonly accepted principle or motivator of human behavior. If you argue, for example, that a sluggish economy is a cause of the increased popularity of taped movie rentals, you are accounting for a particular human behavior: the rental of taped movies. Your claim is a simple claim of cause, with a fact at the causal end and an action (also a fact) at the effect end.

Sluggish economy   Increase in movie rentals
(cause)   (effect)

This causal proposition is plausible only if its two sides are linked by some acceptable motive. Why would people rent more movies for home viewing in a sluggish economy? What motive or need would urge them to react to a particular condition with a particular behavior? In this case, a linking motivation is easy to identify: in tight times, people need to economize, and it is considerably cheaper to watch rented movies at home than to pay high prices in a theater. The cause and the resulting behavior can be linked by a motivation that everyone can understand and identify with:

Sluggish economy.................Increase in movie rentals
{Desire to economize in tight times}

Identifying this motivation doesn't tell you whether this is the only sufficient cause, but it will reassure you that the link between this cause and the effect is plausible. If you can supply no such motivation between cause and effect, your theory is probably not plausible, and it's time to look for another cause.

Applying the Toulmin Model

The Toulmin model discussed in Chapter 5 is particularly useful when you are composing causal arguments. Indeed, the relationship just presented among possible cause, existing effect, and linking principle fits perfectly into Toulmin's data-claim-warrant formula. Here is the example about increased movie rentals translated into the Toulmin model:

In this case, the warrant is that general behavioral principle that connects the cause, which is placed in the data position, and the effect, which is placed under "claim" (even though the actual claim of the argument is the causal relationship between data and claim). When you are trying to identify sufficient causes for a particular effect, you may find it useful to apply the Toulmin model to your cause and effect, making sure that you can provide a warrant that would be widely acceptable to your readers. Remember that in many cases, the warrant will not be acceptable without further support, or what Toulmin calls *backing*. In those cases, the warrant and its backing will need to be provided explicitly in the argument. If the warrant does seem immediately acceptable, it need not be stated outright.

ACTIVITIES (7.2)

1. With three or four other students, study the following effects and possible causes. For each effect, which of the possible causes, if any, do you think are necessary? Which would you class as sufficient? Make sure you can defend your choices.
   a. **Effect:** John's car accident.
      Possible causes: John was driving at night on a poorly lit road; the road was wet from rain; John had taken a very difficult exam that morning; John was driving ten miles per hour over the speed limit.
   b. **Effect:** The dramatic increase in the use of VCRs in the last few years.
      Possible causes: The cost of VCRs is now at an affordable level for most Americans; videotapes of films are increasingly available; viewers can choose what films they will watch with the VCR; many Americans have a large amount of leisure time available.
   c. **Effect:** The decline in oil and gasoline prices in the mid 1980s.
      Possible causes: On the average, cars were more fuel-efficient than they had been ten years before; there was a growing awareness that petroleum

was a nonrenewable resource; the oil-exporting countries were producing more oil than the world consumed.

d. **Effect:** Louise's winning of an award for the best violin recital at the music festival.

Possible causes: Louise practices the violin three hours each day; Louise's parents found the city's best violin teacher for her when she was five; from a very early age, it was obvious that Louise was talented musically; Louise prefers Mozart to any other composer.

e. **Effect:** Charles's favorite hobby is cross-country skiing.

Possible causes: Charles wants to stay in shape, and cross-country skiing is very good for the cardiovascular system; he likes winter and being out-of-doors; he is on a tight budget and cannot afford downhill skiing this year; he was once injured while downhill skiing; in high school, he won prizes in cross-country ski races.

2. For each following pair below, place the cause and the effect within the Toulmin model and supply a warrant that links the data and the claim acceptably. For which warrants should you also supply backing? What would that backing be?

a. **Cause:** Increased leisure time
   Effect: More participation in sports like skiing and windsurfing
b. **Cause:** Fifteen percent increase in tuition
   Effect: Decrease in enrollment
c. **Cause:** Special incentives that reduce the price of automobiles
   Effect: Higher automobile sales
d. **Cause:** More women receiving professional degrees
   Effect: A rise in the average age of women having first children
e. **Cause:** The banning of a book
   Effect: Increased demand for the book

DISTINGUISHING AMONG SUFFICIENT CAUSES

Sometimes, in analyzing causes, you will discover a number of possible sufficient causes for an effect and not know which were actually operating. In these cases, you will need other methods for determining probable cause. The following strategies were formulated by the nineteenth-century philosopher John Stuart Mill to determine cause in such situations. While Mill was looking for ways to establish cause with scientific certainty, his methods are also very useful in situations where certainty is unreachable.

Method of Agreement

The method of agreement is useful when you are investigating the cause of *two or more* similar effects. In these instances, you determine what the sets of events preceding each effect have in common; you are looking for a single sufficient cause that operated in all these similar cases.

If you were investigating the reason or reasons for the success of the five best-selling hardbound books of the year, you would list all the factors that might have contributed to the success of each book—that is, the significant characteristics of each. If all the books center on the subject of personal relationships in the 1990s, you could safely identify subject matter as a leading cause of the books' success. Sometimes you will not discover a factor common to all your effects; perhaps the five best-sellers have no single common characteristic, so that a number of sufficient causes are operating in these instances.

Method of Difference

Mill's method of difference can be used to determine why two essentially similar situations turned out very differently. If you want to know why one self-help book succeeded while another failed, why one calculus class with Professor Jones was interesting while another was boring, or why the Confederate army lost the battle of Gettysburg but won the battles of Bull Run, you can apply the difference method by looking for the factor present in one case but absent in the other. If the only difference between your two calculus classes with Professor Jones was that the subject matter of the second class was more advanced, that could well be the reason for your unhappiness in the second class.

This method will work only when you are examining truly similar situations that share a number of common factors. If you were trying to account for the difference between your career choice and that of one of your grandparents, the situations would be too dissimilar for the method of difference to tell you anything; your grandparents faced an entirely different range of career choices than you did.

Method of Proportional Correlation

The method of proportional correlation is useful in determining the cause of an effect that is continuing and varied: the movement of the Dow-Jones industrial average, the increase and occasional decrease in the gross national product, the enrollment of college students in certain kinds of majors. In trying to identify possible causes of such measurable trends, you should look for conditions preceding the trends that vary and persist proportionally. In considering the reasons for the rise in the divorce rate since the 1960s, you might discover that there has been a congruent increase in the number of two-income families over the same time period—that is, that there has been an increase in the number of married women who are economically self-sustaining. This increasing economic independence of women is a plausible explanation of the increased divorce rate if it satisfies the following three conditions: (1) if it is truly independent of the effect (not a result of the same cause); (2) if the two trends, with all their fluctuations, are truly proportional; and (3) if the cause and effect are plausibly linked by an accepted behavioral principle—in this case, the principle or motive of independence or self-reliance. If these three conditions are satisfied, we would accept that the economic independence of wives is a sufficient cause of divorce.

ACTIVITIES (7.3)

1. Take a group of at least three of your classmates or friends who share a common trait, such as their academic major, a hobby, or some other favorite activity, and try to determine what sufficient cause made each member of the group have this trait. Try to find a common sufficient cause for the entire group, but be prepared to end up with different sufficient causes if a common cause does not reveal itself. Write a one- to two-page essay describing the results of your investigation.

2. Compare two classes you have taken sometime in your education, one that you liked and one that you disliked. The two classes should be as similar as possible in subject matter and level of difficulty. What made the one class likable, while the other was not? Write a one- to two-page essay addressing this question.

3. For the next week, compare fluctuations in two phenomena that you believe may be related, such as the weather and attendance at one of your classes. Make a chart comparing the movement of these two phenomena, and then see if any proportional correlation exists between the two. If there is such a correlation, ask yourself if the two are the result of the same cause and if some plausible behavioral principle links the two. Write a one- to two-page analysis of your study. Be sure to give your instructor the chart you have created.

CAUSAL CHAINS

Some effects are best understood in terms of a directly related series of causes, like links in a single chain, or a row of sequentially falling dominoes. In these cases, identifying the entire chain of causes is far more useful than isolating those causes that are closest to the effect, or isolating the more remote cause that originally set the chain in motion.

If someone told you that closed captioning of television shows (where subtitles can be seen on specially equipped televisions) is a result of the rubella epidemic in the United States during the 1960s, you might initially reject the connection as utterly implausible. What you have been given is the first cause and the final effect in a causal chain; if the links in the causal chain are filled in, the connection is reasonable. In the 1960s, there *was* a widespread outbreak of rubella, or German measles (at the time, there was no rubella inoculation). Rubella is a relatively harmless disease except to the fetuses of pregnant women; babies whose mothers contract rubella during pregnancy often suffer birth defects, one of which is deafness. Because of the epidemic, huge numbers of babies were born deaf. In the last 30 years, as these children have grown, we have seen increased sensitivity to the needs of the hearing-impaired, one of the most notable being the media's provision of closed captioning for television. With all the links in the chain identified, the causal connection between a common virus and closed captioning is no longer implausible, though there were other factors at work, including the increasing emphasis on the rights of the handicapped in the last 30 years.

The constellation leading to Emma's planned withdrawal from college contains a causal chain. Beginning with her decision to withdraw, we can move straight back as far as her parents' lack of a college education. The chain works as follows: Emma plans to withdraw from college because she doesn't like it. She doesn't like it because she feels low self-esteem in this setting. This low self-esteem is a result of poor grades, which at least in part have been caused by the enormous pressure she has been under to do well. This pressure comes from her parents, who, because they have never been to college, desperately want Emma to be the first in the family to get a college degree. Not all of the points in the constellation we identified earlier appear in this chain. So while the chain explains much about the evolution of Emma's decision, it does not explain everything, just as the chain linking the rubella epidemic with closed captioning is not the fullest possible explanation of the situation.

CONTRIBUTING FACTORS

In analyzing causes, we occasionally find a circumstance that is neither necessary nor sufficient yet is somehow relevant. This type of circumstance is labeled a *contributing factor*. If Kathy continues to jog even when she is run-down and then catches a virus, her jogging is not a sufficient cause of her illness; the presence of the virus without sufficient antibodies to combat it is the sufficient cause. Nor is the jogging a necessary cause, since she might have gotten the virus even without jogging. Yet her pushing herself while not feeling "100 percent" certainly didn't help and may have made her more susceptible to disease. In this case, we can label the jogging as a probable contributing factor.

Emma's situation contains at least one contributing factor: her lack of a close role model. Clearly, this factor is not necessary to the effect, nor is it sufficiently influential to have caused her decision to withdraw. Yet it has made a bad situation worse, depriving Emma of any positive example from which to take heart. Contributing factors are present in most complicated situations; if your goal is a thorough analysis of cause, you need to take contributing factors into account.

ACTIVITIES (7.4)

1. For two of the following causes and remote effects, find a plausible causal chain that links the cause with the remote effect.
   a. **Cause:** The rise of industrialization
      Effect: The growth of the conservation movement
   b. **Cause:** The invention of gunpowder
      Effect: The decline of knighthood
   c. **Cause:** Jane's high absenteeism in third grade
      Effect: Jane's difficulty with cursive writing
   d. **Cause:** The invention of printing
      Effect: The growth of democracy in Europe and America
   e. **Cause:** Jack's love of parties
      Effect: Jack's becoming the mayor of his city

2. In Activities (7.2), review the clusters of causes presented in Number 1 and identify possible contributing factors for each cluster.

SUMMARY

Determining Cause

- Because causality is always multifaceted, keep your mind open to all possibilities early in your causal investigations.

- The ultimate purpose of your argument (to explain, instruct, or designate responsibility) will determine which causes you will concentrate on in your argument.

- To determine the most influential causes for your effect, you need to be able to identify the necessary and sufficient causes. A *necessary cause* is a cause without which the effect could not have occurred; a *sufficient cause* is one that by itself is capable of producing the effect.

- Where human behavior is concerned, sufficient causes must be linked to their effect through an assumable motive.

- When you have a number of potential sufficient causes for an effect, use the following methods to determine the most probable cause or causes: the method of *agreement,* which will help you determine the cause of similar effects; the method of *difference,* which will help you determine why two similar situations turned out differently; the method of *proportional correlation,* which will help you determine the cause of an effect that varies over time.

- Some effects are best explained by a chain of causes, often originating at a time remote from the effect.

- Thorough causal arguments may also identify *contributing factors* to the effect—circumstances that are neither necessary nor sufficient causes but do play a role in creating an event or condition.

SUPPORTING CAUSAL CLAIMS

You support most causal claims by (1) establishing the factuality of the effect(s) and cause(s) you present; (2) identifying, sometimes only implicitly, an acceptable motive in arguments involving human action; (3) in some cases, describing the process that helped you validate a causal candidate (method of difference, agreement, or proportional correlation); and (4) qualifying the degree of certainty your argument claims.

Establishing Factuality

Facts are the foundations of causal argument. While in most causal arguments you will write, the causal relationship you propose between two events will rarely be certain and verifiable, there can be no room to doubt the certainty of the events you are linking; they *must* be true if your argument is to be meaningful and plausible. If you exaggerate, understate, or misstate the effect, your identification of cause is useless; you are explaining something that didn't actually occur.

If an article in a campus newspaper claims that the firing of a popular hockey coach has resulted in lower student attendance at home hockey games, the reporter needs to be absolutely sure that (1) the coach *was* fired (perhaps this is only a campus rumor and the coach got a job offer elsewhere) and (2) student attendance at home games really has declined since the coach's departure. Both cause and effect need to be presented and, if necessary, supported as individual factual claims before their causal relationship can be explored (see Chapter 6 for supporting factual claims).

Identifying an Acceptable Motivation

When you're dealing with human behavior as either cause or effect, your argument should suggest a common human motive. If a generally acceptable linking motive is obvious, you probably won't need to identify it explicitly. For example, if you are arguing that a decrease in DWI arrests is a consequence of tougher DWI laws, you don't have to point to people's unwillingness to risk the new penalites as the linking motivator between cause and effect; it is so obvious that it can merely be implied.

But let's take a more complicated example: an argument accounting for the increased divorce rate since the 1960s by a proportional rise in two-career families. Here, you would want to state the motive linking the proposed cause and effect, because it may not be immediately obvious to your readers: women who have some degree of financial independence and employment security are more likely to leave unhappy marriages than women who are financially dependent on their spouses. If the motive you identify may not be immediately acceptable to your audience, you will have to provide some backing for it.

There is a tendency among student writers to omit identifying the linking motivation when they should include it; that is, they find obvious what may not be so obvious to their readers. So if you have any doubt about whether or not to include this explanation in your argument, go ahead and provide it. It is usually better to err on the side of too much information than too little.

Describing the Process of Validation

In arguments where John Stuart Mill's processes of determination have been useful to you, you can support your claim by reporting in your argument how the method was applied. You don't need to use the formal terms *method of agreement* and so on, but you should provide a summary, a kind of narrative of your investigation.

If you were to identify the reasons for the failure of four different food concession stands at your school, you would make use of the method of agreement, because you are looking for a single explanation common to the closing of all four
operations. Your report of the process might read something like this:

> Between 1996 and 2000, four different concession stands have been
> opened in the foyer of the Student Union. Not one of these stands was
> able to draw enough customers to keep operating; each closed within five
> months of its opening.
>
> The stands had little in common. One was run by students from the
> hotel program and sold gourmet coffee and pastries; one was a national
> fast-food franchise; one was a "mom-and-pop" frozen yogurt stand; and
> the fourth was a minideli operated by campus food services. Prices at the
> gourmet coffee stand were slightly on the high side, so when it failed, it
> was replaced by the inexpensive fast-food stand. Frozen yogurt from the
> yogurt stand was competitively priced, and it was the only frozen yogurt
> available on campus. Finally, the deli offered the most choice to cus-
> tomers, with food ranging from sandwiches to chips to pasta salads to
> drinks.
>
> The stands operated at different times of the day: the coffee stand in
> the mornings between 7 A.M. and 11 A.M.; the fast-food concession
> between 11 A.M. and 2 P.M.; the yogurt stand in the afternoons from 1 to 5;
> and the deli between 11 A.M. and 3 P.M.
>
> In short, campus food services tried very hard to learn from its mis-
> takes, trying to eliminate every reason for failure. But the one factor
> common to all four concerns that they did not address was *location*. All
> were set up in exactly the same spot in the foyer of the Student Union.
> The thinking was that since this space saw more daytime student traffic
> than anywhere else on campus, food sales would be brisk. But the prob-
> lem with this particular space in the union is that it is very close to the
> student-faculty cafeteria (on the same floor and open during lunchtime),
> and to the large student snack bar (in the basement of the union and
> open for lunch and dinner). It is reasonable to conclude that the food
> market in this heavily trafficked building was already saturated; if food
> services wants to make a success of the "portable food" idea, it will have
> to locate the next food stand in another area of campus.

As indicated in the preceding section on determining cause, some of Mill's
methods of determination carry particular risks that you'll want to avoid. The difference method, for example, is reliable only if the effects you examine are truly
comparable. And when using the method of proportional correlation, you'll need to
be sure that the trends you identify are independent—that is, that they are neither
effects of another cause nor mutually contributing (for example, bad tempers causing quarrels and quarrels exacerbating bad tempers).

It's a good idea when supporting your causal argument to point out that your
use of a particular method of determination has avoided the associated pitfalls.
For example, if you use the difference method to determine why you like golf but
your friend with similar athletic ability and experience in golf does not, you

should demonstrate that the apparent differences between you and your friend—family background, interest in other sports—are not significant in terms of your argument.

Qualifying Your Argument

Since certainty is rare in causal arguments, you must not mislead your reader and thereby undermine your own credibility by claiming more certainty for your argument than is warranted by its support. You have a wide range of words indicating degrees of causality to choose from, so make sure you use language that accurately reflects your level of certainty. If you are very certain about your causal proposition, you can use such definite words as the following:

necessitated

caused

resulted in

attributable to

produced

created

brought about

was responsible for

But use these words with caution. Without qualifiers like "may have," "probably," "seems to have," and so on, they claim a certainty that may be difficult to document.

The words listed in the following group also indicate causality, but a causality that is clearly qualified:

contributed to

is associated with

is a function of

facilitated

enabled

influenced

increased

decreased

improved

You are better off using words such as these when the causality you propose is not certain. By using such terms, you are both indicating causality and admitting *some* degree of uncertainty.

ACTIVITIES (7.5)

For two of the following examples, write a paragraph on each indicating what would be needed to make the causal argument more convincing. This additional material may include establishing facts, reporting the process of determination, describing motives, demonstrating the independence of two elements in a proportional correlation, or adding qualifying language, though other steps may also be necessary to make the argument credible.

1. Bill's alleged cheating on the exam was certainly a result of his low grades early in the semester and his desire to be accepted into a reputable law school.

2. Police report the arrest of Hubert Midas, the oil and gas billionaire, for shoplifting a thirty-five-dollar shirt from a downtown department store. Midas must have forgotten to pay for the shirt.

3. As more women have entered the workforce, the number of families without children has risen proportionally. The increasing number of women in the workforce has caused this rise in childless families.

4. Without Martin Luther King, Jr.'s charismatic personality, the civil rights movement of the 1960s would not have had the impact it did.

5. The Roman Empire fell because of the moral decadence of many of its citizens.

SUMMARY

Supporting Causal Claims

- To support a cause, you must establish the factuality of cause and effect; identify an acceptable motivation in cases where human actions are at least part of the cause; usually report how you determined the causes; if necessary, qualify your assertions about the certainty of your argument.

ARGUING EFFECTS

Because arguments of effect are concerned with the future, with events that haven't yet occurred, their claim to certainty is even less absolute than arguments of cause. Even the most carefully constructed argument of effect, one firmly grounded in the principles of causality and in experience in the relevant field, can go awry. We have only to look at the accuracy rate of weather forecasters and political analysts to recognize how frequently the future refuses to cooperate with our plans for it. But if executed carefully and according to certain principles, arguments of effect *can* be reasonable and convincing, serving as useful guidelines for many courses of action.

Claims of arguments of effect can be stated in a number of ways, as in the following:

1. If John continues to drink heavily and drive, it's only a matter of time before he will have a serious accident.

2. The number of high school graduates will continue to decline for the next five years, then begin to stabilize.

3. I will not see a woman president in my lifetime.

4. Consumers are so comfortable with certain companies that they will buy almost anything carrying those companies' logos.

While they may seem quite different, these four claims share certain features common to all arguments of effect. Most obviously, all predict that something will happen in the future (or in the case of the third claim, that something will not happen). Claims 1 and 4—John's heavy drinking, and brand appeal—also identify a causal relationship between a current condition and a future event. Claims 2 and 3 don't identify a current condition that will lead to the effect the writer predicts. In order to make them qualify as arguments of effect rather than mere assertions, the writer will have to identify current conditions that might lead to these effects and claim that the conditions and effects are causally linked. For Claim 2, those conditions could be certain demographic trends that have persisted over time; for Claim 3, those conditions could be the conservative disposition of most voters, or perhaps a poll indicating strong opposition to a woman president among teenagers and young voters. These current conditions and trends set the ground for an argument of effect. An argument of effect demonstrates that the existence of these conditions and trends is enough to cause a particular future effect. Lacking identified causes, these kinds of claims are nothing more than random predictions, similar to the bizarre predictions on the covers of the sensational magazines found in supermarkets: "Psychic Foresees Economic Collapse Following Landing of Martians on White House Lawn!"

Determining and Supporting a Probable Effect

The processes of determining and supporting a probable effect overlap considerably. If you identify a future effect through sound methods, the best supporting strategy will be to report these methods, which we discuss in the following paragraphs.

Applying the Principles of Causality.   To argue an effect, you need to identify a sufficient cause for the effect and prove that this cause exists or could exist. Are the causes that are currently operating (or that might be set in place) enough to bring about the effect? If you can identify an existing sufficient cause or causes for the effect, your prediction is probably a good one.

Let's take the case of a publishing house editor trying to decide whether to publish a book submitted to her on personal relationships. The editor will accept the book if she thinks it will sell well; her job is to decide whether current circumstances will make the book a best-seller. In other words, the projected effect is excellent sales. The circumstances operating are as follows: the market for books on this topic has been very strong; the writer has written popular books on this subject before; the book itself, in the view of this experienced editor, is interesting, original, and provocative. An analysis of these circumstances reveals that all are sufficient causes; in the absence of the other two, one cause alone would be sufficient to create the effect. The editor's experience with bookselling makes her a good judge of the sufficiency of these causes. She also knows how important these three circumstances are because she has seen them again and again. In projecting any effect, the arguer must understand the principles of the subject matter.

Missing from this list of current circumstances is a necessary cause, one that has to operate in order for the effect to occur. The absence of a necessary cause does not make the projected effect implausible; often it is the sufficient causes that create the necessary cause. In this example, the necessary cause of high sales would simply be that people buy the book, and they will buy the book in the presence of one or more of these sufficient causes.

Causal Chains.   In some situations, you can argue a future effect by revealing a chain of causes that plausibly connects Cause A with Future Effect D. To demonstrate the connection between a past or present cause and a future effect, you need to make a series of arguments of effect; if A is the remote cause and D the predicted effect, you will argue that A will cause B, which will cause C, which finally will cause D.

The field of economics often uses causal chains as a basis for future action. A classic example is the Federal Reserve Bank's setting of interest rates on money it lends to banks, which in turn affects the interest rates banks and other financial institutions charge customers on mortgages and other loans and the interest they pay to customers for savings and other deposits. One key step the Federal Reserve Bank can take to reduce consumer spending is to raise its interest rates, which means the banks will raise their rates, and customers will find that it costs more to get a mortgage on a house, to finance a car loan, or to buy other items on credit. Faced with these rising costs, consumers will decide to spend less. Also, because these same banks are now paying more interest for deposits, consumers have an incentive to save rather than spend—another reason why they will reduce spending. Visually, the causal chain looks like this:

(A) higher government interest rates⟶(B) higher bank interest rates⟶
(C) lower consumer spending

This causal chain can be extended, since lower consumer spending may lead to a lower inflation rate or to less importing of consumer goods from other countries. With causal chains, however, the greater the length of the chain, the less predictable become the effects.

Sometimes causal chains simply don't work the way they are supposed to. When Prohibition became law in 1919, its proponents predicted that alcohol consumption would decrease and along with it a host of evils, including crime, broken homes, and absenteeism from work. They did not foresee a roaring 14 years of speakeasies, bathtub gin, and bootleg whiskey before Prohibition was abolished in 1933. Especially when trying to predict human behavior through elaborate causal chains, you should always keep in mind the adage about the road to hell being paved with good intentions.

Comparable Situations.   You can also determine the probable future result of current conditions by examining comparable situations in which this cause and effect have already occurred. In trying to raise the educational standards of American primary and secondary schools, teachers, school administrators, and government policymakers look to the experience of other countries. The average scores of students from some other industrialized countries are higher than the average scores of American students on certain standardized achievement tests in areas such as math and science. In some of these countries, notably Japan, children spend much more of the year in school, and the schools introduce rigorous academic material earlier in the student's academic career. Some proponents of reform argue that the same methods used here will improve students' performance.

This comparison method will work only if the situations being compared are *significantly* similar. In arguing that the United States should follow Japan's example, advocates of these changes also need to look carefully at what each country expects from its schools and how these expectations relate to the general culture. What seems comparable at first may turn out to be more complicated on closer inspection, since the American and Japanese cultures have very different expectations about the role of the individual in society.

The more comparable the situations you find, the more convincing your argument of effect will be. If you can demonstrate that a certain cause has had the same result over and over again, and that the current conditions you are considering are truly similar to these other causes, your identification of effect will be well supported.

ACTIVITIES (7.6)

1. For two of the following actions, project two effects that might be caused by the action. State whether the action would be necessary or sufficient to the effect.
   Example action: Graduating *summa cum laude.*
   Possible effects: Being accepted into a prestigious graduate school (sufficient); receiving eight job offers (sufficient).
   a. Getting an A in a course
   b. Arranging a date with someone you don't know
   c. Reducing the danger of theft at your college or in your community
   d. Finding a good place to live
   e. Being stopped by the police for speeding

2. Write a two- to three-page essay describing a causal chain for some area or activity with which you are familiar (for example, gaining or losing weight, saving money, raising your grades).

3. For the following five predictions, cite a truly comparable activity or situation that can be used to support your prediction.
   Example: Extending the academic year in primary and secondary education in the United States. A comparable situation could be the long academic year in Japan, to support the prediction of higher test scores for American students.
   a. Being governor of a state
   b. Student success in graduate school
   c. Decreasing alcohol consumption at fraternity parties at your school
   d. Being removed from academic probation
   e. Making the varsity lacrosse team

SUMMARY

Determining and Arguing a Probable Effect

- To argue an effect, you need to identify a sufficient cause for the effect and prove that this cause exists or could exist.

- You can argue that a certain effect is likely if you can create a causal chain that demonstrates how you move from one cause to an effect that is the cause of the next effect, and so forth. The longer your chain, however, the less likely it is that the chain will perform as predicted.

- You can demonstrate that an effect is likely in a situation if you can prove that a similar situation produced a similar effect.

TWO SAMPLE CAUSAL ARGUMENTS

The following argument is a sample of causal analysis. Based on an essay written by college student Michele Statt, the essay considers possible causes of the recent growth of student interest in liberal arts majors. The essay is not an elaborate and definitive causal argument, but it is a good example of an exploration of the possible causes of an interesting phenomenon (note the qualification of Michele's causal claims). As you study the essay, see if you can locate where Michele establishes the factuality of her cause and effect. Does she report on a process of determination used to test her main cause? What is it? Do you find any reference to a common human motivation?

THE NEW INTEREST IN THE LIBERAL ARTS

In 1978, only 443 students were enrolled in liberal arts majors at my college. Today, with the recent establishment of new liberal arts majors, 604 students are enrolled in these majors. (In the same period, the total enrollment at my college has decreased by 40 students.) Many other schools have also reported that interest in liberal arts majors has been increasing. According to Michael Useem, Director of Boston University's Center for Applied Social Science, across the nation "the proportion of baccalaureate degrees in the liberal arts in 1986 was the largest in four years, and the proportion of first-year college students reporting an interest in a liberal arts major in 1987 was the highest in 10 years" (46).

Several causes may have influenced this increase in interest. Many students entering college are unsure of their career choice and gravitate to the liberal arts because such programs typically do not insist on early declaration of a major. Even if the undecided student then chooses to pursue a major outside the liberal arts, she will find that her liberal arts courses can be applied to her new major. However, having started in the liberal arts, she is likely to find a liberal arts major that appeals to her.

Another cause probably associated with this increase is the growing emphasis on career training within the liberal arts majors themselves. At my college the liberal arts majors include such programs as economics, school psychology, criminal justice, and communications—all of which include a significant element of career preparation that appeals to today's college students. Several of these programs at my college are relatively new. Their existence as additional options for students certainly helps to explain the growth in liberal arts enrollment here.

Liberal arts enrollment, however, has been increasing throughout the country, even at institutions that have not added many new liberal arts programs. The central cause of this growth is very likely the increasing demand for liberal arts majors in the job market. Michael Useem's article, based on research supported by the Corporate Council on the Liberal Arts and the President's Committee on the Arts and Humanities, states that since the early 1980s, many business leaders have stressed the importance of the liberal arts as preparation for a career in business (46). Useem received responses to his survey from 535 large and mid-sized American corporations. The results indicated that corporations do indeed hire liberal arts graduates, with 44 percent of the respondents recruiting liberal arts graduates on campus and 47 percent hiring such students for internships and cooperative education programs; 29 percent reported other efforts to recruit liberal arts graduates, and 61 percent have created programs to train liberal arts graduates for jobs in their corporations (47).

Students are becoming aware of this demand for liberal arts graduates. I chose my field of communication both because of my interest in it and because I was aware of job possibilities after graduation. Twelve students that I talked to said that career preparation was one of the two major causes of their choosing a liberal arts major, the other being their interest in the subject. These results are hardly scientific proof, but they are another piece of evidence demonstrating the importance of the job market in rising liberal arts enrollments.

Useem's study also notes that although many companies hire liberal arts graduates, they are often looking for accomplishments in addition to a liberal arts major, including campus or community involvement and a good grade point average. Another important requirement of most of these corporations was exposure to business courses or experience in business before graduation (47-48, 50-51). The increasing emphasis on career training in at least some liberal arts majors undoubtedly enhances the attractiveness of these majors to employers.

Ten or fifteen years ago, many college students felt that they were forced to make a choice between a liberal arts major or preparing themselves for a career. Because they wanted to find a good job, some of these students chose a program outside of the liberal arts even when they really preferred a liberal arts major. Today's students are more fortunate. They know that in choosing a liberal arts major, they can also prepare themselves for their future after college.

WORKS CITED

Useem, Michael. "The Corporate View of Liberal Arts."
     Journal of Career Planning and Employment. (Summer
     1988): 46-51.

The following argument, "I, Too, Am a Good Parent," combines elements of a causal argument and a recommendation. The author, Dorsett Bennett, claims that the continuing custom of granting child custody to the mother is a result of the prejudice of older male judges who continue to dominate the courts. Is the cause Bennett identifies necessary or sufficient? Is it adequately supported by facts and examples? Do you find any further causal arguments embedded in the essay? What are they?

I, TOO, AM A GOOD PARENT

Dads Should Not Be Discriminated Against

DORSETT BENNETT

Divorce is a fact of modern life. A great number of people simply decide that they do not wish to stay married to their spouse. A divorce is not a tremendously difficult situation unless there are minor children born to the couple. If there are no minor children you simply divide the assets and debts. But you cannot divide a child. The child needs to be placed with the appropriate parent.

In my own case, my former wife chose not to remain married to me. That is her right and I do not fault her decision. My problem is that I do not believe it is her right to deny me the privilege of raising our children. Some fathers want to go to the parent/teacher conferences, school plays, carnivals, and to help their kids with homework. I have always looked forward to participating on a daily basis in my children's lives. I can no longer enjoy that privilege—the children live with their mother, who has moved to a northern Midwest state.

I tried so hard to gain custody of my children. I believe the evidence is uncontradicted as to what an excellent father (and more important, parent) I am. My ex-wife is a fairly good mother, but unbiased opinions unanimously agreed I was the better parent. Testimonials were videotaped from witnesses who could not attend the out-of-state custody hearing. I choose to be a fa-

ther. When I was 3 years old, my own father left my family. While I've loved my father for many years, I did and still do reject his parental pattern.

A couple of centuries ago, a father and mother might have shared equally in the care and raising of children above the age of infancy. But with the coming of the Industrial Revolution the father went to work during the day, leaving the full-time care of the young to the mother, who stayed at home. It was easier to decide who should get child custody under those circumstances. That would be true today even if the mother were put into the position of working outside the home after the divorce.

Now, a majority of married mothers are in the workplace—often because the family needs the second income to survive. With the advent of the working mother, we have also seen a change in child care. Not only have we seen an increase in third-party caregivers; there is a decided difference in how fathers interact with their children. Fathers are even starting to help raise their children. I admit that in a great many families there is an uneven distribution of child-care responsibilities. But there are fathers who do as much to raise the children as the mother, and there are many examples where men are full-time parents.

But, because we have this past history of the mother being the principal child caregiver, the mother has almost always been favored in any contested child-custody case. The law of every state is replete with decisions showing that the mother is the favored custodial parent. The changes in our lifestyles are now being reflected in our laws. In most, if not all, states, the legislature has recognized the change in childcare responsibilities and enacted legislation that is gender blind. The statutes that deal with child custody now say that the children should be placed with the parent whose care and control of the child will be in the child's best interest.

This legislation is enlightened and correct. Society has changed. We no longer bring up our children as we did years ago. But it is still necessary to have someone make the choice in the child's best interest if the parents are divorcing and cannot agree on who takes care of the kids. So we have judges to make that enormous decision.

The state legislature can pass laws that say neither parent is favored because of their gender. But it is judges who make the ultimate choice. And those judges are usually *older males* who practiced law during the time when mothers were the favored guardians under the law. These same judges mostly come from a background where mothers stayed home and were the primary caregivers. By training and by personal experience they have a strong natural bias in favor of the mother in a child-custody case. That belief is regressive and fails to acknowledge the changed realities of our present way of life. Someone must be appointed to render a decision when parents cannot agree. I would ask that those judges who make these critical decisions re-examine their attitudes and prejudices against placing children with fathers.

After the videotaped testimony was completed, one of my lawyers said he had "never seen a father put together a better custody case." "But," he asked me, "can you prove she is unfit?" A father should not be placed in the position of having to prove the mother is unfit in order to gain custody. He should not have to prove that she has two heads, participates in child sacrifice, or eats live snakes. The father should only have to prove that he is the more suitable parent.

Fathers should not be discriminated against as I was. It took me three years to get a trial on the merits in the Minnesota court. And Minnesota has a law directing its courts to give a high priority to child-custody cases. What was even worse was that the judge seemed to ignore the overwhelming weight of the evidence and granted custody to my ex-wife. At the trial, her argument was, "I am their mother." Other than that statement she hardly put on a case. Being the mother of the children was apparently deemed enough to outweigh evidence that all the witnesses who knew us both felt I was the better parent; that those witnesses who knew only me said what an excellent parent I was; that our children's behavior always improved dramatically after spending time with me; that my daughter wished to live with me; and that I had a better child-custody evaluation than my wife.

So I say to the trial judges who decide these cases: "Become part of the solution to this dilemma of child custody. Don't remain part of the problem." It is too late for me. If this backward way of thinking is changed, then perhaps it won't be too late for other fathers who should have custody of their children.

Source: *Newsweek,* July 4, 1994.

SUGGESTIONS FOR WRITING (7.7)

1. Write an essay describing the necessary and sufficient causes for a major event in your life. Be sure to indicate to the reader how you determined that

these causes were operating. Make the essay as long as necessary to describe fully the causes of this event.

2. Analyze at least three persons or organizations that share major common traits, and determine what similar causes, if any, made them the way they are. As examples, you could analyze successful or unsuccessful teams in some sport, or successful or unsuccessful television shows. Report your analysis in an essay of approximately four pages.

3. Analyze two persons or situations that share significant traits but that have ended up differing in some major way. What caused this major difference? For this essay, you might analyze why you and a close friend or a sibling chose different colleges or majors or why you performed differently in two similar classes. Report your analysis in an essay of approximately four pages.

4. Examine two trends that you believe may be causally related to see if there is any proportional correlation between them. An example might be the national crime rate and the national unemployment rate, or the national unemployment rate and the inflation rate. If you expect to find a correlation and you do not, speculate on why the correlation is not present. For the most current information available, your library will probably have the *Statistical Abstracts of the United States* in database format, but you may also be able to retrieve any government statistical data you may need through the Web site at http://www.census.gov/statab/www/ . Report your analysis in an essay of approximately four pages.

5. Fewer and fewer college students are completing bachelor's degrees in the traditional four-year period. Do some research at your own institution, and find out the average time students are taking to graduate. Then write a four- to five-page essay that explores possible causes of this phenomenon. Make sure that the causes you suggest originate in the same time period as the effect.

8

Arguing Evaluations

EVALUATIVE SUBJECTS AND TERMS

All evaluations include a subject to be judged and an evaluative term that is applied to the subject. In the claim "John is a good writer," *John* is the subject, and *good writer* is the evaluative term; in "Tracy Chapman is a gifted musician," *Tracy Chapman* is the subject and *gifted musician* the evaluative term. Some evaluative claims include only partial evaluative terms, but their context should suggest the missing parts. In the claim "Capital punishment is immoral," the full evaluative term is *immoral act,* and in "Rembrandt was a master," the evaluative term is *master painter.*

To make a successful evaluative argument, you need to lay some careful groundwork. First, you must define the evaluative term. In the claim "John is a good writer," where *good writer* could mean different things to different people, you'll want to specify your understanding of the term. In many cases, you can do this by a shorthand definition: "John is a good writer; he communicates ideas clearly and gracefully" (see Chapter 4 for a discussion of shorthand definitions). This definition establishes clarity and grace in the communication as the criteria by which John's writing will be judged.

Sometimes evaluations are expressed negatively, as in "John is a poor writer," or "The instructions for this camera are useless." A negative evaluation can either imply its opposite as the standard of judgment or establish a definition of the negative term itself. The writer of the claim "William Faulkner's *Fable* is a failed novel" could work from a definition of *successful novel,* showing how this novel falls short of that definition, or could establish criteria for the term *failed novel* and apply those to the subject.

The second piece of groundwork necessary to most successful evaluations is gaining your readers' agreement about your definition of the evaluative term. If your readers' understanding of the criteria for good writing do not agree with yours, however clearly you have presented them, your argument won't get very far. Perhaps they agree that John's writing is clear and graceful, but because their understanding of good writing includes rich ideas and original expression, they will never be convinced by your argument that John is a good writer. In this situation, and in many evaluations, you will need to argue the definition of your evaluative term, convincing your readers that the criteria by which you define the term are reasonable and complete. Only then can you proceed to the heart of your evaluation: demonstrating the match between your subject and your evaluative term.

ACTIVITIES (8.1)

1. What is the evaluative term (implied or stated) in the following assertions?
   a. Mark Twain's *Adventures of Huckleberry Finn* is an American classic.
   b. When Roger Bannister broke the four-minute mile barrier in 1954, he accomplished one of the greatest athletic feats of this century.
   c. Calvin Coolidge was a mediocre president.
   d. Calculators are a real boon to mathematics students.
   e. The terrible losses in wars in the twentieth century show the bankruptcy of nations' using war as an extension of foreign policy.
2. Write a paragraph giving a brief definition of one of the evaluative terms you identified in Activity 1.

ESTABLISHING THE DEFINITION OF THE EVALUATIVE TERM

How much space and energy you devote to establishing your term's definition will depend on your audience and the nature of the term. There is so little dispute about some terms that an extensive definition is unnecessary—an honest bank teller, for example, or a reliable car. And in cases where you are very confident about your readers' values, about what is important to them and why, you may not need to argue or even propose a definition. A doctor writing to other doctors about the unprofessional behavior of a certain physician could probably assume agreement among her readers about the definition of unprofessional behavior. But when the following conditions apply, you should define your evaluative term and argue its definition:

- When your audience consists of people with expertise and/or values different from yours
- When your definition of the evaluative term is unconventional or controversial
- When there are different definitions of the term

Whether or not you define the evaluative term explicitly, remember that very vague or inflated evaluations are usually harder to argue than those that are limited and precise. It would be far easier to convince an audience that "Indigo Girls are ingenious lyricists" than that "Indigo Girls are the best songwriters ever."

Presenting the Definition

In most cases, the actual definition of the term can be stated quite briefly, usually as part of or directly following the claim: "Alison is the ideal management trainee: she is intelligent, ambitious, congenial, and hardworking"; "In his highly original and influential reflections on the American spirit, reflections that affected common citizens as well as fellow philosophers, Ralph Waldo Emerson proved himself to be a great thinker."

When defining an evaluative term, you are proposing a *stipulative* definition—a definition that restricts the understanding of a term to a particular meaning appropriate to your context. (See Chapter 4 for a full discussion of definition.) In the argument about John's writing skills, the definition of good writing as the clear and graceful communication of ideas is stipulative: it asks readers to accept this particular and limited definition of the term for the context of this argument. In most cases, your definition will take the shorthand, sentence form identified in Chapter 4, although if the term is very difficult, you might want to provide an extended definition.

As in all definitions, the explanation you offer must be clear and precise. Your definition will be useless if it offers only broad or abstract generalizations. If you write, "The brilliance of the film *Citizen Kane* lies in its wonderful structure," but you fail to define *wonderful structure,* you will leave readers guessing. Try also to avoid definitions that include highly subjective terms. If you define a "talented soprano" as one whose voice is beautiful at all points in her vocal range, you have not done much to clarify the evaluative term. What is beautiful to one listener may be mediocre, or heavy, or thin to another; "beautiful" is a measurement that frequently provokes disagreement. So if you wish the term to be useful, define it by offering comparatively objective standards, like fullness, or clarity, or fluidity. While these, too, are subjective terms, they are more precise and are less a matter of personal taste than a term like *beautiful.*

The following are three examples of promising opening definitions; each is clear, precise, and informative.

- A good argument is one that directly identifies its central proposition; supports that proposition with reasonable, relevant, and concrete evidence; and admits the possibility of alternative points of view.
- A dedicated mother devotes herself to her children because she knows she should; a good mother devotes herself to her children because she can't imagine doing otherwise.
- A good education will prepare a student not only for a career but for a fulfilling life outside a career. As important as careers are in our lives, they do not and should not occupy all of our time and energy. The well-educated person is the one who can view life outside work with zest, knowing that there are many other interests aside from a career.

While the qualities included in your proposed definition should be as clear and precise as possible, the very nature of evaluations will not always allow you to avoid subjective terms. In the last of the three preceding examples, the term *fulfilling life* is inherently subjective, yet it is not meaningless. There are certain qualities and activities we can identify that constitute a fulfilling life, including having friends, having hobbies or other recreational interests, and being curious about the past, the future, and the world. It may not be easy to measure each of these qualities or activities precisely, but they do exist, and they can be gauged on some comparative scale.

ACTIVITIES (8.2)

Using the preceding definitions as a model, give a brief but useful definition of the following. After you have written your definitions, compare them with the definitions written by two other students in your class. How much agreement is there among your definitions? How do you account for the differences that exist?

1. A safe automobile
2. An inspiring professor
3. An honest politician
4. A natural athlete
5. The perfect roommate

Arguing the Definition

Based on your assessment of their backgrounds, needs, and values, you may conclude that your readers will not automatically agree with your definition of the evaluative term. In such cases, you have one more job before you move to the evaluation per se: to *argue* that your definition is just, that the criteria you have assigned to a term such as *necessary war, master craftsman,* or *inspired teacher* are reasonable and complete. You can argue the justness of your definition using any of the methods for supporting definitions presented in Chapter 4, including appeal to assumed values, identification of effect, appeal to authority, and comparison.

To illustrate the application of these methods, let's work with the following example: as a branch manager for a local bank, you are asked to write a formal evaluation of three new management trainees. Your reader will be the bank's vice president of personnel. There is no fixed evaluation form or criteria to work from; *you* must decide which qualities constitute promising performance in a new trainee. The qualities you settle on (in unranked order) are (1) honesty, (2) the ability to foresee the consequences of decisions, (3) attention to detail, and (4) courtesy to customers. Because you have created this list, you will need to justify it, however briefly, to the vice president. Your justification for each item on the list could use the following methods of argument:

- *Honesty:* appeal to assumed value. You wouldn't have to say much about this quality. For obvious reasons, bankers place a premium on honesty in their employees.
- *Ability to foresee the consequences of decisions:* identification of effect. This criterion may not be as obvious as the first, but bankers must base decisions about lending money, setting interest rates, and making investments on the probable consequences of these decisions. You could briefly point out the positive results of having this ability and the negative results of lacking it.

- *Attention to detail:* appeal to assumed value. Like honesty, the importance of this quality doesn't have to be argued to bankers.
- *Courtesy to customers:* identification of effect. You can easily demonstrate that good customer relations lead to good business. For many bankers, this criterion would be an assumed value.

You can buttress these criteria with other support. To bolster the third criterion, attention to detail, you might cite recognized authorities who stress this quality and the grave risks banks run when they hire employees who lack it. To support the fourth criterion, courtesy to customers, you might use the method of comparison, pointing to the success of a competing bank that stresses good customer relations.

If you can make a reasonable argument for your definition of the evaluative term, your readers are likely to accept the qualities you cite. But they may still object to your definition on the basis of omission: your definition is acceptable as far as it goes, but you have omitted one quality critical to them. Without the inclusion of that quality, they cannot accept your evaluation of the subject. So, in formulating your definition, try to anticipate the reactions of your readers; if they are likely to be concerned about the omission of a certain quality, you must explain why you chose to omit it. Any of the methods previously identified will help you make this explanation. For example, you could justify your omission of a knowledge of computer programming as a criterion for judging trainees by using the identification of effect, pointing out that few bank employees do any programming anyway and that it is cheaper and more efficient to hire outside programming experts when they are needed. In this case, you are pointing out that no bad effects are caused by these trainees' inexperience with programming.

Ranking the Qualities in Your Definition

In some evaluative arguments, it is not enough to establish a list of qualities constituting your evaluative term; often you will need to indicate the relative importance of these qualities by ranking them. Ranking is almost always necessary in evaluations of multiple subjects. If you are evaluating four models of home coffee brewers, for example, you might establish the following qualities as essential: reasonable price, good-tasting coffee, a quick-brew cycle, and an automatic timer. A reader may agree with each of these qualities yet disagree with your final choice of brewer. The reason for the disagreement would be that you and your reader rank the four qualities differently. If a quick-brew cycle is most important to you but least important to your reader, he or she will not accept your final evaluation of the three machines.

In some evaluations, particularly those that are likely to directly affect your reader, you may have to justify the relative value you place on each quality. If you are evaluating dormitory life as a valuable freshman experience, you will let your readers (incoming freshmen) know which of the criteria you cite is most important and which is least important. Suppose you rank the qualities as follows: (1) quiet study atmosphere, (2) good social opportunities, (3) proximity to campus, and (4) comfortable surroundings. You could argue the importance of the first quality, a quiet study atmosphere, by a number of familiar methods: appeals to value or authority, comparison, or identification of effect. Regardless of the method you choose, you must be able to demonstrate that without a quiet study atmosphere, one that allows students to work hard and succeed academically, all of the other qualities are meaningless. If a student flunks out of school the first year, the other three qualities will have been useless. Thus the first quality is the most important because, in your view, it is the *essential* quality.

ACTIVITIES (8.3)

For one of the following subjects, list in order of importance the criteria you would include in its definition. Compare your definition with your classmates' criteria, and based on any disagreement you find, write a two-page essay justifying your selection and ranking of the criteria.

1. A college or university
2. A musical concert
3. A campus newspaper
4. A church or synagogue
5. A textbook for a college course

ARGUING THE EVALUATION

Having laid the necessary foundation for a successful evaluation, you're ready to make the evaluative argument.

The evaluation itself will be largely *factual*. By verifying data and presenting concrete examples, you will argue that your subject possesses the criteria you have cited. Establishing this match is especially important when your subject is a service—a travel agency, a long-distance phone service—or a functional object, such as a coffee brewer or a pickup truck. In these cases, where the evaluative term is defined by objectively measurable qualities (for example, speed, efficiency, accuracy, and price), your job is to verify the existence of those qualities in your subject.

Suppose you were evaluating portable MP3 players. For college preparation, your grandparents offered to purchase a portable CD player in the $150 price range. You don't want to take all of your CDs to your dorm room because you won't have enough storage space, and you are worried about some of your favorites disappearing. Your computer has enough memory to store your CDs and a good speaker system, so you really don't need a portable CD player, but you would like to have a stable MP3 player that will allow you to listen to music while you are in the library or walking to class. You see an ad for a *Walkme3* that is comparable in price to the CD player your grandparents suggested. You don't want to hurt their feelings because they thought they were being "hip" by offering to purchase the CD player, and they are not completely "up" on computers. So you prepare an evaluation to show them how the MP3 player will benefit you and provide you with the listening pleasure that they want you to have. Your evaluation will be convincing if the MP3 player will be better for you than a CD player. You evaluate the Euphony "Walkme3" as a *good portable MP3 player.* Your evaluation will be convincing as long as you can establish the following three facts: the suggested retail price of the Walkme3 is below $150; it offers good quality sound; it holds a reasonable number of songs.

These facts can be convincingly established through reference to your own experience, provided you present yourself as reliable and objective. (Other supporting sources—the experience of friends or impartial analyses of the Walkme3 found in consumer guides—could be referred to as well.) You could cite the actual price of the Walkme3 at three local stores to verify the first fact. The second, which is the most subjective, can be verified by your physical description of the Walkme3's sound quality—full tones, adjustable balance treble and bass levels, clear reproduction of the original CDs—a description of what you require for your listening pleasure. The third fact can also be established by reference to the number of songs you want to be able to select. "When I'm studying at home in my own room, I like familiar classical music that doesn't interfere with my reading. But when I'm walking around, I like a wide variety, including folk, rock, alternative, and even heavy metal on occasion. I need enough storage space for at least three hours of listening, and the Walkme3 provides four hours of storage." As with all factual arguments, the key to success in arguing evaluations is to cite reliable and authoritative experience and observations and to include specific, concrete examples of general statements. Your grandparents will happily support your choice, allowing you to purchase the Walkme3 player instead of a CD player.

Not all evaluations are as neat and objective as the preceding example. Let's look at a very different example involving more subjective measurement and see how the principles of factual argument apply. This evaluation argues that your friend Ellen knows how to be a good friend: she respects her friends, accepting and loving them for who they are, and she expects the same treatment from them. Because the definition included in the claim is not a standard definition of friendship, it requires some preliminary support (see the preceding section on "Arguing the Definition").

Once supported, the definition must be applied to the subject, your friend Ellen. The quality of respecting others—a key criterion of your evaluative term—cannot be measured as objectively or established as definitively as the price of a radio or the fuel efficiency of an automobile. Yet general agreement exists about what constitutes respectful behavior: it is attentive, considerate, accepting behavior. The best way to demonstrate the applicability of the quality to your subject is through specific examples illustrating such behavior. As in any factual argument, you must *describe* the experience faithfully and objectively. Because you want to establish that Ellen's respectful treatment of her friends is habitual, not occasional, you should cite a number of examples.

Beyond citing the examples, you might also need to point out what is respectful in the examples cited, particularly if your readers might interpret the behavior differently. But in general, the more concrete and immediate your presentation of examples, the less explicit commentary you will need.

Testing Your Evaluation Through the Syllogism

A good evaluative claim falls very neatly into the basic syllogistic model presented in Chapter 5. Once you have come up with your claim, you can test its reasonableness and completeness by rewriting it in syllogistic terms. The definition of the evaluative term will be the major premise, the application of the defining criteria will be the minor premise, and the claim itself will be the conclusion. The preceding example regarding Ellen's friendship would compose the following syllogism:

> **Major premise:** A good friend respects her friends, accepts them and loves them for who they are, and expects the same treatment from them.
> **Minor premise:** Ellen respects me, accepts me and loves me for who I am, and expects the same from me.
> **Conclusion:** Ellen is a good friend.

The major premise establishes characteristics that constitute friendship; the minor premise applies those same characteristics to Ellen; and the conclusion makes a very specific claim derived from the relationship between the two premises. This syllogism tells us that the claim is valid, but we can accept it as true as well only if the two premises are also true. If the major premise (the definition of friendship) does not appear to be immediately acceptable, it will have to be argued in the ways we have suggested. Similarly the truth (or probability) of the minor premise may have to be established through a factual argument that provides examples of Ellen's behavior toward you. While you may not be able to *prove* the absolute truth of both premises, you can strengthen them by providing appropriate support, thus moving the entire argument much closer to a position of soundness.

ACTIVITIES (8.4)

Working from the definitions you created for Activity (8.2), compose a specific claim from each. Then turn the definition and the claim into a syllogism. To what extent would the major and minor premises of each syllogism need further support?

FURTHER METHODS OF SUPPORTING EVALUATIONS

Definition and factual argument are central to evaluations, but there are other ways to support these arguments. The tactics that follow can be used along with definition and factual arguments or by themselves.

Identification of Effect

Since an action, policy, or object is generally considered valuable if its effects are valuable, a good way to support evaluations is by identifying the positive effects of the subject. Freedom of speech is good because it encourages the widest exchange of ideas, which is more likely to lead to the truth or to solutions to problems.

Child abuse is bad because it causes physical and mental anguish in children. Of course, such a causal support of evaluations will work only if it accords with the principles of causality discussed in Chapter 7, and if your audience agrees with your assessment of the effect. If you anticipate any disagreement from your audience, you'll need to argue, if only briefly, your evaluation of the effect.

Appeal to Authority

You can support any evaluation by appealing to the similar judgment of a recognized authority. If Chris Evert has publicly expressed her admiration for the tennis game of Martina Hingis, this statement would be effective support for your argument that Hingis is the finest tennis player on the women's tour. Just be sure, when you cite the judgment of an expert, that that person truly qualifies as an authority on this particular subject.

Comparison

You can often support your evaluation by showing similarities between your subject and one that your audience is likely to evaluate in the same way. For example, many feminists have supported their arguments against sexual discrimination by comparing it to racial discrimination. The two forms of discrimination are similar in many ways: both base inequitable treatment on irrelevant and immutable characteristics—race and gender. An audience that would object to racial discrimination would, when the similarities were pointed out, be likely to object to sexual discrimination as well. But as with any comparative argument, make sure the similarities between the two subjects are essential, not peripheral.

ACTIVITIES (8.5)

With a small group of your classmates, identify which kinds of support (factual argument, identification of effect, appeal to authority, comparison) would be most appropriate for two of the following evaluative claims. Discuss your reasons for choosing each form of support.

1. Shakespeare is one of the world's greatest writers.
2. Mercedes-Benz makes many of the world's best cars.
3. Failure to build a water treatment plant for the city would be a serious mistake.
4. Strato Airlines has the best customer service record of any airline in America.
5. Military involvements by major powers in small countries are usually unwise in terms of lives lost, money wasted, and the increased suspicion of other small countries.

THE VARIETIES OF EVALUATIONS

By now, you realize that different kinds of evaluations demand different kinds of support. While there are no hard-and-fast rules in this area, if you can identify the *kind* of evaluation you're arguing, you'll have a better sense of how to support it. Evaluations usually fall into one of three main categories: ethical, aesthetic, or functional. Included in this section is a fourth subclass as well: the interpretation. Strictly speaking, interpretations are not evaluative arguments, but since they are argued in much the same way as evaluations, they are addressed here.

Ethical Evaluations

The word *ethical* is one of those terms that we all understand in a vague way yet might be hard pressed to define precisely. To avoid confusion, consider the following definition: *ethical* describes behavior that conforms to an ideal code of moral principles—principles of right and wrong, good and evil. That code may be derived from any number of cultures: religious, professional, national, or political.

All of us operate within many cultures: we are members of families, communities, organizations, religions, professions, and nations. Each one of these cultures has its own set of ethical standards. For example, among the many ethical principles of Judaism and Christianity are the Ten Commandments. As United States citizens, we are subject to other standards of conduct, such as those recorded in the Constitution—including the Bill of Rights—and the Declaration of Independence. Your college also operates by certain standards that it expects its members to follow: respect for school property, respect for faculty, and academic honesty. In most cultures, these standards are formally recorded, but in some instances they remain implicit. There also exist certain ethical ideals common to virtually all cultures—ideals such as fair play, kindness, and respect for others.

Because individuals are tied to a number of different cultures, clashes between standards are inevitable. Some pacifist groups, for example, see a clash between the religious commandment "Thou shall not kill" and the government's standard that citizens must be prepared to defend their country in time of war. Sometimes conflicts occur between standards of the same culture. Such clashes are commonplace in law. What happens, for example, when the right of free speech collides with the right of a person to be free from libel? Free speech cannot mean that someone has a right to say anything about another person, regardless of how untrue or harmful it is. On the other hand, protection from libel cannot mean protection from the truth being told about mistakes or misdeeds, particularly when they have some impact on the public. Throughout our history, the courts have struggled to find a balance between these two competing claims, sometimes slightly favoring one value, sometimes the other, but always denying that either value can have absolute sway over the other.

Defining the Evaluative Term in Ethical Arguments. Whenever you evaluate a subject in terms of right or wrong conduct, you'll be appealing to certain ethical values or standards that you believe your audience holds. When asserting that "Hitler was an evil man," or "Ms. Mead is an honorable lawyer," or "The coach used unfair tactics," you are assuming that your readers both *understand* what you mean by the evaluative term and *agree* with that meaning. As in all evaluations, if you have reason to doubt your readers' understanding of the term, you'll have to define it, and if you're uncertain about their agreement with the definition, you'll have to support it.

The Argument in Ethical Evaluations.   Most ethical arguments concentrate on demonstrating what is unethical or immoral about the subject being evaluated. At the center of these evaluations, then, is a factual argument. In arguing that Hitler was evil, your focus would be on documenting the behavior you identify as evil, and on demonstrating that your evaluative term fits the examples you are citing.

You can also strengthen your evaluation through other supporting methods, including comparison (Hitler was as bad as or worse than certain other dictators) or identification of effect (in addition to all of the bad he did in his life, the war Hitler started led to the division of Europe into two opposing camps, or to a pervasive sense of victimization among Jews of later generations).

ACTIVITIES (8.6)

Using one of the following evaluative assertions (from Activities 8.5) as your claim, write a two-page "Letter to the Editor" of your local city newspaper. Or create your own claim derived from a current local or national controversy.

1. Shakespeare is one of the world's greatest writers.
2. Mercedes-Benz makes many of the world's best cars.
3. Failure to build a water treatment plant for the city would be a serious mistake.
4. Strato Airlines has the best customer service record of any airline in America.

Aesthetic Evaluations

Writing a convincing evaluation of a work of art—a poem, an opera, a painting—is not as futile a task as many believe, provided you understand the goals of such an argument. Just as personal tastes in clothes or food are usually immune to reasonable argument, aesthetic preferences—liking Chopin's music and despising Mahler's—are often too much matters of personal taste to be arguable. There is much truth in the Latin saying *De gustibus non est disputandum:* there is no arguing about taste. Nevertheless, while changing aesthetic tastes or opinions is difficult, it is possible and often useful to convince an audience to *appreciate* the strengths or weaknesses of a work of art by giving them a greater understanding of it. A successful aesthetic evaluation may not convince a reader to like Rubens or to dislike Lichtenstein, but it will at least give a reader reasons for approving of or objecting to a work.

All artistic fields have their own sets of standards for excellence, standards about which there is surprising conformity among experts in the field. Most literary critics, for example, would agree on the standards for a successful short story: coherence of the story, careful selection of detail, avoidance of digression, an interesting style. When critics disagree, and of course they do so regularly, they usually disagree not about identified standards of excellence but about the application of those standards. Often such disagreements are matters of a personal preference for one kind of artist over another. Even professional critics are not immune to the influence of their personal tastes.

When you argue an aesthetic evaluation, you should work from standards currently accepted within the field, though you may not have to do more than briefly or implicitly refer to them. Your evaluation is likely to fail if you ignore these standards, or if you try to effect an overnight revolution in them. Like ethical standards, aesthetic standards usually change gradually, though there have been periods of revolutionary change, as occurred in artistic tastes in the early twentieth century.

Usually, then, your chief task is to demonstrate that these standards apply (or don't apply) to your subject. This demonstration consists of careful description and concrete examples, as in the following excerpt from an essay on the famous comedians the Marx Brothers ("From Sweet Anarchy to Stupid Pet Tricks"). In this excerpt, Mark Edmundson gives a description and examples from a particular scene in a Marx Brothers film and then presents his criteria for rich "antiestablishment comedy."

> Groucho always rebels against his own success. When it seems that Trentino might treat him on equal terms, as a gentleman, Groucho stages an imagined encounter between himself and the Sylvanian ambassador that ends in disaster. "I'll be only too happy," Groucho pledges in most statesmanlike tones, "to meet Ambassador Trentino and offer him, on behalf of my country, the right hand of good fellowship." But then, Groucho worries, maybe the ambassador will snub him (stranger things have happened). "A fine thing that'll be! I hold out my hand and he refuses to accept it! That'll add a lot to my prestige, won't it? Me, the head of a country, snubbed by a foreign ambassador! Who does he think he is that he can come here and make a sap out of me in front of all my people?" Then, rising to a boil, "Think of it! I hold out my hand and that hyena refuses to accept it! . . . He'll never get away with it, I tell you! . . . He'll never get away with it."
>
> Enter Trentino, looking haughty. Groucho, raging now, "So! You refuse to shake hands with me, eh?" Groucho slaps Trentino with his gloves. This means war!
>
> It's Groucho's contempt for his own high-mindedness and posing—"I'll be happy to meet Ambassador Trentino and offer him the right hand," blah, blah, blah—that sends him into a spin. Groucho was about to act decorously, something for which he cannot forgive himself. As his predecessor Thoreau put it, "What demon possessed me that I behaved so well?"
>
> Our current outsider comics—Roseanne, Eddie Murphy, Martin Lawrence—attack incessantly, and they sometimes score. But what they don't generally do is what Groucho does so superbly, turn the lens back, dramatize their own flaws. The richness of Groucho's antiestablishment comedy is that it compels us not only to challenge social hypocrisy but to

consider our own. And it's that double vision, it seems to me, that helps make Groucho and the Marx Brothers as indispensable now as they were in the 1930s.

Edmundson's chief measure of the success of antiestablishment comedians is what he calls their "double vision," their ability to "turn the lens back, dramatize their own flaws." With the criterion clearly identified, the reader can discover it easily in the detailed description of the film scene.

As with all arguments, when composing an aesthetic evaluation, be sure to consider your readers' level of knowledge—both of the subject being evaluated and of the field in general (comedy, tragedy, jazz, autobiographies, etc.) Edmundson assumes that his readers are familiar with Marx Brothers' films, but he also reviews individual scenes in some detail to ensure that his points are made. In cases where your subject and your evaluative criteria may be less familiar to your audience, you may want to offer not only a careful description of the subject, but also a lucid explanation of the criteria. People often fail to appreciate what they don't understand, so if your evaluation can teach them about the standards of a particular field, it will have a better chance of convincing them that your subject meets (or fails to meet) those standards.

Another useful tactic when arguing a positive evaluation to an inexperienced audience is to relate your subject to one with which they are more familiar. If, for example, you want to convince an audience familiar with and appreciative of modern abstract art that the art of ancient Egypt is also interesting, you might point out the similarities between the two: "Although they are widely separated in time, modern abstract art and ancient Egyptian art both concentrate on the essence of a person or object, not the surface appearance." In taking this approach, you are borrowing from your readers' appreciation of modern abstract art, shining its positive light onto the subject of your evaluation.

ACTIVITIES (8.7)

For each of the following forms of art or entertainment, list at least three standards by which you would judge the quality of a specific work of this type. Then, for one of the categories, write a two- to three-page essay demonstrating how a specific work of that type does or does not fit your standards of excellence. (You should make these standards explicit in your essay.)

1. An action film
2. A mystery novel
3. A jazz recording
4. A portrait photograph
5. An abstract painting

Functional Evaluations

Functional evaluations stand a better chance of changing readers' minds than do ethical and aesthetic evaluations. It is easier to convince a reader that her views about turbo engine cars are inaccurate than that her views about abortion are wrong. While people do form sentimental attachments to objects and machines, they can usually be convinced that however powerful that attachment, it has nothing to do with the subject's actual performance; an audience's preconceptions about performance quality are less matters of cultural values and personal tastes than of practical experience, assumptions, or hearsay.

Functional evaluations always work from a definition of ideal standards: like evaluating MP3s, you can't demonstrate that Sony makes an excellent CD player without some criteria for measuring the player's performance. Some functional evaluations require an explicit presentation of evaluative criteria and some can safely assume reader familiarity with the relevant criteria. Certainly, if your criteria are unusual or innovative ("The most important feature of a car for me is that it *look* good"), you'll have to state them explicitly and argue their relevance and completeness (using any of the methods discussed earlier in this chapter).

Sometimes functional evaluations work best from a ranked list of criteria. For example, a lawnmower can be evaluated in terms of safety features, cost, and noise, but the three criteria may not be equally important. To justify your evaluation, you should explain and support the relative weights you've assigned to each criterion.

Any of the other supporting methods discussed earlier in this chapter (identification of effect, appeal to authority, comparison) can also be used in a performance evaluation. Of these, the most valuable is identification of effect. "Virginia Wensel is a good violin teacher" because she has produced a number of fine players; "My college provides an excellent education" because 85 percent of its graduates go on to graduate school. In each case, the subject is judged in terms of its positive effects. Note that sometimes the effect you identify as an evaluative criterion must be argued. Why, for example, does acceptance into graduate school mean you have received an excellent undergraduate education?

If the effect you are citing has already occurred, your support will be a factual argument. In arguing that "Virginia Wensel is a good violin teacher," you would cite the number of fine players she has produced and briefly support your positive judgment of those players. In other cases, where the effect has not yet occurred, your argument is necessarily more speculative: "Based on the evidence we have, this car is likely to give you years of reliable service."

ACTIVITIES (8.8)

List in ranked order at least three standards by which you would judge the performance of the following. Then, for one of the categories, write a two- to three-page essay demonstrating how well one person or object in that category meets your standards of performance.

1. An automobile for a family with three small children
2. A president of a college or university
3. A personal computer
4. A United States senator
5. A college reference librarian

Interpretations

The purpose of an interpretation is to disclose the meaning of a particular subject—often a meaning not immediately obvious to a casual observer or reader. At some time or other, all students must practice interpretive arguments in literature classes. The following are examples of possible claims for literary interpretations: "Beneath the apparently modest and conventional surface of Christina Rossetti's lyrics lie fiery manifestoes of independence and rebellion"; "In placing the last scene of *Tess of the d'Urbervilles* at Stonehenge, Thomas Hardy reminds us that Tess is a pagan, not a Christian, heroine." But interpretations are not solely the province of literature; we make interpretive arguments all the time about the behavior of people we know ("Paul says he craves a close relationship with a woman, but it's easy to see he's terrified of intimacy") and about the productions of popular culture ("Television advertisements are selling one thing: sex").

Interpretations are often paired with explanatory causal arguments. In claiming that "Hamlet's indecisiveness is a symptom of his unresolved Oedipal complex," we are really making two claims, both of which propose an increased understanding of the play *Hamlet*. First, we are identifying the *cause* of Hamlet's indecisive behavior (his unresolved Oedipal complex), and second, we are claiming that an unresolved Oedipal complex can be discovered within Hamlet's character. Now, if you've read the play, you know that Shakespeare is never explicit about the oddities of Hamlet's relationship with his mother. No character ever says to Hamlet, "Oh Hamlet, cast thy infantile and possessive love of thy mother off." But keen readers who recognize some of the telltale symptoms of the Oedipal complex detect one in Hamlet's words and actions. And that detection is the interpretive argument: the demonstration of meaning beneath the surface. You will remember that causal claims are always somewhat speculative; this brand of causal claim is even more so, because the cause it identifies is interpretive, not factual.

Interpretations can imply a positive or a negative evaluation, but they are not evaluations per se. Nevertheless, the processes for arguing the two are very similar. The subject of an interpretive argument is the visible surface we wish to understand or explore further; it is the behavior, data, or event that openly exists for all to observe. The interpretive term is the summarized explanation of the reality beneath the visible surface. In the interpretive claim "The current baseball cap craze among boys expresses their rejection of tradition and authority," the subject is *current baseball cap craze among boys,* and the interpretive term is *rejection of tradition and authority.*

As in evaluations, your central task in interpretive arguments is to demonstrate a match between the subject and the interpretive term. But also as in evaluations, you will need to lay some groundwork. Most solid interpretations satisfy the following requirements: (1) the interpretive term is clearly defined; (2) the interpretive term and the subject are matched—that is, demonstrated to be equivalent or coincident; and (3) evidence is supplied to support the interpretation.

Defining the Interpretive Term.   Like evaluative arguments, interpretations work from assumptions about definition—about what elements make up a certain condition or reality. In interpretations, we are stating that X (the subject) is Y (the interpretation). To prove or support this assertion, we must define Y in such a way that it restates X or restate X in such a way that it coincides with Y. In the interpretive claim "Television news broadcasting is no longer news; it is entertainment," we must demonstrate the coincidence of our definition of entertainment on the one hand with what we see of television news on the other.

In the following passage, we see a similar assertion of coincidence, where Sigmund Freud equates literature (the subject) with the play of children:

> Now the writer does the same as the child at play; he creates a world of phantasy which he takes very seriously; that is, he invests it with a great deal of affect, while separating it sharply from reality. Language has preserved this relationship between children's play and poetic creation. It designates certain kinds of imaginative creation, concerned with tangible objects and capable of representation, as "plays"; the people who present them are called "players."

The first step in assembling an interpretive argument is to consider whether to define the interpretive term and argue your definition. As with evaluative arguments, you should define the term if you are using it in an unusual or controversial way, and you should justify that definition if you think your audience is likely to object to it. In the first example, the term *entertainment* probably should be defined, as it is a very broad and even subjective term. You might define the term as "any brief, self-contained, sensually pleasing performance that amuses but does not challenge." If your audience is likely to disagree with this definition, you will have to support it with the methods discussed in the preceding section titled "Arguing the Definition" in this chapter.

Of course, you can work from an unstated definition, provided your argument clearly reveals the elements of that definition. The following example illustrates this tactic:

> Much of television news broadcasting is no longer news; it is entertainment. Most local and national news broadcasts, news shows like *60 Minutes* and *20/20,* and even public television news are putting out slick, superficial performances that are usually neither challenging nor controversial, but that capture huge audience shares.

Here the definition of entertainment is contained in the characterization of television news.

Extensive interpretations of a series of events or continuing behavior work somewhat differently, though the basic principles are the same. In these cases— for example, an interpretation of a character's actions in a novel or of quarterly stock market activity—the subjects are usually explained in terms of a coherent and preestablished theory, system of thought, or belief. Instead of demonstrating the coincidence or equivalence of the subject and a single concept (like children's play or entertainment), these more ambitious interpretations reveal the existence of a series of related concepts—an entire system—behind the visible activity of the subject. The system identified could be Christianity, Marxism, Jungian psychology, feminism, Freudian drive theory, capitalism, semiotics—virtually any set of facts or principles logically connected to form a coherent view of the world.

Examples of this kind of systematic interpretation are especially prevalent in artistic and literary interpretations, though they are not limited to these contexts. A feminist interpretation of a literary figure like Emily Dickinson would work from a thorough understanding of feminist theory. The interpretation might explain Dickinson's poems in terms of the tension between her vocation as a poet and the very different expectations that nineteenth-century society had for women.

However compelling such an interpretation, readers are not likely to be swayed if they strongly object to the interpretive system—to the Freudian, or Marxist, or feminist model of human behavior. Even if the construct used to explain the subject is not formally named, the principles contained in that construct must seem at least plausible to your readers. If you interpret modern American history on the basis of tensions and conflicts between different social and economic classes, your readers may not give your interpretation fair consideration if they are opposed to this set of principles. On the other hand, a good interpretation often helps readers gain sympathy for a philosophy or point of view they were previously hostile to or ignorant of. When you write interpretations, you should be sensitive to your audience's beliefs and prepared at least to acknowledge their probable objections as you proceed. In doing so, you may convince some hostile readers, bringing them to accept not only your interpretation but also at least some aspects of your underlying point of view.

Establishing Coincidence. All interpretations must demonstrate coincidence between the subject and the interpretive term. *Coincidence* in this context can mean equivalence (as in "Television news is the same as entertainment"), substitution ("Although marriage looks like a romantic partnership, it is often a formalization of female dependence"), or revelation ("Behind Jack's warmth and friendliness is a cold and impenetrable shield of defenses"). The challenge of interpretations is in demonstrating these coincidences.

When the interpretive term is concrete, this task is comparatively easy. We recognize such concepts as entertainment or economic dependence; they are verifiable. Once we agree on the meaning of the term, a simple factual argument will demonstrate the applicability of the term to the subject. If we know what economic dependence is, we can detect it in a relationship with little difficulty or little guesswork, provided we have the necessary facts.

But what about detecting a "cold and impenetrable shield of defenses" in an acquaintance? There is no sure way to verify the existence of such a "shield," so how do we argue its existence? Remember in Chapter 7 on causal arguments the principle of a generally accepted link between cause and effect? Just as a cause and its effect must be linked by some acceptable motivational principle that agrees with human experience and observation, so must the interpretation (the less visible reality) relate to the subject (the visible reality) according to an acknowledged principle of experience.

Let's take the case of Jack's misleading warmth and friendliness. Basically we want to demonstrate that his apparent friendliness is an expression of his need to protect himself. First, we'll have to recast the subject or the interpretive term so that the two are shown to be equivalent. We can do this by elaborating on the friendliness: "Jack is as friendly to a grocery clerk as he is to a lifelong friend. He is completely indiscriminate in how he relates to people. This may be good for the grocery clerk, who enjoys Jack's friendly manner, but not so good for the friend, who, in fact, has never gotten to know Jack any better than the grocery clerk has," and so forth. Having established the coincidence or equivalence of this brand of friendliness and defensiveness, you'll want to assure yourself (and your readers, if necessary) that the equivalence you cite agrees with the principles of human behavior that we generally accept: indiscriminate behavior (even friendliness) often expresses its opposite.

Documenting the Interpretation.   Interpretations need documentation, or evidence. As well as explaining your subject through an acceptable principle of experience, you'll have to document your claim through examples taken from your subject. Different arguments will provide different kinds of evidence, so it is difficult to generalize about the best kind of evidence. In literature papers, professors are looking for examples from the literary work that support the claim. For example, in a paper arguing, "Behind Othello's seeming self-confidence is a collection of debilitating insecurities," the student would need to cite a number of passages in the play that suggest these insecurities. In the student paper at the end of this chapter, an interpretation of popular media, the writer documents his interpretation of a magazine ad by carefully describing the visual details of the ad.

The Possibility of Multiple Interpretations.   Most subjects lend themselves to a number of different interpretations, and these interpretations are not necessarily mutually exclusive. Widely varied and equally convincing interpretations of Shakespeare's *Hamlet* have been written through the centuries; it is a testament to the brilliance of the play that it can accommodate so many different readings. Because of the likelihood of multiple interpretations of any subject, try to resist adopting a dogmatic and inflexible tone in your arguments. You don't need to constantly acknowledge the possibility of other interpretations, nor should you present your own interpretation too tentatively; on the other hand, don't lay out your argument as if it were immutable, inarguable dogma.

ACTIVITIES (8.9)

1. Write a brief interpretation (approximately one page) of a recent event. Your interpretation should include the interpretive term, the kind of coincidence, and the supporting evidence. Then write a second interpretation of the same event, again including all the necessary elements of an interpretation. Give both essays to a classmate to read, and then discuss with him or her which is the most plausible interpretation and why. Some possible events: a recent election, a political scandal, a friend's recent success or failure in some endeavor, an athletic contest.

2. Find in a magazine an interpretation of a film that you have seen recently. Many magazines that offer movie reviews and criticisms can be found

online: *Boxoffice, Entertainment Weekly, Premiere, Film Journal, FilmMaker: The Magazine of Independent Film, Shock Cinema, MovieMaker,* and *Beatdown: British Film Magazine* are just a few. Be sure to support your argument with concrete references to the film itself. (Give your instructor a copy of the magazine review whether you found the review online or in hardcopy.)

SUMMARY

Arguing Evaluations

- All evaluations include a subject to be judged and an evaluative term applied to the subject.

- Before you argue the evaluation, consider whether your readers will recognize and accept your definition of the evaluative term. When their acceptance seems questionable, you'll want to argue your particular definition. Definitions can be argued by appeals to assumed reader values, appeals to authority, identification of effect, and comparison. When evaluating more than one subject against a single set of criteria, you may have to rank the criteria and justify that ranking.

- Applying the syllogistic model to your evaluative claim can help you test its reasonableness.

- Evaluations are made in ethical, aesthetic, or functional terms. *Ethical* evaluations focus on applying the ethical standard (evaluative term) to the subject, or on arguing a stipulative definition of that standard. *Aesthetic* evaluations typically work from standards currently accepted within the field, demonstrating their applicability to your subject. *Functional* evaluations typically work from a number of ranked criteria in terms of which the subject is measured.

- *Interpretations* closely resemble evaluations in structure. They establish coincidence or equivalence between the subject and the interpretive term by linking them through an acknowledged principle of experience.

SAMPLE ETHICAL EVALUATION

The following essay on homosexual marriages, written by college student Douglas Edwards, is an example of an ethical evaluation. After carefully reading the argument, collaborate with a small group of your classmates in answering the questions following the essay.

CRITICALLY ANALYZING THE DEFENSE OF MARRIAGE ACT:

A MATTER OF LOVE

One in ten people is gay or lesbian (Marcus 8). When
the United States passed the Defense of Marriage Act, the
government violated the rights of approximately 25 million
Americans ("United States"). Succumbing to myths and
stereotypes about homosexuals, politicians denied gays and
lesbians federal recognition of marriage. However, they
were denying the ultimate expression of commitment. The
Defense of Marriage Act violates the Constitution and
basic human rights and must be overturned.

Introduced by Georgia Representative Bob Barr, the
Defense of Marriage Act gives federal recognition to
heterosexual marriages only and allows a state to refuse
to recognize a homosexual marriage conducted in another
state ("Defense"). However, before we examine this law, we
must address certain popular and erroneous beliefs about
homosexuals. No one chooses homosexuality just as no one
chooses heterosexuality (Marcus 9). Both are natural
tendencies with origins scientists do not understand. As
author Eric Marcus explains:

> Homosexual people come in all shapes and sizes and
> from all walks of life, just like heterosexual
> people do. Some are single, and some are involved
> in long-term, loving relationships with same-sex
> partners . . . Homosexual people are a part of
> every community and every family, which means that
> everyone knows someone who is homosexual. (1-2)

Throughout history, homosexuality and marriage have
been discussed in virtually every culture. The ancient
Greeks saw homosexual love as normal and acceptable.
Although virtually every Christian or Jewish religion
condemns homosexuality and/or homosexual acts, literally
or loosely interpreting the Bible does not support
fundamentalists' arguments. According to Baptist minister
and Plummer Professor of Christian Morals at Harvard,

Peter J. Gomes, Leviticus 18:19-23 and Leviticus 20:10-16 ban homosexual acts *and* tattoos, eating raw meat, wearing garments made of two types of yarn, planting two different seeds in the same field, and sexual intercourse during a woman's menstrual period. The Gospels do not mention homosexuality, and St. Paul condemned lust and sensuality in anyone (Marcus 132). Homosexuality and AIDS educator Ann Northrup asks if marriage's purpose is children, should sterile couples be denied marriage (17)? Before the Civil War, blacks could not marry since that made them " . . . less marketable" (Troy). Psychologist Dr. Evelyn Hooker demonstrated in the 1950s that heterosexual and homosexual men were not different psychologically, and the American Psychiatric Association does not consider homosexuality a mental illness (Marcus 11-12).

Based on the previously mentioned stereotypes and false beliefs, the Defense of Marriage Act is unconstitutional. Bound by the Constitution's "full faith and credit," states must honor other states' contracts, including marriage. A federal marriage license does not exist; the federal government recognizes marriages in all 50 states. Adoption, marriage, and divorce are all under the states' jurisdiction, and only 34 have dealt with same-sex marriage ("Defense . . . Fact Sheet"). However, a recent court case may allow same-sex marriages in Hawaii. The following is from a <u>Los Angeles Times</u> article:

> In his opinion, Hawaii Circuit Judge Kevin S.C. Chang said that the state had failed to prove it had a compelling interest in preventing such marriages. He issued an injunction to prevent the State Department of Health from denying licenses solely because applicants are of the same sex, basing his reasoning on the equal protection clause of the state constitution ("Hawaii . . ."). Since the federal government will not recognize these marriages, a complicated state and federal tax network will result causing numerous problems.

If a married couple moved to another state, their
marriage may suddenly not exist ("Defense . . .
Fact Sheet").

Obviously, gays want federal recognition of their
marriages for dignity and respect. However, there are many
financial benefits. Married couples in most states have
legal rights to be on their spouses' insurance and pension
plans, to receive special tax exemptions, to receive
Social Security benefits, and to be the legal "next
of kin." There have been many stories in which gays'
long-term partners could not visit their lovers in the
hospital, make decisions regarding medical care, or become
legal guardians of incapacitated loved ones since the
government did not recognize their relationships (Marcus
83). This is not to suggest that gays are motivated
by financial gains, but these are practical issues that
heterosexuals take for granted. Fortunately, companies
such as IBM, Microsoft, American Express, and Walt Disney
grant benefits to their gay employees' partners, and
other corporations are following their lead (Jones).
These businesses realize that sexual orientation is not
connected with employee performance. Some claim that
gays should not be given special privileges. However,
if heterosexuals can marry but gays cannot, then
heterosexuals are receiving special privileges.

Some politicians suggest that homosexual marriage is
a pressing national priority, but many Americans disagree.
In a Mellman Group poll, only 13% said passing the Defense
of Marriage act was an "important priority"; 73% believe
the nation faced more pressing issues. 37% of Americans
support the law, and only 27% of the public believes gay
marriages threaten families ("Defense . . . Poll"). In a
nation faced with mounting crime and an out-of-control
budget, certainly gay marriages—acts of love—do not
deserve national scrutiny. In a Los Angeles Times article
describing the Hawaiian court decision allowing same-sex
marriages, the author said, "Conservative opponents

condemned the opinion as an outrageous example of a court thumbing its nose at public opinion" ("Hawaii"). However, as mentioned earlier, America does not consider this to be an important issue, and popular opinion is not always right. Slavery was popular in the South, but the public opinion certainly was not correct.

National Gay and Lesbian Task Force Executive Director Melinda Paras says, "While they would have us believe that they seek to 'preserve legalized, traditional marriage,' the truth is that they seek to impose their own narrow agenda on every American by playing on people's real fears and concerns about the changing American family" ("NGLTF"). It is understandable that many people fear gays and they hope this legislation will force them to "not choose this lifestyle"; negative stereotypes instigate prejudice. However, gays do not choose their attractions; someone cannot make a homosexual straight just as a person cannot make a heterosexual gay (Marcus 13). People cannot understand what they do not know; since one out of every 10 people is gay, we all know a gay person whether, we realize it or not. Does Congress want gay people to marry into heterosexual relationships that eventually result in divorces, displaced children, and declining family values? Biracial marriage was illegal in some areas of the United States until a 1967 Supreme Court ruling (Marcus 85), but biracial marriage certainly was not evil or sinful.

Executive Director Barry Wick of the South Dakota Gay, Lesbian, and Bisexual Federation, called the Defense of Marriage Act "patently offensive to anyone who remembers the miscegenation laws of the South that banned inter-racial marriage" (Dunlap). When two gay people commit to each other, it is a *natural* expression of their love as it is when African Americans love white Americans. Denying gays marriage will not force them into isolation; it invigorates their civil rights movement. America's family values need serious examination since heterosexuals

The Constitution guarantees life, liberty, and the pursuit of happiness with no exceptions for homosexuals. By banning federal recognition of gay marriages, the U.S. government demonstrated that it focuses on fiction, not fact. Love will prevail; homosexuals will continue to share their lives together. However, heterosexual love should not be given a higher status; every couple deserves the right to solidify their relationship with marriage.

A version of this essay appeared in the September 4, 1997 issue of the University of Akron's student newspaper, The Buchtelite.

WORKS CITED

"Defense of Marriage Act." n. pag. Online. Internet. 25 Nov. 1996.

    <http://www.hrc.org/issues/leg/doma/billtext.html>.

"Defense of Marriage Act—Fact Sheet." n. pag. Online. Internet. 25 Nov. 1996.

    <http://www.hrc.org/issues/leg/doma/factsheet.html>.

"Defense of Marriage Act—Poll." n. pag. Online. Internet. 25 Nov. 1996.

    HTTP://www.hrc.org/issues/leg/doma/polling.html.

Dunlap, David W. "Some States Trying to Stop Gay Marriages Before They Start." The New York Times. (14 March, 95) n. pag. Online. Internet. 3 Dec. 1996.

    <http://www.cs.cmu.edu/afs/cs.cmu.edu/user/scotts/domesticpartners/NYTimes-Same-sex-couples.txt>.

"Hawaii Judge ends ban on gay marriages." Los Angeles Times. Rpt. in The Plain Dealer. 4 Dec. 1996: 1A, 28A.

Jones, Del. "IBM gives gay/lesbian partners health benefits." USA Today. 20 Sept. 1996: 10A.

Marcus, Eric. "Is It A Choice?". San Francisco: Harper Collins, 1993.

"NGLTF Condemns Federal Anti-Marriage Legislation." National Gay and Lesbian Task Force. n. pag. Online. Internet. 25 Nov. 1996.

<http://www.ngltf.org/news/release.cfm?releaseID=205>.

Troy, David C. "Baltimore & the Fifteenth Amendment, May
    19, 1870." <u>Celebrating Rights and Responsibilities</u>.
    n. pag. Online. Internet. 3 Dec. 1996. Available
    <http://www.toad.net/~dave/project/>.
"United States." <u>Microsoft Encarta</u> n. pag. CD-ROM. 1995

DISCUSSION QUESTIONS

1. What are the subject and evaluative term of Doug's argument?
2. Why do you think he provides a definition of the evaluative term?
3. Through what methods does Doug support his evaluation. Are these effective? Why or why not?
4. Identify and discuss the placement of the argument's claim.

SAMPLE INTERPRETATION

The following is an essay by first-year student Kevin Maloney on "Reading Popular Culture." Read it through carefully, then answer the questions that follow the essay. Compare your answers with those of your classmates.

READING POPULAR CULTURE

    Hidden within the productions of popular culture are
quiet endorsements of specific values or attitudes. Such
attitudes are projected not only in print, but in music,
advertisements, and television programs. Just as it is
important to be able to read the written word, it is also
vital to know how to read these other forms of expression.
Being unable to recognize the sometimes hidden messages of
these forms of expression is like being in a foreign
country where you don't speak the language. In both cases,
you can easily fall prey to individuals eager to take
advantage of your ignorance, to manipulate you into doing
what they want you to do.

    Often, the skill of discovering the values or
attitudes promoted in popular culture involves nothing
more than stepping back and seeing "the big picture,"
recognizing what is really pretty obvious. Take, for
example, the popular sitcom *Seinfeld*. It is possible to

watch and enjoy this show week after week without
realizing how it is dominated by sexually promiscuous
behavior. On a recent episode, Jerry Seinfeld pursued a
female gymnast. His goal was to see if sex with a gymnast
was more exciting and varied than with someone less
physically flexible. Within a week's time, he was sleeping
with the gymnast and joking about their sexual encounters.
By the end of the show, he had broken up with her, merely
because the sex wasn't really all that different.

Elaine, another character on the program, seems to
have new sexual partners almost every episode. Since she
can always find some very superficial reason to break up
with them—she doesn't like one guy's name, another gets a
haircut—none of these relationships lasts. But in show
after show, she persists in her search for "the one."

None of the characters in the show disapprove of
Jerry's and Elaine's promiscuity. In fact, their behavior
is often the source of delight and envy for their friends,
some of whom, like George, try to emulate it. I have
watched the show regularly for at least three years, and I
realize that I have never seen sex presented as anything
other than a joke. The program never explicitly says that
viewers should lead a promiscuous life, but that lifestyle
is repeated again and again. And this is one way that
cultural values are constructed and instilled—through
repeated themes and behavior in television programming
(George and Trimbur 228). Whenever a behavior—in the case
of Seinfeld, sexual promiscuity—is repeated, the viewer is
asked to accept it as a norm.

Television is not the only form of popular culture
that promotes promiscuity as a norm. Magazine advertising
does the same. As Jean Kilbourne says, these ads "sell a
great deal more than products" (152).

Take the example of an ad from a recent computer
magazine. A scantily clad woman stands in the middle of
the page, her perfect body more prominent than anything
else in the ad. She is wearing spotted, tight-fitting

pants; her skin-tight T-shirt bares most of her abdomen; her shirt is covered by suggestive fishnet mesh; and a navel ring adorns her trim stomach. Apparently the waitress in this diner, she wears a pair of in-line skates and holds a tray. Everything about this woman suggests available sexuality.

And why is this ad set in a diner with a waitress as its focal point? The answers to these questions don't have much to do with computers, but they do have a lot to do with sex. As a waitress, the woman's job is to bring her customers what they want, and her dress suggests that this means anything. The table closest to the camera has partially empty cups sitting on it; clearly other customers have dined here before. And if they left something in their cups, they must have left satisfied—another instance of the advertisement's sexual insinuations. The text beneath the photograph tells us "Monday's Chef's Special" is "the obvious choice." What this woman can bring you is obviously what you want. And the sexual innuendoes go on and on.

Popular music also frequently contains implicit endorsements of sexual promiscuity. The words are often camouflaged by a good beat, a nice voice, and interesting harmonies, but their message is there.

Pop singer Bruce Springsteen has a song called "Secret Garden." The title suggests something pure and natural, but take a look at the lyrics: "She'll let you in her house if you come knocking late at night. She'll let you in her mouth if the words you say are right." Apparently these lyrics are about a woman who will engage in oral sex if the man sweet-talks her. The next line is "If you pay the price she'll let you deep inside." Again, sex is the reward for saying the right words to a woman. Later in the song, we hear "She'll let you into the parts of herself that'll bring you down." What is remarkable about these lyrics is how clearly they refer to

promiscuous sex; you don't have to be a Houdini of
interpretation to understand their meaning.

Some might say that such sexually promiscuous TV
characters, sexually suggestive computer ads, and sexually
symbolic song lyrics may represent promiscuous behavior,
but they don't necessarily promote it. Yet the more
behaviors and images are repeated in popular culture, the
more "normal" they begin to seem. If we don't stop to
recognize and evaluate these repeated behaviors and
images, we will find ourselves influenced by their sheer
volume. Without even realizing it, we may feel it's all
right to repeat them in our own lives. So let's learn the
language of cultural manipulation so we can avoid being
its victim.

WORKS CITED

George, Dianna, and John Trimbur, Eds. "Introduction to
    Television Culture." <u>Reading Culture: Contexts for
    Critical Reading and Writing</u>. New York: Harper, 1995.
    228-29.

Kilbourne, Jean. "Beauty...and the Beast of Advertising."
    <u>Reading Culture: Contexts for Critical Reading and
    Writing</u>. Ed. Dianna George and John Trimbur. New
    York: Harper, 1995. 152-54.

Springsteen, Bruce. "Secret Garden" <u>Bruce Springsteen:
    Greatest Hits</u>. Recording. Columbia, 1995.

DISCUSSION QUESTIONS

1. What is Kevin interpreting in this essay, and what is his interpretive term?
2. Do you agree with Kevin's decision about providing an explicit definition of the interpretive term?
3. Kevin does not address the possibility that the *Seinfeld* show is satirical, that it presents certain shallow and irresponsible behaviors to criticize or poke fun at them. With a group of your classmates who know the show, consider this possibility and how it would affect Kevin's argument.
4. Discuss the evidence offered as support of the claim. Is it relevant and sufficient? Are you convinced by the argument?

SUGGESTIONS FOR WRITING (8.10)

1. Write a two- to three-page evaluation of a course you have taken or are taking in college. Your evaluation will be primarily a functional evaluation, one of the crucial questions being whether the course actually achieves its intended goals.

2. Write a three- to four-page argument for or against a subject that requires evaluation—i.e., sexual harassment policies, ethnicity issues, Distance Learning, or even euthanasia—based on your reading of the sample student paper at the end of the section on evaluation. Have you established a clear definition? What about the other supporting arguments? Are there other arguments for the stand you have taken or do you have what you believe are more powerful arguments against it?

3. Write a combination interpretation and evaluation (three to four pages) of a recent artistic or entertainment event you enjoyed: a film, play, novel, concert, or something similar. Your evaluation will be primarily aesthetic, but it may be ethical as well.

9

Arguing Recommendations

At one time or another, most of us—whether student, professional, or concerned citizen—will have to argue a *recommendation* (sometimes called a *proposal*). A recommendation is a written request for change of some sort: cable TV in the dorms, paternity leave in a company, or a new major in a university. Recommendations vary in format from a simple one-page letter to an elaborate minivolume with strictly prescribed components. But despite the many variations in format, all recommendations argue for change.

Recommendations are the hybrids of argument, drawing on the principles and practices of factual, causal, and evaluative arguments. So, for the most part, writing a successful recommendation is a question of applying what you have already learned about the different kinds of argument and their support.

All recommendations establish a current situation (how things are now) and a probable future situation (how they would be if the change were instituted). In other words, recommendations rely on arguments of fact and arguments of effect. How central either type of argument is to your recommendation will depend on the emphasis demanded by the particular situation.

If you focus on the current situation, which usually means showing that things have gotten so bad that change must be considered, much of your argument will be factual. Let's say you want to impress the authorities with the inadequacy of parking facilities at your commuter campus. You figure it's up to them to come up with the answer to the problem, but you know they won't do it without being convinced that a serious problem *does* exits. In this case, your recommendation would begin with a factual argument that establishes exactly what the current situation is.

But if you are the contractor asked to submit a proposal for new parking lots, your focus will be on the future effects of your particular plan and predicting its ability to solve the current problem. In this case, the recommendation will be largely causal, establishing the probable effects of the implemented recommendation.

Regardless of their emphases, all recommendations also make evaluative arguments; they include a judgment of the current situation (the parking situation is inadequate or unfair) and/or an evaluation of the proposed change (parking will be more available, more convenient, etc.).

AUDIENCE NEEDS AND VALUES

By now you've learned how important it is when making any kind of argument to know as much about your audience as possible. Nowhere is this knowledge more critical than in writing recommendations. Most recommendations asks readers to *do* something, not merely to give their armchair agreement to a claim. Human nature being what it is, people are more likely to take action if there is a possibility that the action will benefit them in some way. Thus, a powerful way to support any recommendation is to appeal to the needs, values, and desires that you have identified in your readers. Making such an appeal means paying particular attention to the early stage of audience consideration: who is your audience? what are their needs and values likely to be regarding your claim? can you responsibly appeal to these in your recommendation? Luckily, it is usually fairly easy to answer these questions when you're preparing a recommendation, because in most cases, you're addressing a very specific audience (often a single individual).

For example, suppose your favorite professor is denied tenure, and you and a number of other students write a letter to the dean arguing for a reconsideration of the decision. What kinds of appeals would most likely move the dean? To answer the question, you have to know what the dean's priorities and responsibilities are, which, in fact, you're never thought about. In speaking with faculty members, you learn that your dean is determined to enhance the academic reputation of the college as a way of attracting and retaining good students. Knowing this, you're not going to get far arguing that Professor Morris be granted tenure because he's a good shortstop on the faculty-student softball team or an easy grader. You'll need to find a way to demonstrate just how valuable Professor Morris is to students in the *classroom,* perhaps including testimonials from students.

Though you'll always need to be aware of the needs and values of your readers, you will rarely identify them explicitly in the recommendation. In the case of Professor Morris's tenure, you will identify the positive effects on students of granting him tenure, but you probably won't need to identify which of the dean's needs or priorities will be addressed by this action. Provided your assumption about these priorities is correct, you can trust her to recognize that the change you are proposing would satisfy them.

When Your Values Differ from Assumed Reader Values

Recommendations actually work with two sets of values: the reader's *and* the writer's. While a successful recommendation must appeal to the appropriate reader values, it will originate in values held by the writer. Indeed, most recommendations are born in the writer's experience of *dissonance,* that sense of mismatch between one's values and a current situation (see Chapter 2).

Often the values that move you to recommend a certain change will be the same as those that will move your reader to accept your recommendation. But sometimes writer and reader values do not coincide. Usually, as long as the two values or sets of values are somehow related and not directly opposed, their lack of coincidence will not weaken your recommendation. But you do need to be aware of the difference between them.

Suppose you are a commuter student who takes the city bus to get to campus each day. This term, you have an 8 A.M. class, the early bus from your stop has been overcrowded and unreliable, and you have been late to class a number of times. You decide to write a letter to the local transit authority recommending improvements in bus service. Your letter derives from your own experience of dissonance—your frustration at not making it to class on time—and it seeks to satisfy your rights to good service as a paying customer (your needs and values).

But you realize that these values are not necessarily going to move your audience—the transit authority—to make the necessary improvements to the service. The manager of customer service may not care much about your rights as a paying customer, but he does care about the value of *customer satisfaction*. No business, even one that holds a virtual monopoly, as most transit authorities do, can afford to ignore the importance of customer satisfaction.

In this example, the values of customer rights and customer satisfaction are not identical, but they can comfortably coexist in the recommendation because they are not in conflict, and they are *causally* connected: if your rights are being served, you will be satisfied.

Your letter to the transit authority might look like this:

Mr. Brian Rose
Manager, Customer Service
Metro Transit Authority
Collegetown, USA

Dear Mr. Rose:

I am writing to complain about the quality of the morning bus service on Bus 15, which runs from Main and Winton to the community college. By the time the bus scheduled to stop at 7:21 A.M. gets to the stop at Main and Winton, it is usually late (in October, by an average of 15 minutes) and always overcrowded, with standing room only. Two days in October (the ninth and the fifteenth) the bus was so crowded that some people could not get on at all. I have tried to take the 7:04 bus, but the situation is essentially the same, and I cannot take a later bus because I have an 8:00 A.M. class at the college.

I and a number of others who rely on bus service are very unhappy. We are being cheated of the service we deserve, given the high fares we pay, and we would like some action taken to improve the situation. I am enclosing with this letter a petition signed by eight other students who depend on Bus 15 to get them to campus.

Now that you are aware of this problem, I hope you will take action to correct it. I look forward to hearing from you about what that action might be.

Very truly yours,

Patrick Booth

This letter has a good chance of influencing its reader because the values from which it is written and the values to which it appeals are related and compatible. In cases where there is clear conflict between your values and your readers', you must search for other values to appeal to. You couldn't convince an audience of cigarette smokers that cigarette sales should be restricted because smoking is, as you believe, a stinking, filthy habit. But you might make some headway with an argument citing the risks of secondary smoke to loved ones—a risk that might concern even the most committed of smokers.

ACTIVITIES (9.1)

1. In each of the following cases, the value cited to win the audience's acceptance of the recommendation is not appropriate. With a small group of your classmates, identify alternative values that are more appropriate. Then discuss your list with the entire class.
   Sample recommendation: A longer school year for elementary and secondary students
   Audience: Elementary and secondary teachers
   Inappropriate value: More work from teachers
   Alternative value: A greater opportunity to ensure students' mastery of skills
   a. **Recommendation:** Earlier closing of a college cafeteria
      Audience: College students
      Inappropriate value: Shorter hours and fewer headaches for cafeteria staff
   b. **Recommendation:** A new federal tax on gasoline
      Audience: Truck drivers
      Inappropriate value: Reduced reliance on trucks for transporting goods
   c. **Recommendation:** A curfew for everybody under the age of sixteen
      Audience: Those under sixteen
      Inappropriate value: Those under sixteen can't be trusted
   d. **Recommendation:** A law requiring motorcyclists to wear helmets
      Audience: Motorcyclists
      Inappropriate value: Reduced claims against insurance companies and therefore increased profits for insurance companies
   e. **Recommendation:** A shorter work week
      Audience: Employers
      Inappropriate value: More leisure time for employees
2. With the same small group of classmates, identify values that would be shared by the following pairs, or that would be compatible.
   Example: Republicans and Democrats
   Common value: Concern for the national interest—the country as a whole
   a. Planners of a new highway; homeowners whose property is in the path of the new highway
   b. Managers of a company; workers on strike against that company

c. Parents planning to take away a child's allowance as punishment for bad behavior; the child in question
d. Planners of a large rock concert; neighborhood groups opposed to the concert because of noise
e. Proponents of legislation restricting the use of handguns; opponents of this legislation

RECOMMENDATIONS EMPHASIZING THE PRESENT

Some recommendations, like Patrick Booth's letter to the transit authority, concentrate on problems in a current situation, leaving a detailed proposal for change to another argument. The goal of such arguments is to demonstrate more *that* something needs to be done than *what* exactly that something is.

To accept this kind of recommendation, your readers need an accurate and, usually, detailed picture of the current situation. They must grasp the situation as it is before they can agree or disagree with your evaluation of it. Recommendations emphasizing the present usually open with a factual argument.

Establishing the Current Situation

Patrick's letter to the transit authority does a good job establishing the current situation through facts and figures that Patrick collected: the average tardiness of the bus, the number of times the bus had to leave customers behind, and so on. Establishing these details is critical to the recommendation for a couple of reasons. First, readers are likely to take exact figures more seriously than irate vagueness. Exaggerations like "Huge numbers of people are regularly prevented from riding the 7:21 bus" are far less effective than exact figures.

Second, misrepresenting the facts, whether intentionally to strengthen your case or negligently through sloppy research, will be detected. The recipient of any recommendation is going to investigate the situation before taking action, and if the results of that investigation differ substantially from your figures, your recommendation will have reached a dead end.

Evaluating the Current Situation

All recommendations contain some evaluative elements. In recommendations emphasizing the present, the subject of the evaluation is the current situation. If you have a good understanding of your audience and their needs and values, you probably won't need to write a full-blown evaluation complete with a defined evaluative term. The transit authority letter, for example, doesn't require an explicit judgment of the situation presented. Any reader, whether an official of the transit authority or an occasional passenger, will recognize that the conditions described are undesirable. You could point to this fact for rhetorical emphasis, but the judgment is implicit within the factual presentation.

Sometimes your recommendation will be addressed to readers who may not immediately recognize the problems in the current situation. In these cases, you'd be wise to identify *what* is wrong by providing a clear and limited evaluative term. For example, a professor's schedule of assignments on a syllabus is unfair to students or hopelessly unrealistic. You can then proceed to match the subject (the syllabus) with the evaluative term according to the suggestions in Chapter 8, remembering the importance of considering audience needs and values.

Applying the Toulmin Model

The Toulmin logical model is especially useful when you're composing a recommendation. Placing your claim and support in the Toulmin paradigm (see Chapter 5) will help you detect any weaknesses of reasoning or wording in your argument and will suggest the secondary claims you'll need to support the central claim. Assume that an outside consultant, hired to analyze the employee benefits package of Quick-Stop Copy (the current situation), recommends that the company provide a benefits package more competitive with those of comparable companies (central claim). The consultant's recommendation would fit into the Toulmin model as follows:

Data
The current benefit package at Quick-Stop Copy is not competitive with those of comparable companies.

Claim
Quick-Stop Copy should institute a more competitive benefits package.

Warrant
Companies should have competitive benefits packages.

Remember that in the Toulmin model, the warrant is equivalent to the major premise in a syllogism; it is the general statement about a class that enables the data (or the minor premise in a syllogism) to justify the claim (or conclusion in a syllogism). As noted in Chapter 5, sometimes both data and warrant need further support. Indeed, one of the virtues of the Toulmin system is that once you have stated your argument in its terms, you can recognize what further support (backing) your argument will need. In this example, you realize that the argument will need a breakdown of facts and figures to back the data (i.e., how the Quick-Stop package actually compares with those of other companies). And you should recognize as well that the warrant will need further backing if it is not self-evident to the reader that companies should have competitive benefits packages. Depending on the reader's point of view, the consultant may want to strengthen the warrant by supporting it with a secondary argument of effect—that is, demonstrating the negative results of the inferior benefits package to employees and to the company.

ACTIVITIES (9.2)

1. For two of the following current situations, what kind of facts would be necessary to convince readers that some change is necessary? Make a list of all the kinds of factual evidence you can think of.
   a. Traffic at an intersection
   b. Someone's physical appearance
   c. A friend's choice of career
   d. A company's health care benefits
   e. The local court system

2. Using the material you developed for Activity 1, create two claims of recommendation. Then state your argument in terms of the Toulmin model, indicating what additional support or backing is necessary.

RECOMMENDATIONS EMPHASIZING THE FUTURE

When your recommendation emphasizes the probable future effects of its proposed changes, you'll have to move beyond the current problems and the general claim that something must be done; you'll also have to identify, reasonably and convincingly, *what* that something is. A recommendation emphasizing the future will be effective if it can demonstrate (1) that your proposal is likely to produce desirable effects and (2) that the proposal is feasible.

Presenting the Recommendation

The recommendation itself—the proposed plan for change—must be crystal clear. Obviously, readers can't agree with a plan they don't understand. Some situations will call for a rather general recommendation, leaving the details to others, whereas in other cases, particularly when you have some responsibility for implementing the plan, a detailed recommendation will be necessary.

Kate Quill is a second-year student at Carlson College, a small liberal arts college in Maine. Carlson has operated on a trimester calendar for years, with three ten-week terms per academic year. It is common knowledge at Carlson that many students are unhappy with the trimester system: they feel rushed and overworked by the short terms. Kate and a number of her friends think it's time to do something about this dissatisfaction, so they decide to write a letter to the college administration recommending that a committee of faculty and students look at alternatives to the trimester calendar. The letter they write, which follows, is an example of a *general* recommendation emphasizing the future.

Dr. Dale Hill
President, Carlson College
Carlson, Maine

Dear Dr. Hill:

It should be no surprise to you that students feel considerable dissatisfaction with the trimester calendar used at Carlson. Faculty report that students have complained about the excessively fast pace of courses for years. Given this long history of dissatisfaction, we feel it is time for a formal examination of alternative calendars. Such an analysis should determine once and for all whether our current trimester calendar is the best system for Carlson.

We recommend that you put together a calendar committee consisting of students, faculty, and administration to conduct such an examination. This group could research the calendars used by comparable institutions, determining the advantages and disadvantages of each case. If the committee concludes that our current system is the best, we believe that the current level of student dissatisfaction would be reduced. Similarly, if a different calendar more suitable to Carlson were discovered and implemented, students would be much happier.

Any of the students signing this letter would be eager to serve on such a committee. We appreciate your time in considering this proposal.

Very truly yours,

Kate Quill and Carlson Students

Let's assume that President Hill has been hearing complaints about the trimesters for years and decides, on reading this letter, to take its recommendation seriously. After consulting with the deans and vice presidents, the president decides to constitute a "blue ribbon" committee to investigate the calendar issue. While Kate's recommendation was appropriately general (it's not a student's job to dictate details to a college president), the review process President Hill recommends to the chairperson of the Calendar Committee must be detailed and specific. This letter might read as follows:

Professor Rachel Eisenberg
Chair, Calendar Committee
Department of English
Carlson College

Dear Rachel:

Thank you for agreeing to serve as chair of the Calendar Committee. As you know, the calendar issue is extremely controversial; it is my hope that under your competent leadership the committee will put to rest once and for all the question of what calendar is the most appropriate for Carlson.

It is not my intention to direct the committee's work, but I hope you will allow a few suggestions about process and objectives:

- It will be critical to your deliberations to identify and verify the most common student complaints about our trimester system and the most common faculty complaints. This information can be obtained through survey instruments and through individual or group interviews.
- When exploring the alternative calendars currently used by other colleges, you should try to select schools whose size and mission are closely comparable to Carlson's.
- Please do not forget to factor in the budgetary implications of the various alternatives. While our primary concern should be with the quality of the education we deliver, an extremely costly calendar implementation could actually jeopardize our educational quality.
- While the final action taken on the basis of your report will be determined by the Carlson Board of Trustees, it would be helpful if the report included a ranking of the alternative calendars.
- The format and style of the final report I leave up to the committee, but bear in mind that it will be distributed to a number of different campus groups, so brevity and readability will be important.

Again, I thank you for agreeing to take on this challenging and important task. If there is any way that my office can help the work of the committee, don't hesitate to let me know.

Very truly yours,

Dale Hill

President

The preceding examples illustrate only two possibilities; recommendations can be more or less detailed than the second example. Generally, the more concrete your recommendation, the more effective it will be, provided your plan reflects a sound understanding of the operations of the group that will implement it. But there are times when a great deal of detail is inappropriate. Most editorials make recommendations without much detail; most politicians give few details in their speeches to general audiences. In deciding how much detail to include, be sure to consider your audience's capacity for and interest in the details, as well as their proposed role in carrying out the recommendation.

ACTIVITIES (9.3)

1. The following sample recommendations are extremely general. The writers have given no indication of how they expect their plans to be implemented. For each, provide at least three specific recommendations that will help an audience understand how the plans can be carried out. If you like, instead of working with the claims provided, create your own general recommendations (the kind that might come out of a conversation with friends), and then provide more specific recommendations for each.
   Example: We need a city with cleaner air.
   Specific recommendations: (1) Encouragement of "park-and-ride" lots for commuters to decrease automobile traffic, (2) tighter inspection standards for automobiles' exhaust emission systems, and (3) restrictions on the burning of leaves and trash.
      After you have made this list of recommendations, write a short essay (250–500 words) briefly explaining each of the recommendations and how they relate to the general recommendation.
   a. Our college needs more school spirit.
   b. Americans need to be more tolerant of racial and ethnic diversity.
   c. Adolescents must be made more aware of the dangers of alcohol.
   d. American industry needs to put more emphasis on the quality of its products.
   e. Students and professors must learn to see each other as human beings.

2. In your student or local newspaper, find an example of a recommendation that you think is good, but that is too general to be implemented. Write a letter to the editor suggesting specific ways that the recommendation might be developed further.

Arguing the Effects of Your Recommendation

Recommendations with future emphasis always identify and evaluate the probable effects of the proposed plan. Identifying probable effects will take the form of an *argument of effect* and will follow the steps presented in Chapter 7. This part of your recommendation will be strong if you can show that the proposed changes (the causes) are related to the results you predict (the effects) through established causal principles.

In the example of the Carlson College calendar, the Calendar Committee might predict the following short causal chain: converting to a semester calendar (cause) will give students more classroom contact with their faculty (first effect), which in turn is likely to make students feel more satisfied with their college experience (second effect). Readers would be likely to accept the first causal link: a semester course meets something like 45 hours per term, whereas a trimester course meets approximately 30 hours per term. Unless faculty use the additional time showing films and bringing in guest lecturers, the increase in hours will result in increased contact with faculty.

To support the second link in the chain, the committee needs to identify a linking behavioral principle. In this case, the principle linking increased student-faculty contact and student satisfaction has to be spelled out explicitly. That principle might be stated as follows: young people go to college to receive an education and to become adults; faculty not only provide that education but offer a new brand of adult relationship based on mature, intellectual foundations. Thus, substantial contact with faculty will meet a primary objective of many students. The committee report might also want to support this second effect in the chain by citing existing higher education studies that have discovered this connection between student-faculty contact and student satisfaction.

ACTIVITIES (9.4)

With a small group of your classmates, discuss the likelihood of the projected results of the following three recommendations. Have one student write up the reasons for your judgment of each. Submit this write-up to your instructor.

1. **Recommendation:** Increase the price of tickets to films at the college theater from $2.00 to $2.50.
   Projected results: No significant decline in attendance; more revenue from tickets to allow the theater to rent better films, which will eventually lead to higher attendance.

2. **Recommendation:** Allow students to take one course pass-fail.
   Projected results: Students will feel under less pressure about grades and more willing to take tough courses; the students will work just as hard in the courses they take pass-fail as they would have if they had taken the course for a regular grade.

3. **Recommendation:** Increase school taxes to subsidize new athletic facilities at the high school.
   Projected results: Greater community involvement in and identification with high school athletic teams; improvement in high school image; increased student enrollment.

Judging Effects in Terms of Assumed Needs and Values

In developing your recommendation, you will probably identify several probable effects, only some of which will meet the needs and values of your readers. Suppose you support your recommendation to faculty of a pass-fail grading option by predicting the effect of students' doing less work in their courses. Such an effect isn't likely to appeal to faculty values. This does not mean that you should deny the effect if it seems probable, but at the same time, there is no reason to emphasize it.

You may not always have to evaluate the probable effects explicitly nor identify the needs and values that those effects will satisfy. But at a minimum, you must be aware of the values that the probable effects of your implemented recommendation will satisfy.

When Some Effects Are Undesirable.   Few recommendations can promise exclusively positive results. But as long as the desirable effects outweigh the undesirable ones, your recommendation is worth making. When you know that along with the positive effects there may be some less desirable repercussions, you should acknowledge them in your argument. Provided you can demonstrate that the negative effects are less significant than the positive ones, you will not weaken your argument by mentioning them. In fact, an argument that acknowledges and measures its own weaknesses is usually more effective than one that fails to admit what any intelligent reader will recognize.

If you are on a committee recommending the building of a new expressway, you should admit that the building of the new expressway, whatever its ultimate advantages, will cause inconveniences. This is a more effective and responsible approach than ignoring altogether the obvious negative consequences of your recommendation. You will enhance your credibility by admitting what many people will know or suspect anyway.

Implementation.   To be successful, your recommendation must pass one further test: it must be feasible. Even the most brilliant recommendation will be rejected if its implementation is fraught with difficulties. While a detailed implementation plan is not required of all recommendations, some indication of the feasibility of your plan will strengthen your argument. At the least, you must provide a general indication that the recommendation *is* feasible. There is no point in advancing a recommendation that your audience will see as totally impractical, regardless of how desirable the results might be. Sometimes, your audience will expect a very detailed implementation plan, including a list of activities and the name of the person responsible for each activity, the dates for beginning and completing each activity, and the likely costs of each activity.

A crucial element of a general or detailed implementation plan is an analysis of costs. Many great ideas born in the heat of inspiration have failed to materialize because of a lack of cold cash; programs that many judge worthwhile (such as human exploration of Mars) have been delayed because of their expense. Whenever you present a proposal and outline its benefits, you also need to project its costs as accurately as you can. Remember that these costs often include not only the expense of constructing a new building or starting a new program but also the continuing costs once the proposal is a reality. Your community may need a new and larger airport, or a new bus service for the elderly, or new day care facilities, but once these are established, there may be additional costs of keeping the services going from day to day. The new and larger airport, for example, may need more employees to maintain it and may cost more to heat and cool than the old one did. These continuing expenses are easy to overlook or to minimize; the great temptation in making a recommendation that you believe in strongly is to overstate the benefits and understate the costs.

You need to fight this temptation, remembering that some of your readers will be expecting just such a miscalculation.

People tend to accept recommendations that can be implemented within existing systems more readily than those requiring radical changes. Most of us are reluctant to make major changes on the strength of what *might* happen, however convincingly the probabilities are argued. Other things being equal, people usually prefer the least disruptive course of action.

On the other hand, sometimes existing structures need to be shaken up and disruptive measures taken. Much of our world, including the very existence of this country, is a result of radical changes. You should at least consider whether a drastic change will not be more effective ultimately and easier to implement than a piecemeal one. Sometimes piecemeal recommendations are like putting money into an old car that is going to break down anyway, or like eighteenth-century Americans hoping King George III and the British government would see the error of their ways. One test here, though a difficult one, is whether the piecemeal changes will improve the situation enough to justify the time and cost of the changes: the old car may not be worth keeping; on balance, it was easier to leave King George than to reform him.

Applying the Toulmin Model

The Toulmin model will help you evaluate the reasonableness and completeness of recommendations emphasizing the future. Applying the Toulmin format to the Carlson College example, we get a look at what kinds of secondary arguments the recommendation calls for.

Data	**Claim**
Carlson College does not operate on a semester calendar.	Carlson College should adopt a semester calendar to achieve greater opportunities for student-faculty contact.

Warrant
Colleges operating on semester calendars provide the most opportunities for student-faculty contact.

Laying the recommendation out this way shows us what additional support the argument will need. The data in this case will need minimal backing (all the readers will accept it as true), but the warrant is clearly not self-evident and thus calls for backing. Depending on your assessment of the readers' needs, that backing may follow at least two directions. On the one hand, you'll probably want to support the generalization with a secondary factual argument that compares the number of student-faculty contact hours in semester and trimester systems: "Students at Rusk College, which operates on a semester system, meet in class with their course faculty four hours per week for fourteen weeks, as opposed to Carlson's three hours per week for ten weeks."

A second issue raised by the warrant is the unstated assumption that student-faculty contact is a good thing. If you think your readers need to be convinced of this assumption, then you'll want to provide a secondary evaluative and/or causal argument demonstrating the positive elements and results of student-faculty contact. Here, you can resort to anecdotal evidence, but your best bet is to cite some of those higher education studies demonstrating the merits of this contact.

ACTIVITIES (9.5)

1. The following are recommendations that many believe are good ideas. For at least two of these claims, make a list of possible drawbacks to the recommendation that the writer would need to admit. Compare your list with those of some of your classmates. If you like, you may come up with your own recommendations—changes you would like to see occur—and consider the possible drawbacks.
   a. Sending astronauts to explore Mars
   b. Passing elementary and secondary students from one grade to another only after they have passed strict competency tests
   c. Prohibiting smoking in all public facilities
   d. Increasing the school year by an average of one month for all elementary and secondary schoolchildren
   e. Abolishing fraternities and sororities on your campus

2. Prepare an implementation plan for some change you would like to make in your own life, such as studying harder, learning a new sport or hobby, or exploring a possible career. Your implementation plan should include the sequence of activities you will undertake, the dates you plan to begin and end each activity, and the costs, if any, of the project. See the recommendation report "A Proposal for a Computer Facility in Marshall Dormitory" at the end of this chapter for a sample implementation plan.

3. Derive a claim of recommendation from three issues that you feel strongly about. Then place each claim within the Toulmin model, providing data and warrant. For each claim, where will you need additional backing? On the basis of your answer to this question, prepare an outline of a four- to five-page paper that would argue this recommendation.
   Example: Our staggering divorce rate suggests that a course in marriage and relationships should be mandatory for all high school students.

RECOMMENDATIONS THAT CONSIDER PRESENT AND FUTURE

The two types of recommendations we have discussed rarely occur in pure form; many recommendations contain some discussion of both the current situation and the future possibilities. Obviously, such recommendations combine the strategies discussed in this chapter: they present and evaluate the current situation, lay out the recommendation, and finally identify and evaluate the probable results of the recommendation. Because these arguments consider what currently exists and what could exist, they provide the groundwork for a useful comparative evaluation. After you have examined both the present and future elements of your argument, you may wish to compare the two explicitly—to demonstrate that the probable effects will be preferable to the current situation. If you have an accurate grasp of your audience's needs and values, you should be able to make this comparison effectively.

SUMMARY

Arguing Recommendations

- Recommendations emphasizing present conditions include the following:
  - A presentation of the current situation, policy, and or practice (a factual argument).
  - An evaluation of this situation in terms of the values and needs important to your audience. The judgment expressed and the value appealed to may be stated or implied.
  - When applicable, a presentation of the existing effects (causal argument) and a judgment of these effects.
  - When applicable, a presentation of the probable future effects (argument of effect) and a judgment of these effects.

- Applying the Toulmin model will help you identify the supporting secondary claims your argument will need to make.

- Recommendations emphasizing the future include the following:
  - Presentation of the recommendation. The degree of detail in this presentation is usually dictated by your degree of responsibility for implementing the recommendation.
  - Identification of probable effects of your recommendation if it is implemented.
  - Evaluation of these effects (both desirable and undesirable) in terms of audience needs and values.
  - In some cases, a suggested implementation plan and an analysis of costs.

    Whether or not you include such a plan, those recommendations requiring minor changes to existing structures are generally more acceptable, though not necessarily more valuable, than those requiring radical restructuring.

- Recommendations considering present and future include the following:
  - Presentation and evaluation of the current situation.
  - Presentation of the recommendation.

– Identification and evaluation of the probable results of the recommendation.

– In many cases, a demonstration that the probable effects of the implemented recommendation will be preferable to the current situation.

TWO SAMPLE RECOMMENDATIONS

The following sample recommendation report considers both the current situation and probable results of its implementation. The report is an example of what a student might include in a recommendation for a computer room in the dormitory. The format of the report, outlined here, is one of several possible formats for a recommendation report:

    I. STATEMENT OF PROBLEM
   II. STATEMENT OF RECOMMENDATION
  III. ADVANTAGES OF RECOMMENDATION
  IV. DISADVANTAGES OF RECOMMENDATION
   V. COSTS AND IMPLEMENTATION PLAN

Many organizations and many professors have a preferred format for such reports; you would be wise to check whether there are such preferred formats before you begin to write this kind of report either at work or for a class.

This recommendation is briefer and more general than many. If a report with the same proposal were prepared by the university's office of computing, it would undoubtedly include more detail on the scheduling of the project, the nature of the renovations, and the kind of equipment that would be purchased. But a recommendation like this one—proposed by a student to an administrator—need not include an implementation plan (although some suggestions about implementation might impress the audience with how carefully the writer has thought about her recommendation).

```
        A PROPOSAL FOR A COMPUTER FACILITY IN MARSHALL DORMITORY

                          Prepared for

                       Dr. Hector Martinez,

               Assistant Vice President for Student Life

                        by Elaine Weston,

          Chair, Marshall Dormitory Student Committee

                      February 13, 1998

                       Statement of Problem


         Currently many students living in Marshall Dormitory

     have difficulty getting access to a computer. The college's

     main computer facility is located over a mile away on the

     other end of campus, and that facility is often overcrowded;

     many students find that they can use a computer only after
```

eleven at night or before ten in the morning. Some students bring their own computers with them to college, but not all students here can afford their own computers. I surveyed all students living on the third floor of Marshall and found that only 25 percent had their own computers, while another 50 percent said they use computers frequently for course work. Of this 50 percent, 45 percent said that they have sometimes found it hard to get access to one of the college's computers, and 35 percent frequently had this problem. Clearly, this lack of access to needed computers is a serious problem for Marshall students. When I spoke with Helen Borshoff, the Vice President for Computing, she confirmed the severity of the problem and said that her organization is trying to deal with the problem within the constraints of its limited resources.

RECOMMENDATION

We recommend that the Office of Student Life work with the Office of Computing to convert the student lounge at the west end of the second floor of Marshall into a computer facility equipped with seven PCs connected to the central campus computer system and three printers: our discussions with the Office of Computing indicate that the number of computers and printers is the maximum that would fit into the amount of space available and that this range of equipment would be most appropriate for student needs. Since the need for more computers and more access to computers is so pressing, we recommend that the necessary renovations take place this summer so that the facility will be ready by the beginning of the next academic year on September 6, 1998.

ADVANTAGES OF RECOMMENDATION

If our recommendation is implemented, students who live in Marshall will be able to use college-owned computers without having to go all the way to the college facility. There will also be more computers available than there are now, and students without the means to buy their own computers will be at less of a disadvantage than they currently are. For students, then, there are significant educational advantages if this proposal is implemented.

For the administration, there are several other advantages as well. Construction of this facility will alleviate at least some of the overwhelming pressure on the main computer facility. Since the space for this new facility already exists, renovating this space will be less costly than adding new space somewhere on campus. This new facility will also show the administration's concern about increasing student access to computers, and it will therefore help to reduce the growing tension between students and administrators over this issue.

DISADVANTAGES OF RECOMMENDATION

Our recommendation does have some disadvantages. Probably the most significant is the security risk of having a small facility so far removed from the central computer facility, which means that it would not make financial sense to have someone on duty to guard the equipment. Another disadvantage is that some space devoted to student relaxation would be taken and used for another purpose. The placing of a computer facility in a dormitory also raises some new policy questions for the college, including whether only students in the dormitory can use the facility, or whether the facility would be open to all students of the college.

These disadvantages are real, but they can be dealt with. The Vice President for Computing assures us that new electronic security devices reduce the need for security personnel. In a poll taken two weeks ago, the Marshall students indicated that they preferred to see the current lounge converted into a computer facility, with 68 percent expressing this preference, 18 percent opposing it, and 14 percent expressing no opinion. Finally, while this proposal does raise some new questions of policy, these questions must be addressed at some point in the near

future anyway, as computers and computer facilities become
more pervasive in the college.

COSTS AND IMPLEMENTATION PLAN

The following is a tentative and very general outline
of the costs of the project as well as an implementation
plan. These will have to be refined by the Offices of Student
Life and Computing as they begin to work on the project. The
Vice President for Computing has assured us, however, that
the costs and implementation plan we have outlined here seem
reasonable. On her advice, we have not included personnel
costs for the time of administrators, since these costs are
difficult to calculate and are not usually included in the
budgets for small projects of this kind.

Activity	Dates	Costs
Initial planning with students, Student Life, and Computing administrators	March	—
Work requests for construction; orders for equipment	April	—
Renovation of lounge	June–July	$15,000
Installation of security devices	Early August	$ 3,000
Purchase and installation of computer equipment	Late August	$30,000
Total initial costs		$48,000
Ongoing costs; maintenance of equipment		$ 3,000 per year

The following recommendation is a more general argument than the preceding
formal proposal, but like the preceding argument, its central claim calls for a new
course of action.

THE SIDE EFFECTS OF AFFIRMATIVE ACTION

PAMELA J. HSU

In the 1960s, the civil rights movement said people could not be denied things like employment based on race. In the 1970s, affirmative action injected women and minorities into the workplace. In the 1980s, diversity programs stressed appreciating differences among all people. But are we starting to see some negative side effects in the 1990s?

During the past several decades, many programs have promoted the education and employment of women and minorities. Minority scholarships are readily available in just about every field. And most corporations track hiring, retention, and promotion of women and minorities, and aim to improve performance in these areas.

As a 24-year-old Chinese woman, I benefit from these programs. I received a generous minority internship/scholarship package from a major corporation one summer during college. When I applied to graduate school, one university offered me a fellowship specifically for minorities entering that particular field of study.

I know that these opportunities have provided a boost in my career. I appreciate them. But there are times when I wish I could have competed against everyone else. I believe my ability would have made me at least a strong contender against all applicants.

I know we have not reached that ideal scenario. I realize that problems still exist and that economic and social conditions prevent some children from getting any chance at all. But we need to look at some of the actions taken in the name of fighting discrimination and promoting diversity to see if they are solving these problems—or just creating different ones.

I'm noticing a growing number of white males who say they are now being discriminated against. I'm talking about the professor who warns his white male students that a particular graduate program may be difficult to get into because they are favoring women and minority candidates. I'm talking about a former employer who ran a department one person short for months, even though many applied for the job, because the position had to be filled by a minority. There's a difference between fairness and force fitting.

Daniel J. Boorstin, the Pulitzer Prize-winning historian and best-selling author, said it best: "We must give everybody a fresh start and not try to compensate for past injustices by creating present injustices."

A growing number of groups are voluntarily segregating themselves from others to preserve ethnic identity. Just take a look at the average college campus, and you'll find Greek houses for minorities and organized student groups for just about every ethnic population. But some may be developing blanket beliefs about their own ethnic group. I've heard that you aren't being true to yourself if you "act" white or you aren't really happy if you've assimilated. The fact that I'm Chinese in blood and American in behavior rubs some people the wrong way. They dub me a Twinkie—yellow on the outside but white on the inside.

I was raised to assimilate, and I don't regret that. Just because I live an American lifestyle doesn't make me any less Chinese. It's ironic that groups which intend to promote an appreciation of their culture among others sometimes fail to reciprocate the respect among their own.

Competition between minority groups may be breeding another problem. One minority group complains that a university gave such-and-such group this much money, and how come they didn't get the same? Columnist William Raspberry pointed out that more students these days search for "discrimination nuggets" because if they find enough of them, they can trade in at the administration building for an ethnic sensitivity course or a minority student center.

It's time to step back and refocus on our ultimate goal. The idea that minority status equals money needs to change. Financial assistance should be available for those who need a chance. Ethnic groups should preserve traditions but not alienate those who do things differently. Sharing traditions with other people and encouraging those who are interested to get more involved—even if they do not belong to that ethnic group—would truly promote diversity.

Source: *Detroit News*, Sunday, 22 May 1994.

SUGGESTIONS FOR WRITING (9.6)

1. Following the form of the first sample recommendation, write a recommendation report to improve some aspect of your college or university. Possible areas for improvement include dormitories or apartments, the library, the call for more online courses, requiring faculty and students to use laptop computers for class work, the curriculum in your major, or the food service. Make your recommendation as realistic as possible by interviewing people with some responsibility for that area. From these people, you should try to learn why the situation exists in its current form and how feasible your recommendation is as well as to get some sense of the costs of the project. The length of this report will vary with the complexity of the problem and your recommendation, though it might be wise to limit yourself to a maximum of approximately ten pages.

2. Almost every community has its share of white elephants: elaborate projects or expensive buildings that ultimately had to be abandoned or converted to some alternative use because their cost greatly exceeded their benefit to the community. Look for a white elephant in your community and analyze why the project never met its original intentions. Your professor can help you get started. You will almost certainly have to consult the local newspapers and then perhaps the local archives. Since your time is limited and there may be a great deal of documentation, you might have to restrict your research to newspaper accounts of what happened and why. As with Suggestion 1, the maximum length should be approximately ten pages.

3. Working from the outline you prepared for Activity (9.5.3), write a four- to five-page general recommendation emphasizing the future (along the lines of the preceding Hsu sample above). Be sure to include and support all the secondary claims suggested by the Toulmin model.

10

Writing and Image

In our contemporary society of sound bites and spin doctors, the concept of *image* has developed something of a negative flavor, suggesting superficiality and deceit. Public personalities pay a great deal of money to have distinctive images packaged and popularized—images that may bring them enormous success but that bear little relationship to the real people behind them.

This book uses the term *image* differently and more positively, to suggest the ways in which writing honestly reflects to the reader the kind of person the writer is. In successful arguments, writers project an image of intelligence, probity, and trustworthiness. There is nothing false or superficial about this kind of image: these qualities cannot be created out of thin air; they must be true *reflections* of the writer and thus are developed over time and through experience. But whenever you write, you should strive to project such an image, while also being aware that this image will need to be slightly adjusted to fit the context of a given argument.

Image consists of many elements. Most obviously, the quality of the argument itself—its intelligence, honesty, and accuracy—will impress your readers. But image is projected on a smaller scale as well—by your argument's word choice, sentence construction, and figures of speech; by its spelling, punctuation, and physical format; even by its *sound*.

This chapter focuses on some of the conscious choices you'll be making about your image as a writer of argument—choices about voice, diction, metaphor and analogy, emotive language, and the sound of your prose. As you'll see in this chapter, the choices you make will vary from one argument to the next, depending on your subject, your purpose, and your audience.

THE ROLE OF VOICE

A writer's *voice* is the role that he or she takes for a particular occasion, almost like an actor taking a part in a new play. To many inexperienced writers, voice suggests insincerity or fakery, but all of us continually "play" different roles. We behave one way in a classroom, another way playing basketball; we talk to our parents in one way and to our friends in another. Voice is simply the written manifestation of this adaptability.

The following simple example demonstrates the variability of voice:

```
Dear Mr. Jones:

At the suggestion of Ms. Hawkins, I am writing to inquire
about an opening as an electrical engineer in your firm.


Dear Mom and Dad:

Hi and help! You won't believe this but I'm broke again.
Boy, were my textbooks expensive this quarter!
```

The same student wrote both of these openings and was completely sincere in both cases but the voices differ markedly. In the first case, the student was formal, polite, and restrained. In the second, she was informal and very direct. In cases like these, the choice of a particular voice seems natural; the student did not spend much time or effort choosing these voices. But you can improve your writing by being conscious of the available choices and using them effectively. One crucial choice is between the formal and the informal voices—the voices of the first and second letters, respectively. Using an informal voice in a formal situation may have disastrous effects. What would happen to our student if she wrote to Mr. Jones (whom she presumably does not know) in the following manner?

```
Dear Mr. Jones:

Hi and help! I ran into somebody Hawkins—I forget her
first name—and she says you've got jobs. Boy, do I need
one!
```

The Importance of Ethos

As the Greek philosopher Aristotle noted, a major element of a successful image is the *ethos* projected by the writer. The ethos is the impression of the writer's character that the reader gets; a positive ethos is one reflecting sincerity and trustworthiness. Readers are likely to accept arguments written by someone who comes across as honest, upright, and unselfish; they will distrust the claims of one known to be dishonest or selfish, or whose voice suggests these traits. So, in your own arguments, try to write from the most principled, unselfish part of yourself.

And try not to emulate the ethos projected by the angry writer of the following letter to his campus newspaper:

> The grading policies of this college are rotten, just like everything else here at State. How can the administration put a student on probation for failing a course outside of his major? That's just outrageous. When I got an F in physics, they put me on probation even though I received at least a C in the courses in my major. I didn't want to take physics anyway, and the professor really stunk. Now I'm not eligible to play basketball! When are we students going to force the administration to get rid of this stupid policy?

The reasoning in this letter has many weaknesses, but the writer's failure to establish a respectable ethos also destroys its effectiveness. He presents himself as lacking balance (is *everything* at State rotten?) and as concerned only about himself (what about the effect of the probation policy on others?). Almost all readers, including fellow students, would dismiss this letter as the howl of outrage that it is; certainly they would not be likely to join forces with the writer in an attempt to change school policy.

When Aristotle urged writers of argument to establish an effective ethos, he was not urging hypocrisy. In creating an ethos, you will present your best side, but this side is still part of you; it is not wholly fabricated. Our outraged student in the preceding example is doubtless capable of balance and concern for others. Before writing that letter, he should have given himself the time to move from outrage to a broader perspective, using his anger to inspire dissonance but recognizing that hurt feelings and the impulse to dodge responsibility don't advance arguments.

A writer's ethos can be enhanced by the confidence with which his ideas are expressed. You should always appear confident about your claims, though not more confident than their support warrants. A credible ethos finds a balance between dogmatism and apology. Readers suspect writers, such as our angry student, who make sweeping claims (everything at State is rotten) and writers who make forceful statements that they can't possibly support ("the governor is the dumbest woman in the state"). On the other hand, readers will also suspect arguments that seem too wishy-washy: "I think it is probably true that this policy may lead us in the wrong direction."

Let's take a look at how the disgruntled student might create an ethos that works *for,* rather than *against,* him.

> After a painful experience with the academic probation policy here at State, I have concluded that the college should consider revising it. The policy states that any student whose grades fall below a C average will be placed on probation, so that that student will be ineligible for many extracurricular activities. The policy appears reasonable, but its effect is to place too much emphasis on courses outside a student's major. Many students, including three of my acquaintances, have found themselves ineligible to participate in extracurricular activities even though they were doing solid work in their majors. I now find myself in a similar situation, being ineligible to play basketball yet earning grades of C or higher in my major.

Here, the student comes across as someone who is honest about his own situation and also concerned for others, someone who allows for an apparently reasonable opposing view while remaining firm in his own.

ACTIVITIES (10.1)

1. Write a one-page letter to your parents or a friend asking for a loan to help with college expenses. Then write a letter to your college's financial aid office asking for the same loan. With two to three of your classmates, make a list of the differences in the two letters.

2. Go back to Chapter 8 and reread Kevin Maloney's essay "Reading Popular Culture." In a one- to two-page essay, characterize the argument's ethos. Your instructor may want to devote some class time to a discussion of the effectiveness of Maloney's ethos.

THE VIRTUES AND LIMITATIONS OF PLAIN WRITING

Most writing teachers and most writing textbooks encourage students to make their writing clear and straightforward, without distracting embellishments. Perhaps the most famous advocate of this plain style was British writer George Orwell, who formulated the following six stylistic rules in one of the most famous essays about writing style, "Politics and the English Language":

   (i) Never use a metaphor, simile or other figure of speech which you are used to seeing in print.

  (ii) Never use a long word where a short one will do.

 (iii) If it is possible to cut a word out, always cut it out.

 (iv) Never use the passive where you can use the active.

  (v) Never use a foreign phrase, a scientific word or a jargon word if you can think of any everyday English equivalent.

 (vi) Break any of these rules sooner than say anything outright barbarous.

The plain style Orwell urges arose as a reaction against the bloated and often dishonest prose of modern bureaucratic society, where military first strikes are called "anticipatory retaliations," visual materials in school curricula become "integrated systems learning designs," and simple sentences and direct expression disappear behind clouds of vague pomposity: "Please contact my secretary about an appointment regarding the project slippages in implementing the new on-line system." The writer could have said, "Please see me about the delays in starting the new on-line system," but to too many writers today, the first version seems more official, more important. A plain style of writing is an antidote to this swollen prose.

But plain writing carries its own risks, as Orwell notes in his sixth rule. Writers who use the plain style exclusively risk prose that is clear but undistinguished, serviceable but dull. To help you avoid this extreme, here are some friendly amendments to Orwell's rules:

(i) Don't be afraid to use metaphors, similes, or other figures of speech, provided they are not overworked.
(ii) When a long word is the best one, use it.
(iii) Use long sentences for variety and when they best suit your needs.
(iv) Dare to try something different.
(v) Break any of these rules rather than confuse your reader.

The following passage from Annie Dillard's book *The Writing Life* is a good sample of writing that succeeds by going beyond the plain style. The marginal annotations mark instances of enriched prose.

Effective exaggeration—dare to be different

Varied sentence length

Inventive language

Ironic humor

It should surprise no one that the life of the writer—such as it is—is colorless to the point of sensory deprivation. Many writers do little else but sit in small rooms recalling the real world. This explains why so many books describe the author's childhood. A writer's childhood may well have been the occasion of his only firsthand experience. Writers read literary biography, and surround themselves with other writers, deliberately to enforce in themselves the ludicrous notion that a reasonable option for occupying yourself on the planet until your life span plays itself out is sitting in a small room for the duration, in the company of pieces of paper.

FIGURES OF SPEECH

A figure of speech involves a "turn" on the literal use of words, or using words to suggest something related to but different from their literal meaning. Two of the most common figures of speech are *metaphor* and *analogy*. A metaphor is an implicit comparison of two unlike subjects so that some aspects of one (usually concrete and familiar) illuminate aspects of the other (usually more abstract or unfamiliar). "The twilight of her career" is a metaphor comparing something concrete and familiar, the end of a day, to something more abstract, in this case the end of someone's career. "Global village" is another metaphor, where the abstract concept of the globe or world (the entire population of the earth) is compared to the more familiar and concrete idea of a village. A *simile,* a variant of a metaphor, is an explicit comparison, where the two subjects are linked by *like* or *as:* "Falling in love is like getting caught in a warm spring rain."

Analogy is like metaphor in that dissimilar subjects are compared, but in analogy, the comparison is usually extended through several points. The "global village" becomes an analogy when the world is compared to a village in several respects—for example, the need for certain agreed-upon laws and the importance of communication and cooperation among those in the community.

The following passage by historian Barbara Tuchman shows the value of metaphor in argument. In the first paragraph of "History as Mirror," Tuchman compares history to a mirror reflecting our own image:

> At a time when everyone's mind is on the explosions of the moment, it might seem obtuse of me to discuss the fourteenth century. But I think a backward look at that disordered, violent, bewildered, disintegrating and calamity-prone age can be consoling and possibly instructive in a time of similar disarray. Reflected in a six-hundred-year-old mirror, a more revealing image of ourselves and our species might be seen than is visible in the clutter of circumstances under our noses.

Tuchman could not have made her point about history so succinctly without this metaphor. What aspects of history are clarified through its comparison to a mirror?

The following passage by psychoanalyst Carl Jung contains an effective use of analogy. Here Jung describes the collective mind of twentieth-century humanity through the analogy of a building:

> We have to describe and to explain a building the upper story of which was erected in the nineteenth century; the ground-floor dates from the sixteenth century, and a careful examination of the masonry discloses the fact that it was reconstructed from a dwelling-tower of the eleventh century. In the cellar we discover Roman foundation walls, and under the cellar a filled-in cave, in the floor of which stone tools are found and remnants of glacial fauna in the layers below. That would be a sort of picture of our mental structure.

Of course, Jung could have described the characteristics of the mind in more abstract language, but his description would have been less memorable than this picture of a house with a buried cave underneath. This example demonstrates how analogies crystallize abstract ideas into a sharp picture that both clarifies the ideas and makes them memorable.

Metaphors can also be valuable means of discovery—doors that lead you to important ideas and arguments. We are all naturally disposed to notice correspondences, to see the threads of similarity that unify experience. We have all had the experience of being spontaneously struck by similarities between two seemingly different subjects. Usually our minds hit on such a comparison because it is apt, because it contains a truth that we may not consciously recognize. On close examination, these correspondences or metaphors that come to us may reveal important truths about both subjects and may generate and even structure a theory or argument. When the noted computer scientist Edward Fredkin was struck by the correspondences between the operation of computers and the operation of the universe, he followed up that metaphor, creating a controversial but intriguing theory of digital physics from the implications of a seemingly simple metaphor. Like Fredkin and others, you should be alive to the generating power of your natural metaphor-making tendency, letting it work for you in the ideas you develop and the arguments you write.

Some Cautions About Figures of Speech

Metaphors, similes, and analogies can illuminate and generate ideas, but they can't prove a point; they offer clarification, not evidence. (See Chapter 5 for a discussion of false analogy as an informal fallacy.) Calling the world a village doesn't prove the need for world government. Ultimately all analogies break down if pursued too far; the two subjects of an analogy are, finally, *different* subjects. The world may be a village, but it is a village with more than five billion inhabitants, speaking thousands of different languages and following countless different customs and beliefs. Some village!

Analogies are risky if people take them too literally, as they did the "domino theory" analogy in the 1960s and 1970s. The domino analogy compared countries in Southeast Asia to a row of dominoes. When dominoes are placed on their ends in a row, they will fall down one by one if the first in the series is pushed. According to the domino theory, these countries would fall to communism in the same manner. The domino theory was a major reason for American involvement in Vietnam; American strategists believed that the fall of South Vietnam to the communists would lead to communist control of all of Southeast Asia and perhaps all of Asia. South Vietnam and some other parts of Southeast Asia are now communist, but other countries in Southeast Asia are not and do not seem to be in any danger of falling under such control. The domino theory may not always be this faulty, yet the theory cannot become an excuse for failing to analyze the particular complexities of a specific situation. Real countries are always more complicated than dominoes.

ACTIVITIES (10.2)

1. For one of the following analogies, write a one-page essay analyzing how the analogy illuminates aspects of the situation and how it does not. Our discussion of the "domino theory" in the previous section is one example of this kind of analysis.
   a. Sexual politics
   b. The family of humanity
   c. The game of life
   d. The war of ideas
   e. The corporate ladder

2. Write a paragraph that develops an analogy. You may use one of the analogies in Activity 1, provided it is not the one you used in that exercise. The paragraph by Carl Jung previously cited is one model for this kind of development.

3. Read a classmate's paragraph from Activity 2 while he or she reads yours. Evaluate the effectiveness of the analogy, and discuss your evaluation with your partner.

CONNOTATIVE LANGUAGE AND SLANTING

Good writers must be aware not only of the *denotations* of words but of their *connotations* as well. The denotation of a word is its explicit meaning, its dictionary definition; the connotation of a word is the meaning or meanings suggested by the word, the word's emotional associations. The denotation of the words *apple pie* is a baked food made with apples. In our society, the connotations of "apple pie" are family life, patriotism, and innocence. Writers of arguments need to be sensitive to the connotations of words and to use these connotations appropriately. A writer urging the development of a suburban tract of land for offices and factories is more likely to succeed by describing it as a "high-tech park" than as an "industrial development area"; the term *high-tech* has a certain vogue, while "*industrial development*" smells of factory smokestacks. And have you noticed how frequently suburban office complexes are called something like Corporate Woods, even when there are few trees anywhere in sight? Beyond a certain point, words used for their connotative value cease to have any meaning at all; there are very few woods in Corporate Woods and nothing fresh in "lemony fresh" soap or in "fresh frozen" juice. And what is so natural about many of the products that advertise themselves as "naturally delicious"? Connotation is an inescapable element of argument, but it should not be used without regard to denotation. Some advertising disregards denotation and gets away with it, but most readers demand higher standards for other kinds of written arguments.

Writers are often tempted to use not only connotation but also blatantly emotional terms as illegitimate supports for their arguments. Suppose you were arguing for a new recreation center on your campus. You might refer to the necessity of having a place "where students can use their free time constructively, letting off the frustrations and pressures caused by rigorous scholastic demands." Here you are portraying students and their needs in a positive way: we tend to respect anyone subjected to "rigorous scholastic demands." But if you were arguing against the recreation center, you could completely alter this impression by using words with negative connotations: "Do our spoiled and spoon-fed students really need another service catering to their already well-satisfied needs?" The respectable students of the first argument have become the undeserving parasites of the second. Words like *spoiled, spoon-fed,* and *catering* are negative words, and their application to the students in question affects a reader's impression of the issue. The words used *slant* the argument, even in the absence of sound evidence. As a writer of responsible arguments, *you* must not fall into the trap of letting such language suggest conclusions your argument does not support.

The temptation to slant is probably strongest in arguments of ethical evaluation; of all the arguments you write, these are the most personal, the most self-revealing, and thus the most important to you. For these reasons, they may tempt you to resort to irrational means to convince your audience. You are not likely to invest high emotional stakes in arguing that four-wheel-drive cars are superior to other kinds of cars, but you can be passionately committed to an argument for or against capital punishment or abortion. Slanting, while almost unavoidable in such cases, must not become a substitute for sound support of your argument.

(See Chapter 5 for a discussion of "Emotive Language" and "Circular Argument" as informal fallacies.)

ACTIVITIES (10.3)

With one other student in your class, select a subject to describe. Each of you should then write a description of that subject—one favorable, one unfavorable. Some possible topics are: city life, a particular television show, a book you both have read. Before you write your descriptions, agree on certain qualities to refer to in your descriptions.

THE MUSIC OF LANGUAGE

Any writer who ignores the importance of *sound* in argument is overlooking a valuable tool. We all know the power of advertising's jingles and catch phrases, which linger in our minds even when we wish they wouldn't. Less obvious but powerfully convincing is prose that holds our attention because of a fresh and pleasing combination of sounds. Such prose contains euphony and rhythm.

Euphony, a term that comes from Greek roots meaning "good sound," is a pleasing combination of sounds. We usually think of euphony as a characteristic of poetry or some kinds of prose fiction, but it can and should be present in written arguments as well. Euphony, of course, depends on the ear of the reader or listener, but ears can be trained to become sensitive to this quality of prose, just as we learn to be sensitive to different qualities of music.

Rhythm is a recognizable pattern of sounds through time. In prose, rhythmical units are often divided by grammatical pauses such as commas or periods, though a rhythmical break may also occur at some other place where we would pause to catch our breath if we were reading aloud. "I came, I saw, I conquered" is a simple example of prose rhythm, with three short, rhythmical units divided by commas. All of us have a rhythm to our prose just as we have a rhythm to our breathing or walking, and this rhythm varies with the situation, just as our walking rhythm does. Good prose writers learn to know their prose rhythms, to develop them as they gain experience in writing, and to recognize and use the appropriate rhythm for a specific purpose.

The following passage is from Jeff Greenfield's "The Black and White Truth About Basketball." Note Greenfield's sensitivity to euphony and rhythm:

> Basketball is a struggle for the edge: the half step with which to cut around the defender for a lay-up, the half second of freedom with which to release a jump shot, the instant a head turns allowing a pass to a teammate breaking for the basket. It is an arena for the subtlest of skills: the head fake, the shoulder fake, the shift of body weight to the right and the sudden cut to the left. Deception is crucial to success; and to young men who have learned early and painfully that life is a battle for survival, basketball is one of the few pursuits in which the weapon of deception is a legitimate tactic rather than a source of trouble.

For one thing, this passage makes effective use of the stylistic element of parallelism. Parallelism is the principle that equivalent thoughts demand equivalent expression. Notice how the actions described in the first and second sentences are presented in the same grammatical form: a noun modified by a verbal phrase ("the half step with which to cut around the defender for a layup, the half second of freedom with which to release a jump shot"). In addition to the grammatical parallelism within each of these sentences, Greenfield has made the two sentences parallel to each other: in each, two shorter phrases are followed by a third, longer phrase.

As well as parallelism, Greenfield also makes use of repetition ("half step" and "half second"; "the head fake" and "the shoulder fake") and opposition ("the shift of body weight to the *right* and the sudden cut to the *left*"). The overall effect of these strategies is one of balance—a rhetorical balance that nicely mirrors the physical balance of the intricate choreography of basketball.

The sound of your prose *will* affect how readers react to your argument, even if they are not conscious of the role sound plays in written prose and even if they have not developed the skill to create sound-pleasing prose themselves. As the rhetorician Kenneth Burke has noted, audiences tend to identify with skilled speakers and writers and are likely to be carried along simply by the very structure of the prose. A solid argument that is also aurally effective is hard to beat.

ACTIVITIES (10.4)

Read the following passages and choose the one whose prose style you find most memorable or striking. Write a one- to two-page evaluative argument demonstrating what is effective about the style and why.

1. You know how it is, you want to look and you don't want to look. I can remember the strange feelings I had when I was a kid looking at war photographs in *Life*, the ones that showed dead people or a lot of dead people lying close together in a field or a street, often touching, seeming to hold each other. Even when the picture was sharp and cleanly defined, something wasn't clear at all, something repressed that monitored the images and withheld their essential information. It may have legitimized my fascination, letting me look for as long as I wanted; I didn't have a language for it then, but I remember now the shame I felt, like looking at first porn, all the porn in the world. (Michael Herr. *Dispatches*. London: Picador, 1978. 23.)

2. Commercial exploitation and growing population demands will speed destruction of rain forests as well as oceans, grasslands, lakes, and wetlands. *Pleading ignorance of these vital and fragile ecosystems can only spell global disaster. What can you do?*
   You can accept this invitation to support World Wildlife Fund. *We have a plan for survival. We need your help to make it succeed.* (Letter from the World Wildlife Fund. World Wildlife Fund, 1987. 1.)

3. The stars awaken a certain reverence, because though always present, they are inaccessible; but all natural objects make a kindred impression, when the mind is open to their influence. Nature never wears a mean appearance. Neither does the wisest man extort her secret, and lose his curiosity by find-

ing out all her perfection. Nature never became a toy to a wise spirit. The flowers, the animals, the mountains, reflected the wisdom of his best hour, as much as they had delighted the simplicity of his childhood. (Ralph Waldo Emerson. "Nature." *Essays and Lectures*. Ed. Joel Porte. New York: Library of America, 1983. 9.)

4. Many adults carry high school around with them always. It is a unique, eccentric, and insulated social system, a pressure cooker where teenagers rush from one class to another, shoved into close quarters with twenty-five or thirty others their age they may love, hate, care little about, or hardly know at all. It has its own norms, rituals, vocabulary, and even its own way to tell time— not by the minute and hour but, as sociologist Edgar Friedenberg has pointed out, by periods. As the setting for the adolescent search for identity, high school is, Kurt Vonnegut wrote, "closer to the core of the American experience than anything else I can think of." There is life after high school, but what we do as adults is powerfully shaped by those years. (Myra and David Sadker. *Failing at Fairness: How America's Schools Cheat Girls*. New York: Scribner's, 1994. 99.)

5. Yes, Virginia, there is a Santa Claus. He exists as certainly as love and generosity and devotion exist, and you know that they abound and give your life its highest beauty and joy. Alas! how dreary would be the world if there were no Santa Claus. It would be as dreary as if there were no Virginias. There would be no child-like faith then, no poetry, no romance to make tolerable this existence. We should have no enjoyment, except in sense and sight. The eternal life with which childhood fills the world would be extinguished. (Francis Pharcellus Church. *New York Sun*, 1897.)

SUMMARY

Writing and Image

- The image you project through your writing is the result of a number of conscious choices you make about your style, your voice, and your use of language.

- You should write clearly, but you should also use various strategies to enrich your prose, including metaphors, similes, and other figures of speech, as well as long words and sentences when appropriate. In general, dare to try something different.

- Metaphor and analogy are valuable for illuminating and generating an argument, but they can never prove a point.

- You must be sensitive to the connotations of words, but you must defend your position with adequate support, not merely with connotation or open slanting.

- You should be sensitive to, and use, euphony and rhythm in your prose.

SUGGESTIONS FOR WRITING (10.5)

1. Write a one-page description of a friend for another friend. Then rewrite the description as a speech describing your friend at a ceremony where he or she will be receiving an award. Have a classmate read both versions and identify the stylistic details of each version.

2. Choose a famous brief essay or speech such as Kennedy's Inaugural Address, Lincoln's Gettysburg Address, or Martin Luther King, Jr.'s, "I Have a Dream." Each of these speeches and many others can be found on-line reproduced by reliable sources. Using this essay or speech as a model, try to capture some of the spirit of the original while using your own words and ideas on some topic of your choice in a two- to three-page essay. Pay particular attention to frequently recurring patterns of sentences, and try to use some similar patterns in your own essay. (Give your instructor a copy of the speech you select as a model.)

11

Introductions and Conclusions

Because your argument's introduction and conclusion are the first and last impression you will make on your readers, they require careful attention. Conclusions—whether a general closing or a specialized summary—are, of course, almost always composed late in the writing process, when you know exactly what it is your argument has concluded. Some writers compose introductions before they write the actual argument, but many delay until the last stage of the first draft, when they know more clearly what is to be introduced. This chapter discusses the importance of effective openings and closings and makes some suggestions for writing them.

INTRODUCTIONS

Because it is your readers' initial experience with your argument, your introduction must be particularly appealing to them. Regardless of what form your introduction takes, it is the hook that draws your readers into your argument.

The style and content of your introduction will be influenced by your argument's context (the occasion and audience for which it is written) and by its length, tone, and level of complexity. But no matter how you choose to open your argument, the basic purpose of any introduction is the same: to engage your readers. Usually an introduction succeeds in engaging readers if it is clear and inviting. Of these two features, clarity—the precise and accurate expression of carefully considered ideas—is probably the easiest to achieve, though for many writers it comes only with careful thought and considerable revision. To be inviting, your introduction must stimulate your readers' interest, as well as arouse their curiosity about the rest of the argument. Since being inviting is, for most of us, a learned skill, we offer some strategies for writing engaging introductions.

Strategies for General Introductions

Introduction by Narrative.   Writers of "general interest" arguments (nontechnical arguments intended for a broad audience) often gain their readers' attention by opening their essay with a specific anecdote or short narrative. This kind of opening engages readers in two ways: first, in its narrative approach, it satisfies our delight in being told a story, and second, it gains our interest by its *particularity*—its details about people, places, and events that give readers a firm footing as they enter an unknown text. An essay entitled "Boring from Within," by English professor Wayne C. Booth, begins with the following paragraph:

> Last week I had for about the hundredth time an experience that always disturbs me. Riding on a train, I found myself talking with my seat-mate, who asked me what I did for a living. "I teach English." Do you have any trouble predicting his response? His face fell, and he groaned, "Oh, dear, I'll have to watch my language." In my experience there are only two other possible reactions. The first is even less inspiring: "I hated English in school; it was my worst subject." The second, so rare as to make an honest English teacher almost burst into tears of gratitude when it occurs, is an animated conversation about literature, or ideas, or the American language—the kind of conversation that shows a continuing respect for "English" as something more than being sure about *who* and *whom, lie* and *lay*.

Booth's essay, addressed to high school English teachers, goes on to identify the ways in which English is mis-taught and to suggest alternative teaching methods. As a renowned college professor addressing high school teachers about the problems of high school instruction, Booth must be careful not to alienate his audience by coming across as superior or critical. He does this in part by opening the essay (initially an oral address) with this personal anecdote, which immediately, but tacitly, says "I am one of you." As well as disarming his audience with the personal references, Booth captures their attention with the simultaneous specificity and universality of effective narrative.

Introduction by Generalization.   Good introductions can also begin with a strong, unambiguous generalization related to the readers' experiences, as in the following opening paragraph of an article by David Brown published in a medical society journal:

> Few honorable professions have as much inherent hostility toward one another as medicine and journalism. Ask a doctor to describe journalists and you are likely to hear adjectives such as "negative," "sensationalistic," and "superficial." Ask a journalist about doctors, and you will probably hear about "arrogance," "paternalism," and "jargon."

Broad statements such as this should be limited and developed in succeeding sentences or a succeeding paragraph. In the second paragraph of this essay, the writer both justifies and develops the generalization made in the first paragraph.

The descriptions are the common stereotypes and not wholly inaccurate, for the two professions occupy distant worlds. Physicians are schooled in confidence and collegiality; journalists seek to make knowledge public. Physicians speak the language of science; journalists are largely ignorant of science. Physicians inhabit a world of contingencies and caveats; journalists inhabit a world where time and audience require simplification. Physicians are used to getting their way; journalists are used to getting their story.

This paragraph's development of the idea contained in the initial paragraph is echoed by the writer's syntax (the arrangement of his words): the last four sentences, neatly divided by semicolons into opposing clauses, emphasize the focus on this professional opposition.

Introduction by Quotation.   Some introductions begin with quotations that are eventually connected to the topic of the essay. While perhaps overused and overtaught, this technique *does* work if practiced thoughtfully. The writer using an opening quotation must be sure that it can be made to apply to the subject in an interesting way, and that the quotation is interesting, provocative, or well written (preferably all three). The following paragraph in an essay by Marilyn Yalom is a successful example of this technique:

> When Robert Browning wrote his famous lines "Grow old along with me!/The best is yet to be,/The last of life, for which the first was made," he was undoubtedly not thinking about women. The poet's Victorian optimism is difficult enough to reconcile with the realities of old age for men, and virtually impossible when we consider the condition of older women in the nineteenth century.

As in the article about the antagonism between the medical and journalistic professions, the initial statement here is immediately explained and developed in the succeeding sentence. Here, in fact, the explanatory sentence is also the claim of this essay on the older woman in Victorian England and America.

Other Types of Introductions.   There are a number of other strategies for making arguments inviting to your readers: startling statistics, a brief historical survey of the topic (which can have the same charm as the narrative introduction), a particularly startling or shocking statement (provided, of course, that it is relevant to the content of your argument), and even a direct announcement of the argument's subject (as in "This is an article about bad writing"). Any of these tactics will work as long as it connects in some way with the body of the argument.

Introductions in Professional Writing

Introductions written in a professional context according to established formats don't need to be as inviting as the previous examples, largely because readers of professional reports usually don't have much choice about whether or not to read a given report. Rather than trying to engage their readers, on-the-job writers are concerned about serving the needs of a known audience who will make some use of the report. In these cases, introductions are successful if they accurately represent the report's content. Company policy often dictates the form of a preliminary summary: some companies require an initial outline, others an abstract, still others a summary reflecting both organization and content. When the form is not dictated, the most useful is a simple summary of organization and content.

Take as an example an analysis of problems in customer relations assigned to a customer service representative of a local grocery chain. In her report, the representative first identifies, describes, and documents the different conditions she has found to be damaging to good customer relations: inadequate customer check-cashing privileges, a time-consuming refund policy, impolite carryout personnel, and inaccurate advertising of sale prices. She then estimates the loss of business resulting from each problem. Finally, she recommends possible solutions to the problems she has identified. Her report is clearly written and organized, but it is also lengthy and somewhat complex; it needs an introduction that will prepare its readers not only for the content of the report but also for the arrangement of its material. The preliminary summary will prepare readers for the sequence of the argument's main points, and it will serve as a useful reference should the readers become confused while reading the full report.

Our customer service representative introduces her report with the following preliminary summary:

> This report examines the recent quarterly decline in business at the seven Goodbelly stores. It attributes this loss of revenue to at least four remediable problems in the area of customer relations: (1) inadequate check-cashing privileges, (2) a time-consuming refund policy, (3) lack of concern for customers by carryout personnel, and (4) inaccurate advertising of sale prices. It is estimated that these difficulties may have cost Goodbelly's as much as $300,000 in revenue in the past three months. This report concludes by recommending specific personnel and policy measures to be taken to ease these difficulties and to regain the lost business.

Without being painstakingly mechanical, this brief paragraph identifies the central claim of the report (that the decline in revenue is due to poor customer relations) and prepares the reader for the organization and content of the argument. While an introduction such as this one may not engage a reader who has neither an interest in nor an obligation to the company, its concise and accurate representation of the report's content will be extremely useful to the obligated reader.

General Suggestions About Introductions

Finally, you may find these general suggestions about writing introductions useful:

1. Try writing your introduction *after* you've written your first draft. Often, there's no point in agonizing over a preliminary summary for a professional

report or a catchy introduction for a general interest argument before you know exactly how the argument is going to evolve. Even if you're working from a detailed outline, your organization and content will change as you compose.

2. On those rare occasions when a catchy opening sentence or paragraph comes to you early, giving you a hold on the overall structure, tone, and style of your argument, don't let this opening get away!

3. Don't make your introduction too long. Even the most interesting, captivating introduction is going to seem silly if it's twice as long as the argument itself. The turbot, a variety of anglerfish, has a head that takes up half of its total body length and is one of the silliest looking fish on the planet. Don't follow its example.

4. Make sure your introduction is truly representative of the entire argument. If you are writing a preliminary summary, be sure all the main points of the argument are covered in the introduction. In a less formal argument, don't let your desire to be engaging lure you into writing an introduction that is stylistically or tonally inconsistent with the rest of the argument. In short, the opening paragraph should never look as if it has been tacked on merely to attract reader interest, with no thought about its relationship to what follows. Rather, it should resemble an operatic overture, beautiful in its own right, but always preparing its audience for what is to follow.

ACTIVITIES (11.1)

1. For one of the following writing tasks, write two different introductory paragraphs using two of the tactics discussed in the preceding section: narrative, generalization, quotation, startling statistics, a brief historical survey, a startling statement, or an outright announcement of claim. Then write a two- to three-sentence description of the different effects of the two introductions.
   a. An essay on a relative whom you admire
   b. An essay on a law or policy of the federal government that you strongly support or oppose
   c. An essay on your favorite food
   d. An editorial in your local newspaper opposing teenage curfew
   e. A report to your supervisor (or a parent or a friend) explaining why you have failed to accomplish all the goals you set for yourself six months ago
2. For one of the arguments you have already written for this class, write (or rewrite) an introductory paragraph following the suggestions offered in the preceding discussion.
3. Working on a different argument written for this course, compose an opening paragraph that begins at a general level and ends with the argument's claim.

CONCLUSIONS

Once you have selected and presented the best possible support for your argument, you may feel that you have nothing more to say on the subject. But you're not finished yet. Until you have provided a final closing, a conclusion that rounds out your argument, your argument is incomplete. Most readers need to feel closure in all kinds of writing: letters, imaginative literature, and arguments.

Conclusions are not always easy to write, particularly because by the time we get around to thinking about writing an ending, we're often tired of the whole project. But you don't need to be a master rhetorician to write an effective ending. A conclusion that is direct, precise, and appropriate to the occasion will do the job just fine. Depending on the context, it can be as short as a paragraph or as long as a chapter.

Types of Conclusions

Arguments can have three basic types of conclusions: the findings or results of an investigation, a recommendation or set of recommendations, or a more general closing reflecting on the argument or raising other considerations related to the central claim.

Findings. The findings or results conclusion usually ends an argument of fact, such as the reporting of a scientific experiment or a case study. Some causal arguments, such as certain historical studies, may also end with findings or results. Actually, these findings are the argument's claim, which may be given in general form early in the argument and then with more detail at the end, or they may be given only at the end. The following paragraph (the second-to-last paragraph of an essay titled "Particle Accelerators Test Cosmological Theory") exemplifies the findings type of conclusion:

> Preliminary results from the machines indicate that there are at most five families of elementary particles. David B. Cline of the University of California at Los Angeles and the University of Wisconsin at Madison . . . has shown that the lifetime of the $Z°$ boson [a subatomic particle] is approximately what one would expect with just three families. Experimental uncertainties, however, allow for two additional kinds of neutrinos [another subatomic particle] and hence two additional families. . . . For the first time accelerators are counting neutrino types and getting a small number, one that was predicted by cosmological theory.

Recommendation. Not surprisingly, recommendations typically conclude arguments of recommendation. Their purpose is to tell readers exactly what the argument expects of them. If the findings conclusion tells readers what they should *know*, the recommendation conclusion tells them what they should *do*. An example of this type of conclusion is found at the end of "A Proposal for a Computer Facility in Marshall Dormitory" in Chapter 9 of this book. The proposal ends with a "Costs and Implementation Plan" section that spells out in some detail the actions that need to be taken. In this proposal, the more general recommendations came earlier, so ending with more specific steps is a suitable way to conclude. In many other cases, the most appropriate conclusion is a general recommendation, as in this last paragraph from an essay titled "U.S. Economic Growth":

Only if we increase investment in both capital and technology in all sectors of the U.S. economy (particularly manufacturing) and improve the quality of labor at all levels can the American standard of living rise at an acceptable rate. In the present highly competitive world market, the U.S. has some historically demonstrated advantages, but it must take the longer view and pursue those seemingly trivial increases of a few tenths of a percentage point in growth rate each year.

General Closing.   The general closing is what we usually think of when we think of conclusions. This type of conclusion can work in several ways: it can move from the specific argument to a statement of the argument's broader significance, it can suggest future directions for research, or it can raise related issues. The general closing suggests a movement *onward* (where we go from here) or a movement *outward* (how this specific argument relates to other arguments), though the emphasis in any case will vary between these two elements.

The following paragraph (the closing of Mike Messner's "Sports and the Politics of Inequality") exemplifies a conclusion that moves to a consideration of an argument's broader significance:

> If this discussion of sports and inequality seems to make contradictory points, it is because sports plays a contradictory role in the larger politics of inequality. On an ideological level, sports strengthens and legitimates class and ethnic inequalities in society while simultaneously providing cultural space where ideologies supporting inequalities can be challenged and debunked. And for participants, sports offers a place where class and ethnic antagonisms and prejudices can be destructively played out *and* it can offer a space where participants can experience transcendent moments of play which are relatively free from the larger social inequities. In this space, it is possible to discover ourselves and each other as human beings. What all this means is that the role sports will play in the politics of inequality will be determined by "how we play the game," both individually and collectively.

The final paragraph of "Particle Accelerators Test Cosmological Theory" (cited previously) demonstrates the concluding strategy of pointing to new directions and future possibilities:

> The next step promises to be even more exciting. As new accelerators are completed and begin producing more data with fewer uncertainties, the cosmological limit of three or at most four families will be checked with extreme accuracy....The machines will probe the early universe with an effectiveness that no telescope will ever match.

A conclusion that raises related issues is found in the last two paragraphs of George Orwell's famous essay "Politics and the English Language." Throughout most of the essay, Orwell gives examples of bad English. But toward the end of the essay, he suggests connections between corrupt language and corrupt political systems. The final paragraph addresses this connection directly:

One ought to recognize that the present political chaos is connected with the decay of language, and that one can probably bring about some improvement by starting at the verbal end. If you simplify your English, you are freed from the worst follies of orthodoxy. You cannot speak any of the necessary dialects, and when you make a stupid remark its stupidity will be obvious, even to yourself. Political language—and with variations this is true of all political parties, from Conservatives to Anarchists—is designed to make lies sound truthful and murder respectable, and to give an appearance of solidity to pure wind. One cannot change this all in a moment, but one can at least change one's own habits, and from time to time one can even, if one jeers loudly enough, send some *melting pot, acid test, veritable inferno,* or other lump of verbal refuse—into the dustbin where it belongs.

A conclusion can contain more than one of the three basic types described previously. The second-to-last paragraph of "Particle Accelerators Test Cosmological Theory" presents the results of the research, whereas the very last paragraph presents a statement on the future directions of this research. A results or recommendation conclusion may be supplemented with a more general conclusion that opens the argument outward.

A word of caution about all conclusions: the conclusion must not lie outside the boundaries of what you can legitimately claim in your argument. You should not, for example, turn an argument about the weakness of a certain school's curriculum into a conclusion uniformly condemning all schools, though your conclusion may suggest that the case you have examined is not an isolated one. In other words, don't overgeneralize from the evidence you used to support your argument. Nor should you use your conclusion as the place to launch a whole new argument or to make claims that do not have some basis in what has preceded.

SUMMARIES

A conclusion is different from a *summary,* which is a restatement of the main points of your argument. Most short or medium-length arguments (five hundred to five thousand words) do not require a summary; final summaries are typically found in very long essays, in essays with difficult subject matter, or in books. This book, for example, uses sentence summaries at the end of each chapter to stress certain key points to an audience new to much of this material.

Writers of arguments sometimes provide a summary of the basic points *preceding* the argument. Such summaries are usually either separate from or at the very beginning of the argument. Typically they take one of two forms: the *abstract,* often used in academic or technical research, and the *executive summary,* often used in business reports and proposals.

An abstract is a summary, typically in paragraph form, that states the essential points of the essay so that readers can grasp these points without having to read the essay; in other words, the good abstract can stand alone, being meaningful by itself. If the readers read only the abstract, they will of course miss much of the argument, especially its support, but they will at least know what the argument's main claims are. With the flood of information confronting us all, abstracts have the obvious value of helping us decide what research needs further investigation and what can be left alone.

The following summary by King-Kok Cheung of her essay on Alice Walker's *Color Purple* and Maxine Hong Kingston's *Woman Warrior* is a good example of an abstract for academic writing:

> *The Color Purple* and *The Woman Warrior* exhibit parallel narrative strategies. The respectively black and Chinese American protagonists work their way from speechlessness to eloquence by breaking through the constraints of sex, race, and language. The heroines turn to masculine figures for guidance, to female models for inspiration, and to native idioms for stylistic innovation. Initially unable to speak, they develop distinctive voices by registering their own unspoken grief on paper and, more important, by recording and emulating the voices of women from their respective ethnic communities. Through these testimonies, each written in a bicultural language, Walker and Kingston reveal the obstacles and resources peculiar to minority women. Subverting patriarchal literary traditions by reclaiming a mother tongue that carries a rich oral tradition (of which women are guardians) the authors artfully coordinate the tasks of breaking silence, acknowledging female influence, and redefining while preserving ethnic characteristics.

Here is an example of an abstract introducing a technical argument, "Cutting into Cholesterol," written by Bruce P. Kinosian and John M. Eisenberg:

> We performed an analysis of the cost-effectiveness of treating individuals with significantly elevated levels of total serum cholesterol (>6.85 mmol/L [>265 mg/dL]), comparing treatment with three alternative agents: cholestyramine resin, colestipol, and oat bran (a soluble fiber). We simulated a program for lowering cholesterol levels that was similar to that of the Coronary Primary Prevention Trial, and then used the outcomes of the trial to calculate the incremental cost per year of life saved (YOLS) from the perspective of society. Our findings suggest that the cost per YOLS ranges from $117,400 (cholestyramine resin packets) to $70,900 (colestipol packets) and $17,800 (oat bran). Using bulk drug reduces the cost per YOLS to $65,100 (cholestyramine resin) and $63,900 (colestipol). Targeting bulk colestipol treatment only to smokers has a cost per YOLS of $47,010; the incremental cost of treating nonsmokers would be $89,600 per additional YOLS. Although pharmacologic therapy has substantial costs, it may be more cost-effective when low-cost forms are applied to particular high-risk groups, such as smokers. However, a broad public health approach to lowered cholesterol levels by additional dietary modification, such as with soluble fiber, may be preferred to a medically oriented campaign that focuses on drug therapy.

Executive summaries are often longer than abstracts, though they should not usually be longer than a page. Like abstracts, they give the main points of an argument, but they may also contain some background on why the report was written and on the scope of the original study. If the executive summary is of a recommendation report, the major recommendation should be included in it. Like abstracts, executive summaries should be written to stand alone; readers should be able to get the major points of the report without referring to the report itself.

The following is a sample executive summary with a format that might be used by a group auditing the overall effectiveness of a university computer center:

> The audit completed a review of the Johnston Computer Center in February 1994. The Johnston Computer Center is one of three academic computing centers at the university and contains terminals and microcomputers for up to 200 on-site users, with access also available for up to 50 off-site users, so that it is second largest of such centers at the university.
>
> The objectives of our review were to determine whether present and planned center operations are fulfilling user needs and are in compliance with university policies and procedures for computer security.
>
> In our opinion, the center's operation is satisfactory in meeting the needs of its users and in using its internal resources to meet these needs, but unsatisfactory in meeting security policies and procedures.
>
> Our survey of Johnston Computer Center users indicated that user satisfaction is high and that center personnel are responsive to user needs. While system response time has deteriorated in the last six months because of an unexpected increase in user demand, center management has addressed this problem by encouraging users to use the system during nonpeak hours and by recommending a hardware upgrade to the Vice President for Systems and Computing.
>
> Our review of security showed that unauthorized users could gain access to and change another user's files. Since the center's computers are not directly connected to the university's administrative computers, which do contain other security safeguards, the university does not face a risk to its financial and personnel records because of these deficiencies. The student and faculty academic files contained in the center's computers are at risk, however. The center has reported three instances of tampering in the last six months. Center management is eager to address this problem but will need additional resources to purchase software and to obtain the necessary technical assistance.

Executive summaries have become increasingly common as business executives and other managers find themselves confronted with an overwhelming number of reports to read. The executive summary allows readers to decide if they want to read further, or if the summary alone provides enough information. Unlike abstracts, which are often intended for a specialist audience, executive summaries usually have a nonspecialist audience of higher managers who may be very far removed from the technical details of the report. The executive summary should allow for the audience's lack of familiarity with these details by avoiding specialized vocabulary whenever possible and by defining any specialized terms that are used. In other words, executive summaries demand great attention to the readers' needs and great precision in wording. Typically they are written after the report is finished, when the writer knows all its twists and turns.

ACTIVITIES (11.2)

1. Return to an argument you have written for this course, and write two different conclusions for it: first, a general closing, and second, a conclusion restating the argument's findings or results. Give your argument and these two conclusions to a classmate to read; discuss with him or her which of the two conclusions seems more appropriate to its context.
2. Find a different argument from the one you used in Activity 1, and write a 250-word abstract (one double-spaced page) of the argument.

SUMMARY

Introductions and Conclusions

- The context of your argument will influence the style, content, and length of your introduction, but all introductions should be clear, engaging, and appropriate to the occasion.

- Some useful tactics for general introductions are:
  - Introduction by narrative
  - Introduction by generalization
  - Introduction by quotation

- Introductions of arguments in formal, professional writing should be precisely representative of the content of the report.

- Conclusions are usually one of three basic types: findings or results, a recommendation or set of recommendations, or a general closing. Which type of conclusion you use depends on the type of argument. Findings or results typically conclude reports of scientific experiments or case studies. Recommendations conclude recommendation reports. General closings are used for other types of arguments, especially interpretations and evaluations. The general closing has three subtypes: a statement of significance, suggested directions for research, and a raising of related issues.

- Do not confuse a conclusion with a summary. A summary is a restatement of the main points of your argument. There are three types of summaries: the ending summary, the abstract, and the executive summary. Ending summaries are typically found in books and in very complex or very long essays or reports. Abstracts and executive summaries are typically found at the beginning of or separate from the arguments on which they are based. Readers should be able to understand an abstract or an executive summary without referring to the report or essay on which it is based.

SUGGESTIONS FOR WRITING (11.3)

1. Locate a section of a newspaper or magazine that presents several editorial or opinion essays. The Sunday *New York Times* op-ed page is an excellent source; your local Sunday paper may have its own version. Or, if you choose a reputable newspaper or magazine resource online, note that you need to select their op-ed section for your articles. (This is one exercise that might be easier to conduct using hardcopy because all of the op-ed pieces can usually be found on one or two pages of your newspaper of choice.) Examine the types of conclusions used for three pieces, and write an essay of two to three pages describing the type of each conclusion, its effect on readers, and its overall effectiveness. Which of the three do you find the most effective? Why? Be sure to give your instructor a copy of the op-ed articles you use for this assignment.

2. Write a one-paragraph executive summary using one of your last papers, making sure that your readers will be able to understand the summary without reading the paper. When you hand in this assignment, give your instructor both the summary and the paper on which it is based.

12

Revising

Finally, you've finished your argument. It has an introduction and a conclusion, a claim and appropriate support, and you're ready to hand it over to your instructor with a sigh of relief.

But not so fast. You've certainly earned a break—writing is hard work—but if you want your paper to be as good as it can be, you've got to find the time and the energy for another crucial step in the writing process: revising.

Revising your argument means stepping back from it and seeing it whole. As the word's Latin roots (*re*—"again," and *visere*—"to look at") indicate, to revise is to see again, to have a new vision of the entire work. Sometimes this new vision leads to dramatic changes in any part of the argument, though the more attention you pay to the content and organization of your argument as you're writing the first draft, the fewer the major changes you will need to make (yes, that paper you've just finished is a only a first draft, not a finished argument). But even the most carefully composed first draft will require some changes. So, if you're not in the habit, it's time to make a practice of allowing plenty of time and attention for revision. It will pay off. Some people revise *as* they write, adjusting earlier parts of the argument to fit better with what they've just written or are about to write. This is a perfectly good practice that can save you time later on, but it shouldn't take the place of the revising process outlined in this chapter.

WRITING A FIRST DRAFT, REVISING, AND EDITING

Don't confuse revising with editing. Editing is a careful check of the spelling, grammar, punctuation, and overall consistency of a manuscript. Revising, as noted, is a more profound look at the argument's entire content, shape, and style.

Revising involves considerable judgment on your part, because questions about claim, support, and style rarely have simple right or wrong answers. On the other hand, most questions about editing do have right or wrong answers; there are only so many ways to spell a word or to punctuate a sentence correctly.

Writing your first draft, revising, and editing require different attitudes and use somewhat different skills. Writing the first draft requires energy and egoism to keep you going through the bumpy parts; revising calls for detachment and reflection; and editing demands close attention to detail. Attempting a "perfect" first draft is actually one of the most dangerous and laborious ways to write. It is dangerous because you will lack the necessary distance to judge the quality of your argument, and laborious because you are trying to combine these three separate tasks. To some extent, of course, revising and editing occur during the writing of any draft; we all make minor changes in wording, organization, and mechanics even in the early stage of writing, and sometimes we decide on major changes as we write. Inserting these changes then makes sense, but you still need to set aside time for revising and editing, making each your major preoccupation in a separate review of the manuscript.

Many college students feel that they don't have time for anything but a first draft; in fact, they usually do. Students of roughly equal ability and with roughly the same amount of time available work in amazingly different ways, some finishing their work with plenty of time to spare, others doing everything at the last minute. Most students who claim that they were forced to write their papers just before the due date mean that writing the paper was not their highest priority and they could get motivated to write it only by the pressure of a deadline. Especially with word processing, writers who write a first draft, leave it for a while, and then revise it, do not spend any more time writing than those who try to write just one polished draft.

SOME SUGGESTIONS FOR SUCCESSFUL REVISING

Offered here are some suggestions aimed at making your revising stage as effective as possible. These suggestions are based on years of writing experience, but they are only suggestions, not ironclad rules.

Suggestion 1: Give Yourself Some Breathing Space

After you've finished your first draft, give yourself some time—at least 24 hours—before you begin the revising process. This "breathing space" gives you some distance from your work, which you will need in order to review it objectively. And it gives your unconscious an opportunity to mull over the material, so that when you return to the argument, you'll find you have fresh ideas about how to make it more effective. You've probably had the experience of rereading a graded paper and wondering how you could have missed the problems that seem so obvious to you now (and that were far too obvious to your instructor). Putting some distance between first draft and the revision gives you an opportunity to gain this fresh perspective, and to put it to use *before* your paper is graded.

Suggestion 2: Avoid the Red Pen

As you're reviewing your first draft, avoid the lure of the red pen or typing in any changes if you are reading from the screen—the temptation to make small editorial changes before you have reread and assimilated the argument as a whole. Reread with your hands tied behind your back (figuratively, that is), and you'll get a much better sense of how the draft works as a whole.

Suggestion 3: Review Your Original Purpose and Audience

In writing your first draft, you've been intent on coming up with the right word and composing individual sentences. It's easy at this level to lose touch with your original purpose and intended audience. So an important question to ask yourself as you're rereading and revising is whether you've fulfilled your original purpose for your intended audience (of course, your original purpose and audience may have changed during the first draft, but that should be your conscious choice, not an accident).

It can be helpful to review your argument pretending that you're one of its intended readers. From this perspective, you can ask yourself: do I understand the purpose and claim of this argument? are the vocabulary and specialized terms clear to me? is the argument meaningful to me? am I convinced by the argument?

Suggestion 4: Review Your Organization

In reviewing the effectiveness of your argument, you'll need to consider not only your purpose and audience, but also the overall organization of what you've written, making sure that the parts fit together well and are logically sequenced, that nothing crucial is omitted, and that the structure is lean, with a minimum of repetition. If it's hard to keep the organization in mind, try reproducing it in outline form, as in the following model. Remember, you're outlining what you actually wrote, not what you intended to write. If you actually wrote your draft from an outline, don't look at it until you have completed this new one.

    I. Introduction (if appropriate)
    II. Claim (if appropriate)
    III. Supporting arguments:
        A.
        B.
        C.
        D.
    IV. Conclusion or summary (if appropriate)

If you have trouble constructing this new outline, your argument probably has organizational problems that need attention.

This is also a good time to review the effectiveness of your claim and your introduction. Ask yourself these questions: if I have an explicit claim, is it clearly stated? if it is implied, will my readers recognize it? does my introduction prepare my readers for what follows? should it be more interesting?

Suggestion 5: Review Your Argument's Coherence

Even the most carefully organized argument will puzzle readers if the relationship between its parts is not indicated in some way. In certain professions and businesses, standard formats include headings like "Introduction," "The Problem," "History," and so on. But such headings are inappropriate in many settings. You can make the elements of your argument *coherent*—establish their relationship to one another and to the whole—by using simple transitional words and expressions that indicate the nature of the relationship.

Words like *therefore, thus, so,* and *consequently* identify a conclusion and its evidence. Words like *but, however,* and *on the other* hand indicate exceptions to a stated point. You can alert your reader to the introduction of each new piece of support by using indicators such as *first . . . , second . . . , and furthermore, and finally.* Transitional words and expressions such as these are enormously useful to readers of arguments, particularly when the argument is long or elaborate. They help readers understand how one statement or section that may otherwise seem a digression or an irrelevancy relates to what has gone before or what might come later.

As well as using such brief signposts, you can also be quite direct about the role of different parts of your argument. Public speakers are often very explicit about the function of crucial parts of their speeches: "Let me give you two reasons why this land should be developed," or "To conclude, I'd like to remind you of a few lines by Walt Whitman." Such obvious signs are crucial when there is no written text for an audience to follow and ponder. But indicators such as these can be used in written argument as well, especially when the parts are many and complex.

Suggestion 6: Review Your Style

The revising stage is the time to consider the effectiveness of your argument's style: its tone, word choice, and general treatment of the reader. As discussed in Chapter 10, style is a crucial component of argument, often playing a major role in convincing or alienating readers. Poor style is just as damaging to an argument as a vague or unsupported claim; an effective style is just as convincing as compelling evidence. And while you're considering your style, think about the ethos projected by your argument: does the argument reflect a writer who is fair, open-minded, and appropriately confident?

This is also a good time to ask yourself if you have followed Orwell's rules for clarity, along with the friendly amendments offered in Chapter 10. Finally, check your draft to see if you have (1) used connotation effectively, (2) avoided slanting, (3) used metaphor and analogy effectively, and (4) paid attention to the sounds of words. Some of these questions will naturally occur during your consideration of claim (if you have one) and the organization of its support, as well as during your review of audience and purpose.

Suggestion 7: Review Your Argument for Faulty Reasoning

Chapter 5 introduced some basic principles of logic that will help you set up a reasonable argument. The "informal fallacies" presented there are most easily detected during the revision stage. As a final step in reviewing your argument, read it through to detect any unwitting fallacies, paying special attention to those that are particularly common in the kind of argument you've written.

Suggestion 8: Use a Word Processor

Fortunately (some students would say unfortunately), revising may lead to a drastic overhaul of your argument. But if you want your argument to be as good as it can be, you won't ignore the opportunity to make these major changes. Most students now write their papers on computers, which make large- and small-scale revising much easier than any other method. If you're one of those few people who have resisted the move to computers, we strongly urge you to make the change. With a computer and a good word-processing program, you can switch entire sections of a draft around with ease; change words swiftly and even "globally," so that one word replaces another throughout an entire essay; and make corrections with no trace of erasures or correction fluid. Virtually all campuses have computer labs for their students, which save the expense of purchasing your own computer. And while a computer will not make you a better writer, it will give you the chance to make yourself a better writer. So get wired!

ACTIVITIES (12.1)

1. Write an outline of a paper or a draft of a paper that you have written for this class, using the format given in Suggestion 4. Then exchange this paper or draft with one of your classmates, while keeping your outline. Now prepare an outline of your classmate's paper, again using the same format, and then exchange outlines with your classmate. Compare your classmate's outline with your own. Do the two outlines agree on what the claim is and what the supporting arguments are? If there are disagreements, discuss these with your classmate. Find out why he or she saw your argument working in a different way than you did. Remember that if there is disagreement, you cannot simply assume that your classmate is wrong and you are correct: the purpose of your argument is to convince the reader, not yourself. After this discussion, make a list of the changes or possible changes you would make in your paper in the next draft.
2. Have a classmate read a clean copy of one of the papers you have written for this course. Ask him or her to write a one-page description of the overall image reflected in that paper and a one-page evaluation of that image. Do the same for a paper written by your classmate.

SUMMARY

Revising

- You should plan to spend separate portions of time writing a draft, revising, and editing.

- Allow breathing space between writing a draft and revising it. In your first review of the draft, concentrate on how the draft works as a whole.

- In revising, review your original purpose and audience, your organization, the adequacy and logic of your support, and your style.

- Knowing the principles of logic is a significant help in reviewing your draft.

- Using a word processor makes revising much easier.

AN EXAMPLE OF REVISION

Having read your manuscript all the way through at least once, and preferably twice, you are now ready to make major changes if they are needed. By avoiding the red pen until you have reviewed the entire manuscript, you are more likely to recognize the need for such major changes, and less likely to get lost in grieving over minor errors.

The following sample student essay is a good example of how to correct major problems in an argument. What follows is the first draft of the essay, along with the student's notes for revision, which he wrote in the margins during a second and third reading of the draft.

> When we think about computers, we usually think about how helpful they are to us: they enable us to process huge amounts of data, prepare large written documents with an ease undreamt of even twenty years ago, and by acting as the "brains" of robots, help us perform dangerous or monotonous tasks. But we often fail to think of the negative side of computers, including the threat they pose to our privacy. *Drop this idea not followed up* || Also, in many cases, computers are replacing human labor in factories and offices.
>
> One thing computers are used for is to store information about people. These computers contain databases, which are collections of discrete data that are divided into fields,

such as age, sex, income, and place of residence. A user of a database can pull information out of the database on everyone who fits a category made up of some or all of these fields, such as every male between thirty and forty who earns between thirty and fifty thousand dollars a year and lives in Florida. An example of a database is the Internal Revenue Service's database, which contains basic information on tax returns along with demographic information on those who pay taxes. Other databases contain credit histories. If you have someone's Social Security number, you can find out just about anything you want about that person. Not just anybody can do this, but there are already too many people who can.

overstated →

wordy, vague

A separate point, not related to ¶. Also, I have no proof.

As if it isn't bad enough to have someone go through all the information about you in one database, databases can even be linked to other databases because of the increased networking power of computers today. Having this ability leads to the potential problem of wrong information being kept on a person (especially if no written records are kept). Computers do fail, but the most important reason why a database would contain wrong information about someone would be because someone typed in incorrect information. If the police used computer databases to keep track of criminal records without having another record of them on paper somewhere, anyone could input harmful data on innocent people that could cause them a great deal of misery.

Too many separate ideas in this ¶: networking, human error, lack of paper copies. These need separate treatment.

If the major problem with the accuracy of information in databases is human error, then perhaps new forms of electronic entry of data will eliminate some of these errors. Our phone bills are one example of a completely electronic system. But these phone bills can tell someone who wants to know all the people we called and when we called them. Our phone companies could be recording everything we say as well.

No evidence. Statement undermines my credibility.

In our society, privacy is regarded as a right—a right that is being threatened by the increasing use of databases to maintain large

Ideas need development. Is situation hopeless?

amounts of information on all of us. A number of privacy bills have been passed but are almost useless because they are so hard to enforce. Violating someone's privacy is hard to detect, and successfully prosecuting someone for this offense is harder still.

Not relevant to what I've written.

Is this conclusion justified by what I've written?

Computers are enormously valuable tools, but they can be misused to violate privacy and to manipulate people. We have a population explosion today, and yet we replace people with computers. We must carefully examine the role of computers in our society and learn to control them before they control us.

First drafts (and final drafts, for that matter) are never perfect, as our student has recognized on rereading his. Here is a list of the problems that his review has discovered:

1. *Claim.* I have a combination claim focusing on the privacy issue and the issue of computers replacing human labor, but I do nothing with the second issue. I should drop the second issue and concentrate on the first.

2. *Organization.* My ideas aren't clearly presented and organized, especially in the third paragraph, which talks about the three separate ideas of networking, human data-entry errors, and lack of paper or "hard-copy" backups. All of my paragraphs must be clearly tied to the privacy threat.

3. *Support.* I don't really support my argument because I talk a lot about the threat of invasion of privacy but give no actual cases. I need to distinguish clearly between the potential for abuse and actual cases. Is there a real possibility of abuse? Also, my conclusion about humans controlling computers before they control us isn't warranted by what I've written, since I've offered no suggestions for controlling computers.

4. *Style.* I undermine my credibility with sweeping statements like "If you have someone's Social Security number, you can find out just about anything you want about that person." Some of my writing could be much tighter, including wordy expressions like "As if it isn't bad enough to have someone go through all the information about you in one database . . ."

In his second draft, the student carefully attended to this list, ending up with a much stronger version of the paper. After completing his research, he was able to add authoritative support and documented references, going beyond supposition.

When we think about computers, we usually think about how helpful they are to us: they enable us to process huge

amounts of data, prepare large written documents with an
ease undreamt of even twenty years ago, and by acting as
the "brains" of robots, help us perform dangerous or
monotonous tasks. But we often fail to think of the
negative side of computers, including the threat they pose
to our own privacy. This threat may not seem immediate,
but it is growing with the increasing power of computers,
and so far society has done little to deal with it (Roszak
181).

One thing computers are used for is to store
information about people. Computers often use databases,
which are collections of discrete data that are divided
into fields, such as age, sex, income, and place of
residence. A user of a database can pull information out
of the database on everyone who fits a category made up of
some or all of these fields, such as every male between 30
and 40 who earns between 30 and 50 thousand dollars a year
and lives in Florida. An example of a database is the
Internal Revenue Service's database, which contains basic
information on tax returns along with demographic
information on those who pay taxes. Other databases
contain our credit histories, our history of contributions
to a specific organization, our personnel records with our
employers, and a variety of other information. Businesses
and other organizations already use this information to
bombard us with targeted advertising through the mail; the
information could be used to monitor our opinions and
activities (Roszak 182-87).

Databases can be made even more powerful by being
linked to other databases through networking. The
increasing capabilities of network systems raise the
possibility of a wide variety of information on us being
shared by numerous databases. Such information on specific
individuals would be a boon to marketers trying to find
target audiences, but individuals could end up with
their records of contributions to an organization in
the hands of the IRS, or their IRS files in their

employers' personnel records, without their even
knowing it.

So far at least, cases of deliberate abuse or
manipulation of databases to violate an individual's
privacy have been relatively rare. Far greater problems
have arisen because of errors in the entry of data in
databases, with such undesirable results as individuals'
receiving bad credit ratings because of erroneous reports
of unpaid bills or even some cases of innocent
individuals' being denied government jobs because their
names appeared on computer lists of people belonging to
subversive organizations (Sherman 344). The risk of these
kinds of errors may increase with increasing use of the
"on-line" entry of data into computers, where a paper copy
(called a hard copy in computerese) of the transaction is
not necessary, so that no trace is left outside the
computer system of the source of the error. These errors
threaten our privacy, because this supposedly "private"
information may mislead others, damage our reputation, and
enormously complicate our lives. Common sense suggests
that with the increasing amount of "private" data being
kept on all of us, the likelihood of harmful errors also
increases.

Most such errors are caused by human mistakes, but
even computers can develop "glitches." Furthermore, even
errorless electronically-entered data can pose threats
to our privacy. Our phone bills are one example of a
completely electronic system which is almost always error-
free. Yet these phone bills can tell someone who wants to
know all the people we called and when we called them. The
information may be accurate, but in the wrong hands, it
can be seriously misused.

In our society, privacy is regarded as a right—a
right that is being threatened by the increasing use of
databases to maintain large amounts of information on all
of us. A number of computer privacy laws have been enacted
in the last 20 years, including the Medical Computer

Crimes Act of 1984, the Cable Communications Policy Act of 1984, the Financial Privacy Act of 1978, the Fair Credit Reporting Act of 1974, and the Family Educational Rights and Privacy Act of 1974 (Organization for Economic Co-operation and Development 22). One aspect of all these laws is the protection of individuals from unwarranted use of data about them. But violating someone's privacy is hard to detect, and successfully prosecuting someone for this offense is harder still.

Nevertheless, protecting individual privacy against the threat posed by large databases is not a hopeless cause. The growing list of computer privacy laws indicates that the public is not blind to the threats posed by computers, though much needs to be done to make these laws meaningful. Even consumers can help, by insisting that their names not be sent to others when they subscribe to a magazine or join an organization. Faced with such insistence and the possibility of losing customers or members, many groups will stop sharing these lists.

Computers are enormously valuable tools, but they can be misused to violate our privacy. While the threat to our privacy is real, the situation is not yet severe. We still have the time to control this threat before the threat begins to control us.

WORKS CITED

Organization for Economic Co-operation and Development (OECD). *Computer-Related Crime: Analysis of Legal Policy. Information on Computer Communications Policy* 10. Paris: OECD, 1986.

Roszak, Theodore. *The Cult of Information: The Folklore of Computers and the True Art of Thinking*. New York: Pantheon, 1986.

Sherman, Barrie. *The New Revolution: The Impact of Computers on Society*. Chichester, UK: Wiley, 1985.

Having read this second version carefully, do you think the student has solved the problems he noted in his list? Do you see further changes that he might wish to make before handing the paper in to his instructor?

ACTIVITIES (12.2)

Read the following draft of a student's essay (actually a composite of several essays), and make a list of what you feel the major revisions need to be. Compare your list with those of your classmates; then revise the essay in accordance with your list. Compare your revision with some of those done by your classmates.

STUDENT GOVERNMENT: WHY NO ONE CARES

Being an engineering student here at High Tech, I have very little free time. My time is entirely devoted to academics. Occasionally I will have a few hours free on the weekend, but then I work part time at odd jobs. Tuition here is very high.

I am one of many busy students here who simply doesn't have the time to take an interest in student government. This same fact is true for most of us. Most of us don't even know one person who is in student government and could not tell you what student government actually does.

We are very ignorant about student government and what role we can play in it. Speaking for myself, even if I saw posters announcing a meeting about student government, I would not attend. Most of my fellow students would not either. What can just one student do? None of us has much of a voice in how things are run. The administration really runs the show here at High Tech, not the students. I believe that if the student government started putting up more posters and getting out more publicity about its activities, students would be more interested in its activities even if they did not attend them.

It is a whole lot simpler to just ignore what's going on and to assume that the student government is looking out for our interests than to take the trouble to get

involved. Besides, life isn't all that bad around here, so
why should we spend a lot of time and effort trying to
improve a situation most of us already find satisfactory?
By the time we solved some problem, we would be ready to
graduate anyway.

SUGGESTIONS FOR WRITING (12.3)

1. Revise a paper you wrote earlier in this course, following the advice outlined in this chapter. Make a list of the major differences between the original paper and your new version, and indicate very briefly why you made these changes.

2. For this assignment, the class should be divided into groups of three or four. Each group will collectively write a three- to four-page paper (750 to 1,000 words) on the general question "What are the three things that infuriate me most about this campus?" Each group will brainstorm ideas that lead it to a working claim for an evaluative paper concerning student life at your school. From this working claim, the group will compose an outline; then each student will write a particular section of the paper. When the first draft is written, the group will discuss it and each student will revise his or her own section. Finally, the group will discuss this second draft and choose one student to prepare and edit a final version consistent in style and tone.

3. Write a description of the steps you typically follow when writing arguments. Start with the step of coming up with ideas and move through writing the first draft to whatever steps you take before you arrive at a final edited version. How efficient is this typical process in terms of time spent? How effective is it in helping you compose a convincing argument? Do you think the process can be improved so that you can write better arguments in a reasonable amount of time? Give the description to your instructor for comments and suggestions.

4. If you selected activity number one in this section, write a complete paper incorporating your resources. Be sure to give your instructor copies of your resource materials along with your first draft and notes you made concerning the draft.

Text Credits

page 43　"Letter from Birmingham Jail" by Martin Luther King Jr. Reprinted by arrangement with the Estate of Martin Luther King Jr., c/o Writers House as agent for the proprietor. Copyright © 1963 Martin Luther King Jr., copyright renewed 1991 Coretta Scott King.

page 56　"Ally McBeal's Younger Sister" by Jane Rosenweig. Reprinted with permission from *The American Prospect*, Volume 11, Number 1: November 23, 1999. *The American Prospect*, 5 Broad Street, Boston MA 02109 and the author. All rights reserved.

page 70　"Eating Disorders in Males" by Leslie Knowlton, *Psychiatric Times*, XII, September 1995. Reprinted by permission of the author.

page 91　"'Vonnegut Speech' Circulates on Net" by Dan Mitchell from *Wired* (online), August 4, 1997.

page 113　"I, Too, Am a Good Parent" by Dorsett Bennett. From *Newsweek*, July 4, 1994. All rights reserved. Reprinted by permission.

page 127　"From Sweet Anarchy to Stupid Pet Tricks" by Mark Edmundson as appeared in *Civilization*, December 1996/January 1997, Vol. 3, No. 6.

page 136　Excerpt from "Hawaii Judge Ends Ban on Gay Marriages" as appeared in the *Los Angeles Times*, (Rpt. in *The Plain Dealer*) December 4, 1996, pp. 1a, 28a.

page 164　"The Side Effects of Affirmative Action" by Pamela J. Hsu from *The Detroit News*, May 22, 1994. Reprinted with permission from *The Detroit News*.

page 171　From "History as Mirror" by Barbara W. Tuchman. Reprinted by permission of Russell & Volkening as agents for the author. Copyright© 1973 by Barbara Tuchman.

page 179　From "Medicine and the Media: A Case Study" by David Brown. Copyright © 1984 by Alpha Omega Honor Medical Society, reprinted by permission from *The Pharos*, Vol. 47, Number 3.

page 183　"Particle Accelerators Test Cosmological Theory" by David N. Schramm and Gary Steigman, New York: *Scientific American*, June 1988, Vol. 258, #6.

page 186　From "Cutting into Cholesterol" by Bruce P. Kinosian and John M. Eisenberg, *Journal of American Medical Association*, April 15, 1988, 259; 2249–54. Reprinted by permission of the American Medical Association.

page 186　Reprinted by permission of the Modern Language Association of America from "Don't Tell: Imposed Silences in 'The Color Purple'" by King-Kok Cheung, *PMLA*, 1983.

Index